T0024759

THE SHŌGUN'S LAST
SAMURAI
CORPS

The Bloody Battles and Intrigues of the Shinsengumi

ROMULUS HILLSBOROUGH

TUTTLE Publishing

Tokyo | Rutland, Vermont | Singapore

For Minako and Matthew Ryūnosuké —
In memory of my mother

There are but few important events in the affairs of men brought about by their own choice.
— *Ulysses S. Grant*

Miniature Shinsengumi Banner
(original; courtesy of Hijikata Toshizō Museum)

CONTENTS

List of Photographs

Page 4: Miniature Shinsengumi Banner (original; courtesy of Hijikata Toshizō Museum)

Page 26: Shinsengumi Commander Kondō Isami (Courtesy of the descendants of Satō Hikogorō and Hino-shi Furusato Hakubutsukan Museum)

Page 27: Shinsengumi Vice Commander Hijikata Toshizō (Courtesy of the descendants of Satō Hikogorō and Hino-shi Furusato Hakubutsukan Museum)

Page 28: Shinsengumi Banner (replica; courtesy of Hijikata Toshizō Museum)

Page 52: Kondō Isami's black training robe (original; courtesy of Masataka Kojima)

Japan

RUSSIA

CHINA

Ezo

Hakodate

Tsugaru Strait

Matsumae

Miyako Bay

SEA OF JAPAN

SHONAI

Sendai

KOREA

Yonezawa

Aizu

Kami'ishihara

Utsunomiya

Fukui

Honshu

Nikko

Mito

Hikone

Lake Biwa

Musashi

SHIMOUSA

Otsu, Zeze Han

Hino

Edo

Sasago Pass

Katsunuma

Edo Bay

Kyoto

Kofu

Yokohama

Fushimi

OWARI

Yodogawa

Sunpu

Tama

Shimonoseki

Osaka

Hakone

Hagi

GEISHU

Fujisan

Shimoda

CHOSHU

Izu

Shimonoseki Strait

Kuwana

Peninsula

TOSA

KII

Kochi

Nagasaki

Matsuyama

Koshu-kaido

Uwajima

Road

Shikoku

Yamaguchi

SATSUMA

Kumamoto

PACIFIC OCEAN

Kagoshima

Kyushu

0   50   100   150 mi

0   50 100 150 200 km

EDO AND VICINITY

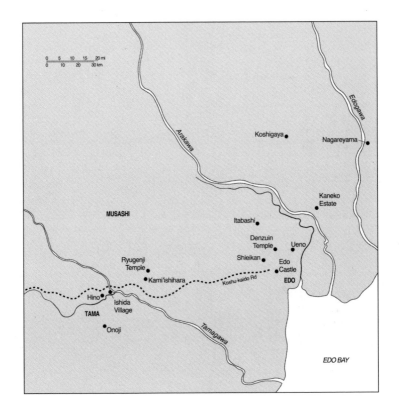

Kyōto

Ezo

SEA OF JAPAN

PACIFIC OCEAN

Washinoki

Futamata

Esashi

Goryokaku

Hakodate

TSUGARU STRAIT

Matsumae

| 0 | 5 | 10 mi |
| 0 | 5 | 10 15 km |

NOTE ON JAPANESE PRONUNCIATION

The pronunciation of vowels and diphthongs are approximated as follows:

a	as in	*car*
e	as in	*pen*
i	as in	*police*
o	as in	*low*
u	as in	*sue*
ai	as in	*sky*
ei	as in	*bay*
au	as in	*now*
ii	There is no English approximation of this sound. There is a slight pause between the first *i* and the second *i*.	

An *e* following a consonant is not a hard sound but rather a soft one. This is indicated by an accent mark (*é*). For example, *saké* is pronounced "sa-kay," and *Ikéda'ya* as "ee-kay-da-ya." An *e* following a vowel is also indicated by an accent mark (*é*) and pronounced similarly. For example, the place name *Uéno* is pronounced "oo-ay-no," and *Iéyasu* as "ee-ay-ya-su." The long vowel sounds (in which *u* or *o* are extended) are indicated by *ū* and *ō*, respectively, as in *Kaishū* and *Kondō*. There are no English approximations of these sounds. They are included to distinguish between the short *u* and *o*, as in *Shinsengumi* and *Edo*.

There are no English approximations for the following sounds. They consist of only one syllable.

ryo
myo
hyo
kyo
ryu
kyu
tsu

There are no English approximations for double consonants, including *kk* (Nikkō), *ss* (Gesshin'in [temple]), *tt* (Hokushin Ittō style [of fencing]), and *nn* (Tennen Rishin style [of fencing]). They are distinguished from single consonants by a slight fricative sound.

AUTHOR'S NOTE

For the sake of authenticity I have placed Japanese family names before given names (except for the names of twentieth-century writers quoted in the text) and have used the Chinese calendar rather than the Gregorian one to preserve the actual feeling of mid-nineteenth-century Japan. For clarity's sake, Japanese dates and era names are generally accompanied by the corresponding years in the Western calendar. For easy reference, I have included a short Table of Era Names and Their Corresponding Years in Western Chronology after the appendixes. I have romanized Japanese terms when I felt that translation would be syntactically awkward or semantically inaccurate. These romanized terms, other than names, are italicized the first time they appear, except for words such as samurai and geisha, which are included in the lexicon of modern American English. I have translated terms, including proper nouns, that I thought would lend themselves favorably to English. I have not necessarily adhered to translations of terms that have been used by other writers. I have not pluralized Japanese terms, but a plural or singular meaning should be clear from the context in which a term is used. For example, a *samurai* is singular, whereas *many samurai* is plural.

I have written a brief Historical Background, preceding the first chapter ("Loyal and Patriotic Corps"), to give readers a basic foundation by which to better comprehend this intricate history. Unlike in my previous books, I have included a bibliography and source notes, although most of my sources are in the Japanese language. All English renderings of historical Japanese documents—including poems, letters, diaries, memoirs, and recollections—are my own translations. For the benefit of readers who have trouble keeping track of

Japanese names and terminology, I have included a Glossary of Japanese Terms after the Table of Era Names.

I express my sincerest appreciation to Mr. George L. Cohen for his invaluable and painstaking work in editing the original manuscript; to Mr. Masataka Kojima, direct descendant of Kojima Shikanosuké and curator of the Kojima Museum, for his kind permission to use the photograph of Kondō Isami's training robe and for providing me with an insight into this history that cannot be had from written materials alone; to Ms. Chié Kimura, direct descendant of Hijikata Toshizō's elder brother, for her permission to use the photo of the original miniature Shinsengumi banner and for her special effort in photographing a replica of the Shinsengumi banner for use herein; to Ms. Fukuko Satō, direct descendant of Satō Hikogorō, for sharing with me an anecdote of Hijikata Toshizō's last days and for her kind permission to use the photos of Kondō Isami and Hijikata Toshizō; to Ms. Mariko Nozaki for her assistance in the translation of archaic Japanese. Finally, I would like to extend special thanks to Mrs. Tae Moriyama, my Japanese teacher, without whose dedicated instruction nearly a quarter century past I might never have gained sufficient knowledge of the Japanese language to comprehend this complicated history; and to Mr. Tsutomu Ohshima, chief instructor of Shotokan Karate of America, whose invaluable teachings over these past three decades have provided me with an occasional and sudden bright flash of insight into the hearts and minds of the samurai depicted herein.

PREFACE

This book is about bloodshed and death and atrocity. It is also about courage and honor and fidelity. It explores some of the darkest regions of the human soul, and some of its most noble parts. The underlying themes in this historical narrative of the Shinsengumi are the extraordinary will to power and sense of self-importance of the leaders of that most lethal samurai corps, and the unsurpassed propensity to kill instilled by them into the rank and file.

The leaders of the Shinsengumi—Kondō Isami and Hijikata Toshizō—are among the most celebrated men in Japanese history. Much has been written about the Shinsengumi, by acclaimed writers of Japanese history and by former Shinsengumi corpsmen. They have also been widely depicted—and romanticized—in numerous novels, period films, and, more recently, comic books and animation. In writing this first English-language narrative of the Shinsengumi, I have given precedence to capturing their essence and the main events of their history, rather than merely rewriting the tedious facts of their history. I have concentrated on the spirit of the Shinsengumi and their place in history, rather than on trivial details, particularly for situations in which my numerous sources contradict one another—with disconcerting frequency.

The causes for such contradictions are inevitable. Much of the information available about the Shinsengumi is fragmentary. Many of the facts regarding the corps have been lost to history. For example, depending on the source, it might or might not have been raining on the night that Serizawa Kamo was assassinated. While the sound of pouring rain adds a certain melodramatic element to the scene, exceedingly more important than the weather are the reasons that Serizawa was assassinated, the circumstances of the bloody incident, and its historical consequences. As another example, the cause of

Okita Sōji's collapse during the furious and bloody battle at the Iké-da'ya inn is uncertain. Whether the cause was a sudden attack of tuberculosis or the intense heat inside the house on that hot summer night in 1864 is of far less importance than the fact that the genius swordsman killed numerous men with his sword before collapsing, and the far-reaching effect of his sword on Japanese history.

In this regard I must mention that this narrative is based entirely on historical documents and records, historical narrative and biographies (including definitive histories of the Shinsengumi and biographies of their men and other contemporaries), letters, diaries, memoirs and recollections (including firsthand and secondhand oral accounts and interviews), and other widely accepted sources. However, to the question of whether this narrative is entirely nonfiction, my answer must be a carefully considered yet resounding *no*. No, because I do not believe that any of my source materials are entirely foolproof—although to the best of my knowledge they are the truest and best available sources on this history. All historical documents and written histories, in that they are recorded after the fact and are not simultaneous depictions of men and events, must be, to a certain extent, flawed. Even eyewitness accounts of events are naturally flawed by biases, preconceptions, and myriad viewpoints, accented by the countless, or perhaps uncountable, perceptions inherent in the individual human mind. Thomas Carlyle, the master historical essayist, summed up this inevitable condition simply but truly: "The old story of Sir Walter Raleigh's looking from his prison window, on some street tumult, which afterwards three witnesses reported in three different ways, himself differing from them all, is still a true lesson for us."*

In this light, I pose a question: Even in this day and age of advanced technology, is there a newspaper account of current events absolutely and undoubtedly free of misinterpretation of human intention or just plain factual error? How could the answer be but *no* at the beginning of the twenty-first century, when deception and lies

---

* Thomas Carlyle, "On History," *Thomas Carlyle: Historical Essays* (University of California Press, 2002), p. 6.

are rampant at the highest levels of government, as they were in Japan during the 1860s and have been among organizations composed of human beings since the beginning of recorded history? Let it suffice to say, then, that this historical narrative is nonfiction in that my intent throughout has been, to the best of my ability, to present a coherent and accurate picture of the men and events of the Shinsengumi.

"Stern Accuracy in inquiring, bold Imagination in expounding … are the two pinions on which History soars," Carlyle wrote.* The gist of this message by the visionary historian is that while we cannot know the certain truth of human events and actions which we ourselves have not witnessed, we can, by force of careful scrutiny, depict a clearer template from an otherwise muddled parade of uncorrelated facts of history and embellish this clarified image with fleeting and boundless leaps of "bold Imagination," to paint a picture that reflects the soul and essence of great human events and actions. This is what I have attempted in these pages. Whether I have succeeded, I leave to the reader to judge.

— *Romulus Hillsborough*
January 2005

---

* Thomas Carlyle, "Count Cagliostro," *Thomas Carlyle: Historical Essays* (University of California Press, 2002), p. 32.

INTRODUCTION

The Shinsengumi was a police force organized in the spring of 1863 to guard the shōgun, quell sedition and restore law and order in the Imperial capital of Kyōto during the upheaval of the 1860s. In this book, previously published under a different title*, I have demonstrated how the Shinsengumi earned its well-deserved reputation as the most feared police force in Japanese history. But the Shinsengumi was much more than that. While this book is a history-in-brief of the Shinsengumi, providing a solid foundation for understanding "the shōgun's last samurai corps" and the complex intricacies of the final years and collapse of the shōgun's regime, further research has led me to write a second book that will be an in-depth history and more complete study of the Shinsengumi.

While readers of the current volume will become familiar with an array of historical figures, including several of the key members of the Shinsengumi, the focal personalities are the commander, Kondō Isami, and the vice commander, Hijikata Toshizō. Kondō was chief instructor of the Tennen Rishin style of *kenjutsu* (Japanese swordsmanship). Since I did not write much on the history of the style in the original publication, the following brief historical background, based on my subsequent research, will benefit readers of this book. Readers will also benefit from a brief comparison between Kondō's and Hijikata's practice of *kenjutsu*, along with a short discussion of the swords that each man favored, both of which, included in this Introduction, are also the result of my subsequent research.

---

* This book was originally published in 2005 under the title *Shinsengumi: The Shōgun's Last Samurai Corps*. There is no change in the contents, other than the addition of this Introduction.

Historical Background of the Tennen Rishin Style

The Tennen Rishin style was established around the end of the 18th century by Kondō Kuranosuké, Isami's predecessor by three genera-tions, of whose background very little is known. He came from the province of Tōtoumi near present-day Hamamatsu. After establish-ing the style, he was based in the shōgun's capital of Edo while also teaching in the rural provinces of Musashi, just east of Edo, and the adjacent Sagami to the south. Originally the Tennen Rishin style was a comprehensive system of martial arts, which, beside *kenjutsu*, in-cluded the arts of *jūjutsu*, *bōjutsu* (staff), and *hōjutsu* (gunnery), among other disciplines. Under Kondō Shūsuké, Isami's adoptive father and immediate predecessor as head of the style, students of Tennen Rishin practiced only *kenjutsu*.

Kondō Shūsuké's immediate predecessor was Kondō Sansuké, born in the Tama district of Musashi in 1774. Sansuké succeeded Kuranosuké upon the latter's death in 1807. Though short and slight, Sansuké was, by all accounts, an exceptionally gifted swordsman, even more skilled than Kuranosuké. But his career as head of the style was cut short after less than twelve years by his untimely death at age forty-six. A successor would not emerge for years.

Kondō Shūsuké was born in 1792, as the third son of the head-man of a local village in Tama. Though one of Sansuké's top students, he was the youngest and least experienced of his peers. Having stud-ied the Tennen Rishin style for only about eight years under Sansuké, he was not qualified to receive *shinan menkyo* (instructor's license) directly from the master. From whom he received it is unknown. Nor is it known just when or under what circumstances he became the third-generation head of the style; but we do know that it was no later than 1829, based on the date of an extant diploma of rank conferred by Kondō Shūsuké. He served as head of the style for no less than thirty-two years, traveling around villages in Tama to teach students mostly from wealthy peasant households, and later at his own dōjō, the Shieikan, in Edo, until his retirement in 1861.

Kondō Shūsuké established the Shieikan in Ichigaya, in the north-western part of Edo, in 1839. The Shieikan flourished, attracting students from surrounding neighborhoods in the city, including the sons of samurai in service of the shōgun. Shūsuké's student roster would eventually exceed one thousand. Beginning in 1848, Shūsuké, with two assistants, traveled to Tama to teach at the homes of wealthy peasants to supplement their income. They continued teaching in Tama until around 1857, when those duties were given to Kondō Shūsuké's prize student, a young man also from the wealthy peasant class named Miyagawa Katsugorō, who, having changed his name to Kondō Isami, would succeed the master as fourth-generation head of the Tennen Rishin style around four years later.*

Comparisons of the *Kenjutsu* Practice of Kondō and Hijikata

The following brief comparison of the *kenjutsu* practice of the two Shinsengumi leaders shed light on a fundamental difference in their personalities. But first some historical background. The great historical novelist Shiba Ryōtarō wrote that the original purpose of the sword was to kill people, though during the centuries of peace under Tokugawa rule "it became a philosophy."† With the enactment of the Code for Warrior Households of Kanbun in the second half of the 17th century (the Kanbun era corresponds to 1661–1673), which included a ban on matches using real swords, *kenjutsu* was treated in some respects as a sport. Starting in the Genroku era (1688–1704), many samurai, especially in Edo, led relatively easy lives as administrators rather than warriors—while form and a beautiful technique took precedence over effectiveness in actual fighting, and theory became more important than ability. But with the renaissance of the martial arts after the arrival of Perry in the summer of 1853, many swordsmen shunned form and beauty for practical techniques that would work in a real fight.‡

In this respect Hijikata Toshizō was very much a man of the times, as demonstrated in his swordsmanship, which, it seems, was more

---

* The historical background of the Tennen Rishin style provided herein is mostly from Kojima Masataka's *Bujutsu: Tennen Rishinryū*.

† Shiba Ryōtarō. *Hitokiri Izō*. Tokyo: Shinchōsha, 1988, p. 83.

‡ Kojima, *Bujutsu Tennen Rishinryū*, p. 2.

practical than philosophical. While Kondō's swordsmanship was "disciplined" and "magnificent," Hijikata practiced to "kill people," recalled Yūki Minizō, who served under both men in early 1868.* "While Kondō, in contrast to his appearance, had a high-pitched, piercing voice when shouting [out commands] and a mild manner of teaching, Hijikata, contrary to his usual demeanor, had a rough manner during *kenjutsu* practice, which filled ... [his students] with fear," said Hijikata Yasushi, grandson of Toshizō's elder brother, Kiroku, in an interview published in 1972.[†]

Swords Favored by Kondō and Hijikata

Both men, it seems, preferred swords of greater than average length. Kondō famously favored blades forged by the smith Kotetsu. In the fall of 1863, Kondō wrote to his student Satō Hikogorō, Hijikata's elder brother-in-law, that he had "long and short Kotetsu swords," and that the short sword was "2 *shaku*, 3 *sun*, 5 *bu*" (about 2 feet, 4 inches), slightly longer than the average long sword, which measured about 2 *shaku*, 3 *sun* (about 2 feet, 2.5 inches). (There were two types of long swords, *chōtō* and *daitō*, though the two terms were used interchangeably. A cutting edge measuring 2 *shaku*, 5 *bu* or greater was classified as a *chōtō* (literally, "long sword"). A *daitō* (literally, "big sword") was over 2 *shaku*. Regarding short swords, Kondō asserted, "The longer the better." His reasoning, it seems, was that in an actual fight his long sword might break, in which case he could depend on his short sword. In the following summer, three days after the Shinsengumi's notorious raid on the Ikéda'ya inn in Kyōto, he reported to his adoptive father that he had used his Kotetsu in the fighting. In the battle at Kōfu in the spring of 1868, Kondō wielded a particularly long sword measuring 2 *shaku*, 8 *sun* (about 2 feet, 9 ½ inches), forged by the smith Munésada, and given him by Itakura Katsukiyo,

---

* In Tani Haruo, "Hino to Shinsengumi (2): Satō Hikorgorō to Hijikata Toshizō," Hino Tōmonkaihō, No. 6, p. 3, which does not cite the source.

† From Shinjinbutsu Ōraisha, ed. *Shinsengumitaishi Retsuden*, Tokyo: Shinjinbutsu Ōraisha, 1972, qtd. in Kimura Sachihiko, *Shiden Hijikata Toshizō*, Tokyo: Gakushū Kenkyūsha, 2001, p. 48.

a former senior councilor to the shōgun, according to Isami's nephew and heir, Kondō Yūgorō.

In the above-cited letter to Satō, Kondō mentioned Hijikata's long and short swords. His short sword, forged by Horikawa Kunihiro, was 1 *shaku*, 9 *sun*, 5 *bu* (just over 1 foot, 11 inches), slightly shorter than a "big sword." Hijikata's "long sword," forged by Izumi-no-Kami Kanésada, was a lengthy 2 *shaku*, 8 *sun*, the same as Kondō's Munésada. Hijikata had at least one other, shorter Kanésada sword, currently housed at his eponymous museum, located at the site of his ancestral home in Hino. Forged in Kyōto in 1867, the length is 2 *shaku*, 3 *sun*, 1 *bu*, 6 *rin* (about 2 feet, 2.5 inches). He had another sword of around the same length forged by Yamato-no-Kami Minamoto-no-Hidékuni, no earlier than the summer of 1866, the year engraved with the smith's signature on the tang. He might have used this sword during the Boshin War, beginning with the Battle at Toba-Fushimi in early 1868, according to the Ryōzen Museum of History, where it is currently housed. Perhaps the longest sword Hijikata carried was one mentioned by Abei Iwané in 1892, formerly a samurai of Nihonmatsu who had seen Hijikata at a war council held among the confederate domains at Sendai Castle in 1868, during the rebellion in the north. In the fall of that year, Abei said, Hijikata, as a condition for accepting the command of confederate troops, demanded the right to use his "sword of 3 *shaku*" to kill anyone who defied his orders.[*]

Romulus Hillsborough
October 2019

---

[*] *Shidankai Sokkiroku*, talk by Abei Iwané, July 11, 1892, in *Shinsengumi Shiryōshū* (Compact). Tokyo: Shinjinbutsu Ōraisha, 1998, p. 262.

Shinsengumi Commander Kondō Isami (Courtesy of the descendants of Satō Hikogorō and Hino-shi Furusato Hakubutsukan Museum)

Shinsengumi Vice Commander Hijikata Toshizō (Courtesy of the descen-dants of Satō Hikogorō and Hino-shi Furusato Hakubutsukan Museum)

PROLOGUE

By the end of 1862 the situation had gotten out of hand. Hordes of renegade samurai had abandoned their clans to fight under the banner of Imperial Loyalism. These warriors, derogatorily called rōnin by the powers that were, had transformed the formerly tranquil streets of the Imperial Capital into a sea of blood. The rōnin were determined to overthrow the shōgun's regime, which had ruled Japan these past two and a half centuries. Screaming "Heaven's Revenge," they wielded their swords with a vengeance upon their enemies. Terror reigned. Assassination was a nightly occurrence. The assassins skewered the heads of their victims onto bamboo stakes. They stuck the stakes into the soft mud along the riverbank. The spectacle by dawn was ghastly.

*Shinsengumi Banner
(replica; courtesy of Hijikata
Toshizō Museum)*

The authorities were determined to rein in the chaos and terror. A band of swordsmen was formed. They were given the name Shinsengumi—Newly Selected Corps—and commissioned to restore law and order to the Imperial Capital. At once reviled and revered, they were known alternately as rōnin hunters, wolves, murderers, thugs, band of assassins, and eventually the most dreaded security force in Japanese history. Their official mission was to protect the shōgun; but their assigned purpose was single and clear—to eliminate the rōnin who would overthrow the shōgun's government. Endowed with an official sanction and unsurpassed propen-

sity to kill, the men of the Shinsengumi swaggered through the ancient city streets. Under their trademark banner of "sincerity," their presence and even their very name evoked terror among the terrorists, as an entire nation reeled around them.

HISTORICAL
BACKGROUND

The fall of the Tokugawa Shogunate in 1868 was one of the great events in Asian and, indeed, world history. The creation of the shogunate over two and a half centuries earlier was the pivotal event in the history of Japan. In 1600 Tokugawa Iéyasu, head of the House of Tokugawa, defeated his enemies in the decisive battle at Sekigahara, the historical and geographical center of Japan. Iéyasu emerged from Sekigahara as the mightiest feudal lord in the empire. In 1603 he was conferred by the emperor with the title *sei'i'taishō-gun*—commander in chief of the expeditionary forces against the barbarians, or simply, shōgun. The new shōgun established his military government in the east, at Edo (modern-day Tōkyō). He and his descendants ruled from Edo Castle, which by the time of the third shōgun of the Tokugawa dynasty* was the largest fortress in Japan. The emperor, meanwhile, remained a powerless figurehead at his palace in Kyōto, the ancient Imperial Capital in the west.

During the Tokugawa Period (1603–1868), Japan was comprised of hundreds of feudal domains. These domains were called *han*. Their number fluctuated slightly, but by the end of the Tokugawa Period there were approximately 260 han. Each han was ruled by a feudal lord, or *daimyō*. The samurai retainers of each daimyō administered the government of their lord's han. In turn, the samurai received annual stipends which were calculated in *koku*—bushels of rice.† The

---

* Tokugawa Iémitsu, ruled 1623–1651.
† 1 koku = 44.8 U.S. gallons.

rice was produced by the peasants, who ranked just below the samurai in the social hierarchy. Beneath the peasants were the artisans and merchants.

The Tokugawa regime, known as the Tokugawa Bakufu, Edo Bakufu, or simply Bakufu, subjugated the han throughout Japan. Shōgun Tokugawa Iéyasu bequeathed upon his favorite sons the great domains of Owari, Kii, and Mito. These became the Three Branch Houses of the Tokugawa. The heads of the Three Branch Houses were the highest-ranking feudal lords under the shōgun. By Iéyasu's provisions, in the event that a shōgun failed to produce an heir, his successor was to be chosen from among the branch houses.* Following in the hierarchy were the twenty Related Houses, descended from Iéyasu's younger sons. Below them were the hereditary lords, whose descendants had aided Iéyasu at Sekigahara. The hereditary lords were direct retainers of the Tokugawa and, generally speaking, occupied the most important governmental posts, including those of regent and senior councilor. During the final years of Tokugawa rule, there were 145 hereditary lords. The progeny of those who either had been defeated by Iéyasu or had not sided with him were the so-called outside lords, of whom there were ninety-eight at the end of the Tokugawa Period. The Yamanouchi of Tosa, the Shimazu of Satsuma, and the Mōri of Chōshū were among the most powerful families of outside lords. From these three han would emerge the leaders in the revolution to overthrow the Bakufu and restore the emperor to his ancient seat of power. This revolution was the Meiji Restoration.

In 1635 the Bakufu initiated the system of alternate attendance, by which all daimyō were required to maintain official residences at Edo and live in them in alternate years. Through this system the Bakufu ensured that half of the feudal lords would always be present in Edo, while the other half were in their respective domains. The vast expense of maintaining Edo residences and traveling back and forth to the shōgun's capital necessarily reduced the amount of money left

---

* Tokugawa Yoshimuné, the eighth shōgun, added three additional branch houses to strengthen the foundation of his family's rule. These were the Hitotsubashi, Tayasu, and Shimizu families. None of these additional three branch families possessed a provincial castle, but rather they lived permanently in Edo.

the feudal lords for military expenditures. Further safeguarding against insurrection in the provinces was the requirement that each daimyō keep his wife and heir at his Edo residence as virtual hostages during his absence from the capital.

The Tokugawa ruled more or less peacefully for the next two and a half centuries. To maintain this peace, the Bakufu had strictly enforced a policy of national isolation since 1635. But the end of this halcyon era approached as the social, political, and economic structures of the outside world underwent major changes. The British colonies in North America declared independence in 1776. The remnants of feudalism in Europe were obliterated by the French Revolution in 1789 and the ensuing Napoleonic Wars. The nineteenth century heralded the age of European and North American capitalism and, with it, rapid advances in science, industry, and technology. The development of the steamship in the early part of the nineteenth century served the expansionist purposes of Western nations. Colonization of Asian countries by European powers surged. In 1818 Great Britain subjugated much of India. Through the Treaty of Nanking, which ended the first Opium War in 1842, the British acquired Hong Kong.

The foreign menace reached Japan on June 3 of the sixth year of the era named Ka'ei—July 8, 1853, on the Gregorian calendar.* It was on that day that Commodore Matthew Perry of the U.S. Navy led a squadron of heavily armed warships into Edo Bay, off the shōgun's capital, eventually forcing an end to Japanese isolation and inciting fifteen years of bloody turmoil across the island nation. Perry carried a letter from President Millard Fillmore demanding a treaty between the United States and Japan. After months of stormy and unprecedented debate among samurai and daimyō both within and outside the Tokugawa camp, and even including members of the general populace, the authorities eventually yielded to Perry's gunboat diplomacy. In March 1854, the first year of the era of Ansei, Japan relinquished its policy of isolationism and signed the so-called Treaty of

---

* New eras were promulgated to mark an extraordinary occasion or occurrence, such as the enthronement of an emperor, a good omen, or a natural disaster. The era name reflects the zeitgeist of the era. (*Kojien*)

Peace and Amity with the Americans.* Similar treaties with England, Holland, France, and Russia followed. Two ports were opened—one at Shimoda, not far from Edo; the other at Hakodaté, on the far-northern island of Ezo.

Samurai throughout Japan were outraged over the humiliation they suffered at the hands of the foreigners. The situation was tersely explained by one who rose above this outrage in order to deal with the unprecedented and pressing dangers facing Japan. "Since the time that the American warships arrived at Uraga† in 1853, public opinion became divided between the advocates of war and peace, so that a decision could not be made either way," Katsu Kaishū wrote four decades later, in a brief chronicle of the origin and downfall of the Tokugawa Bakufu. Kaishū was an expert swordsman who never drew his sword on an adversary. He was a philosopher-statesman, founder of the Japanese navy, and, during those dangerous times, probably the most valuable personage in the entire Edo regime. "At that time the Bakufu decided to open the country, and gradually did so. There were many people, including feudal lords, who resented this. They said that the Bakufu was forced by the barbarians to open the country because of its cowardice and weakness, and that this was why the Bakufu submitted to this humiliation. They no longer believed in the Bakufu. There was heated argument everywhere. People were killing foreigners, and assassinating government officials."

Two schools of thought came to the fore. *Kaikoku* (Open the Country) was the official policy at Edo. *Jōi* (Expel the Barbarians) was violently advocated by the vast majority of samurai throughout Japan. Four domains stood at the vanguard of the antiforeign movement: Mito, Satsuma, Chōshū, and Tosa. As close relatives of the Tokugawa, the Mito rulers would never oppose the Bakufu. (Hitotsubashi Yoshinobu, a son of the Lord of Mito, would become the last shōgun in 1866.) Meanwhile, the antiforeignism embraced by the Imperial Loyalists of Chōshū, Satsuma, and Tosa transformed into an anti-Tokugawa, nationalistic movement. At first they advocated

---

* The Treaty of Peace and Amity is also known as the Treaty of Kanagawa, after the town where it was concluded.
† In Edo Bay.

Sonnō-Jōi (Imperial Reverence and Expel the Barbarians), which they eventually replaced with the more radical battle cry *Kinnō-Tōbaku* (Imperial Loyalism and Down with the Bakufu).

Chōshū, Satsuma, and Tosa were among the most powerful han in Japan. The Mōri family of Chōshū and the Shimazu family of Satsuma were bitter rivals, but they had borne a common and deep resentment of the Tokugawa for these past two and a half centuries. Both had been subjugated by the Tokugawa since Sekigahara. But the rulers of Chōshū had fared much worse at the hands of the victorious shōgun than had their counterparts in Satsuma. The Mōri's vast landholdings had been reduced by two-thirds, while the Shimazu had been permitted to retain their entire domain. Since the income of the samurai was based on the rice yield of their domain, the Chōshū samurai felt the pain of Iéyasu's punishment for the following two and a half centuries. It was probably for this reason that after the fall of the Bakufu, Satsuma tended to favor more lenient treatment of the Tokugawa than did Chōshū. Meanwhile, the Tosa daimyō, Yamanouchi Yōdō, found himself in a unique, if not wholly desirable, situation. He owed his very position as Lord of Tosa to the goodwill of the first Tokugawa Shōgun. Iéyasu had awarded Yōdō's ancestor fifteen generations past with the vast Tosa domain, not for aiding him, but rather for not opposing him. Accordingly, while Lord Yōdō would never officially oppose Tokugawa rule, many Tosa samurai would.*

The majority of antiforeign samurai in Kyōto hailed from Chōshū, Tosa, and Satsuma. These men developed close relationships with radical nobles of the Imperial Court. They advocated Imperial Loyalism and Down with the Bakufu. They rallied around the Son of Heaven, a chronic xenophobe. They murdered Toku-gawa representatives and sympathizers with an equal vengeance. Screaming "*Tenchū*"—Heaven's Revenge—they severed their victims' heads, mounted them atop bamboo stakes, and exposed them to the elements and public derision along the Kamogawa River near Sanjō Bridge.

---

* Among the most prominent leaders of the revolution were Sakamoto Ryōma and Takéchi Hanpeita, both from Tosa. I have written in detail about these and other Tosa men, as well as about the special relationship between the Yamanouchi and the Tokugawa, in *Ryoma—Life of a Renaissance Samurai* and in *Samurai Tales*.

The fear of things foreign among Emperor Kōmei and his court was based on ignorance. They had never been away from the Imperial Capital, and the emperor rarely left the idyllic confines of his palace. None of them had ever seen the ocean or, of course, the great ships that carried the "barbarians" to Japan. They had heard rumors of the foreigners, ridiculous as they were gruesome. Foreigners were monsters with long noses, round eyes, and red or yellow hair, who partook of human flesh and who harbored unholy designs on the sacred empire of Yamato.

Their ignorance notwithstanding, the emperor and his court were painfully aware of the Treaty of Nanking. Neither they nor the Loyalist samurai who revered the emperor believed that the encroachment of Western nations would stop with China. If British warships could bring to its knees the great Middle Kingdom, which had stood at the vanguard of civilization and culture since ancient times, certainly Japan faced similar peril.

Many of the Imperial Loyalists were rōnin, samurai who had quit the service of their lord. They claimed that Emperor Kōmei was the true and rightful ruler of Japan, although his ancestors had not held political power for a thousand years. The Loyalists, self-styled *shishi*—"men of high purpose"*—professed that the Tokugawa Shōgun was merely an imperial agent whose ancestor had been commissioned by the emperor to protect Japan from foreign invasion. But the present shōgun and his councilors had upset the emperor by failing to deal firmly with the foreigners. If the Bakufu was unable to keep the foreigners out, the emperor and his court must be restored to power to save the nation. National politics gradually developed into a twofold structure: while the Bakufu continued to rule at Edo, the Imperial Court underwent a political renaissance at Kyōto.

---

* *Kojien*, the standard Japanese dictionary, defines *shishi* as (1) "a person of high purpose;" (2) "a person of high purpose who risks his own life for the nation or society." Many of the shishi in Kyōto were rōnin. Most of the shishi during the final years of Tokugawa rule hailed from the Chōshū, Tosa, Satsuma, and Higo clans. But the term was by no means limited to Imperial Loyalists. Numerous supporters of the Tokugawa, including samurai of Mito, Fukui, Aizu, and the Shinsengumi, also called themselves shishi. Nor was the title limited to samurai; it was also claimed by peasants, merchants, and clerics who risked their lives on both sides of the revolution.

The situation exploded in June 1858—the fifth year of Ansei—when Edo signed a commercial treaty without imperial sanction. The Loyalists cried lése-majesté. They charged treason. They vowed to punish the wicked Tokugawa officials who were responsible. The man they most hated was the Tokugawa regent, Ii Naosuké, Lord of Hikoné, who had usurped power two months earlier. Just before the subsequent death of the feebleminded Shōgun Tokugawa Iésada, the regent arranged for a twelve-year-old prince of the Kii domain, Tokugawa Iémochi, to succeed him. Under the boy-shōgun, the dictatorial regent ruled with an iron fist.

Regent Ii was determined that his enemies would not interfere with his plans. He unleashed his infamous Ansei Purge, the extent of which was unprecedented in scope and severity. Nearly one hundred shishi were arrested. A number of them were either executed or perished in prison. But Ii was not the devil incarnate his enemies believed he was, as indicated by a document handed down by the Ii family.

Fighting [the foreigners] and being defeated, and [as a result] having our country rent asunder, would bring the worst possible disgrace upon our nation. Which would be the graver—refusing [a treaty] and causing ourselves eternal disgrace, or concluding a treaty without imperial sanction, and so sparing our nation from eternal disgrace? At the present time neither our coastal defenses nor our armaments are sufficient. Our only choice for the time being is to concede [to a treaty], as the lesser of two evils. The aim of the Imperial Court is to avoid national disgrace. The Bakufu has been entrusted with the administration of the country. Those who administer the affairs of state must sometimes act with expediency as occasion demands. However, Naosuké is determined to bear upon himself the responsibilities of the grave crime of not obtaining imperial sanction.

Regent Ii would pay for his "grave crime" the following spring. On the unseasonably snowy morning of March 3, 1860 (the first and only year of the era of Man'en), the regent was assassinated by a band of swordsmen—seventeen from Mito, one from Satsuma—as his palanquin approached Sakurada Gate of Edo Castle. The authority by which the Tokugawa had ruled Japan these past two and a half centuries seemed to evaporate into thin air as the regent's hot blood melted the freshly fallen snow just outside the castle gate and news of the Sakurada Gate Incident shocked the nation. If the most powerful man in Edo could be cut down by a small band of assassins, there was no limit to the havoc that hundreds, or even thousands, of rōnin could wreak throughout Japan.

Loyal and Patriotic Corps

The situation in the Imperial Capital continued to deteriorate. Unruly rōnin flocked to Kyōto. Most were Imperial Loyalists with a vendetta against the Bakufu. All were men of high purpose. They wore two lethal swords at their left hip. They were raring to use their swords to expel the barbarians and punish the shōgun's government for allowing them entrance. In the spring of 1863, as blood flowed and chaos reigned in the Imperial Capital, the shōgun was compelled to visit there—to report to the emperor his promise to expel the barbarians. The Bakufu instituted a new post—the protector of Kyōto. It was the official function of the protector of Kyōto to safeguard the Imperial Capital in preparation for the shōgun's visit; but it was his true purpose to crush the enemies of the Tokugawa. Under the slogan "Loyalty and Patriotism," the Bakufu enlisted rōnin in the east to subdue rōnin in the west. In vain, the government provided each man of the "loyal and patriotic" corps with a pittance of gold—an ill-conceived attempt to gain their loyalty. When the corpsmen proved no less possessed of anti-Tokugawa fervor than those they were commissioned to subdue, the protector of Kyōto and his bewildered allies in Edo balked.

Shōgun Tokugawa Iémochi could not expel the foreigners—his regime, and indeed Japan as a whole, lacked the military means to do so. The bitter truth of Japan's weakness vis-à-vis foreign nations had long been expressed by no less an authority on Western military power than Katsu Kaishū.* A decade earlier, in the face of Perry's gunboat diplomacy and while most men in Japan blindly opposed Open the Country, Kaishū, then an obscure Tokugawa retainer, had submitted a letter to the Bakufu. In this famous document he expressed the urgent and unavoidable necessity for Edo to lift its centuries-old ban on the construction of large oceangoing vessels and to develop a modern navy. To this end, international trade would be imperative to raise capital for building warships and manufacturing Western-style guns. Although these and other of Kaishū's proposals were adopted by the Bakufu during the 1850s, in the spring of 1863—and for years to follow—Japan was still a technologically backward nation. While most of his countrymen ranted and raved about expelling the foreigners through virtue of their "samurai spirit," Katsu Kaishū, always ahead of his time, continued to profess that without foreign assistance—i.e., modern military technology—Japan could not hope to stand up to Great Britain, France, Russia, or the United States. Unless Japan prepared itself for the future, it would share the fate of China and India, under the yoke of foreign subjugation. Kaishū knew, as did a small handful of other farsighted men both within and outside the Tokugawa camp, that Edo's proposed promise to expel the foreigners was at best appeasement, at worst deception, of the Imperial Court.

Lord Matsudaira Katamori was less concerned with the bitter truth of Japan's weakness than with protecting the shōgun. The Matsudaira family of Aizu Han were among the Tokugawa Bakufu's staunchest allies. As one of the Related Houses, their crest displayed the three hollyhock leaves of the Tokugawa. At age twenty-seven, the Edo-born Lord Katamori, head of the House of Matsudaira and daimyō of Aizu, was appointed protector of Kyōto. His first task upon assuming his new post was to safeguard the streets of Kyōto in preparation for Iémochi's visit. At the end of 1862, the second year of the

---

* See Appendix I (1).

era of Bunkyū, the Bakufu authorities had devised a plan to assist him. In former days they would have deployed samurai of the Edo camp to suppress the renegades in Kyōto. But now the authorities came up with a novel idea. For the first time in its history, the Tokugawa Bakufu officially recruited rōnin, whom the authorities generally referred to by the preferred term *rōshi*, to suppress the renegades.* To this end, the Bakufu proclaimed a general amnesty, whereby even incarcerated criminals deemed worthy were set free to enlist. By February hundreds of men, whose majority hailed from the east, had been recruited into the Rōshi Corps to serve the shōgun in the troubled west.

In April of the previous year, Shimazu Hisamitsu, the father of the Satsuma daimyō and de facto ruler of that powerful clan, had led an army of one thousand men into Kyōto in an unprecedented display of military might by an outside lord. Hisamitsu, a sometimes ally of the Tokugawa, urged the Imperial Court to accept Edo's much vaunted call for a Union of Court and Camp. By uniting with Kyōto to shore up national strength against the foreign threat, Edo hoped to regain its unchallenged authority of the past. The reasoning: once the union had been completed, the Imperial Loyalists could no longer oppose the Bakufu, for so doing would be tantamount to siding against the Imperial Court. Lord Hisamitsu, meanwhile, had ulterior motives. In his role as great mediator, he would strengthen his influence at Edo and gain prestige at Kyōto, at the expense of his Chōshū rivals.

Upon his arrival in the Imperial Capital, Lord Hisamitsu, as he fully expected, was commanded by the court to reestablish order there—which, of course, was the paramount desire of Emperor Kō-mei. Lord Hisamitsu was therefore vexed to learn of a planned uprising by radical samurai, including twenty of his own vassals. These radicals would invade the Imperial Palace and assassinate supporters of the Tokugawa, whom they claimed had "infested" the court. They had been waiting for the Satsuma host to arrive, counting on the sup-

---

* The *rō* of both terms literally means "wave" (the gist being "wandering aimlessly"). The *nin* of *rōnin* simply means "person," while the *shi* of *rōshi* means "samurai."

port of Hisamitsu, whom they assumed had come to declare war on the Bakufu. When the rebels learned that they had misjudged Hisamitsu's intent, they gathered at the Terada'ya inn, in the town of Fushimi just south of Kyōto, to finalize their war plans. Hisamitsu appointed a squad of nine Satsuma samurai, all expert swordsmen, to proceed to the Terada'ya and bring their twenty errant brethren back to Satsuma's Kyōto headquarters. The result was the notorious fratricidal sword battle at the Terada'ya inn, the first, though unsuccessful, attempt at a military uprising aimed directly at the Tokugawa Bakufu.*

Among the planners of the failed uprising was a rōnin named Kiyokawa Hachirō. Kiyokawa was the eldest son of a family of wealthy saké brewers of Shōnai Han in northern Japan. He disliked his family business, pursuing instead his passion for the martial and literary arts. He studied at the celebrated Chiba Dōjo, one of the three great fencing academies in Edo,† and became a renowned swordsman licensed to teach the Hokushin Ittō style. Kiyokawa was also a noted Confucian scholar who taught his subject at his private academy in Edo. He was a charismatic speaker, with flashing eyes and a tall, slender frame. He was a man of political ambition who, like many of his peers, censured the Edo regime for its weakness in dealing with foreigners. Kiyokawa was particularly outspoken in his anti-Tokugawa views. He was a man of strong conviction, and it seems that he also had a short temper. One evening at dusk, as he walked through the center of Edo after an afternoon of heavy drinking, he nearly collided with a man coming from the opposite direction. The man carried a walking stick, with which he attempted to strike the samurai. The samurai lost his temper. The next instant he drew his sword, and with one clean stroke beheaded the man with the walking stick.

The local Tokugawa magistrate in Edo had kept a close watch on Kiyokawa. He was aware of Kiyokawa's openly anti-Tokugawa views. The magistrate used the incident of the slaying as an excuse to order Kiyokawa's arrest. But Kiyokawa would not be arrested. Instead, he traveled through western Japan to recruit shishi into the Loyalist fold

---

* For a detailed account of this incident, see *Ryoma—Life of a Renaissance Samurai*.
† See Appendix I (2).

and wielded significant influence among the radicals of Chōshū, Satsuma, and Tosa. Although the uprising in Fushimi had indeed been crushed, Kiyokawa would not abandon his ultimate objective of Imperial Loyalism and Down with the Bakufu.

The plan for the Rōshi Corps was nominally proposed by one Matsudaira Chikaranosuké,* chief fencing instructor at the Bakufu's Military Academy in Edo and close relative of the shōgun. Matsudaira's intentions included reining in the radical elements in and around Edo who threatened the Bakufu. Once these rōnin were in the Tokugawa fold, the Bakufu could more readily effect a Union of Court and Camp. The actual planners of the corps, however, had different ideas. One of them was Kiyokawa. The other was Yamaoka Tetsutarō,† a low-ranking Tokugawa samurai. Kiyokawa and Yamaoka were close friends. The two had studied *kenjutsu* (literally, sword techniques) at the Chiba Dōjo. Shortly after the commercial treaties had been concluded, they formed a subversive political party that advocated Imperial Reverence and Expel the Barbarians. Yamaoka served as assistant kenjutsu instructor at the Bakufu's Military Academy. His loyalty to the Tokugawa was unquestioned; but he was nevertheless Kiyokawa's equal in his reverence for the emperor and resentment of the foreign intruders. Around the same time that Yamaoka received orders from the Bakufu to oversee the Rōshi Corps, Kiyokawa was selected by Matsudaira as the ideal man to attract other rōnin to enlist. Kiyokawa was pardoned of his crime under the general amnesty. With Kiyokawa as the leading member of the corps, its slogan, "Loyalty and Patriotism," became its byname and synonymous with Imperial Reverence and Expel the Barbarians. Kiyokawa recruited other "loyal and patriotic" men. Soon the ranks swelled to 250, as large as the armies of many of the feudal domains.

The first visit to Kyōto by a shōgun in over two centuries demonstrated Edo's diminishing ability to dominate Japan. It served to fur-

---

* Not to be confused with Matsudaira Katamori, Lord of Aizu and protector of Kyōto.
† Later Yamaoka Tesshū.

ther empower the radical elements at the Imperial Court and to embolden the Loyalists. On February 8, 1863, the third year of Bunkyū, the Rōshi Corps left Edo for Kyōto as an advance guard to the shōgun's entourage.

For the time being, Kiyokawa's corps outwardly obeyed the Bakufu's original purpose of protecting the shōgun. They gathered at Denzūin Temple in Edo, the starting point of their three-hundred-mile overland trek. Two weeks later, nine days ahead of the shōgun, they crossed the wooden Sanjō Bridge over the Kamogawa River, which flowed through the eastern side of Kyōto. Few of these warriors from the east had ever laid eyes on the ancient Imperial Capital in the west. It was the height of spring.* The cherries were in full bloom in the green hills in the east of the city. The fallen blossoms covered the lowlands of the town like so much pink and white gossamer. In the distance, on the opposite side of the city, the corpsmen saw the five-tiered pagoda of Tōji Temple, a black monolith rising above the land in the southwest.

Telltale of these troubled times, on the night before the corps reached Kyōto, the heads of three wooden statues at a local Buddhist temple had been severed and displayed along the riverbank. These were images of three shōgun of the Ashikaga regime,† whose tenuous rule of Japan spanned fifteen generations. This symbolic act of Heaven's Revenge was committed only days before Iémochi's arrival at Kyōto, as a direct threat to the Tokugawa Bakufu.

The Rōshi Corps stopped in the western outskirts of the city, north of Tōji and two miles west of the Kamogawa. They set up headquarters at Shintokuji Temple in the village of Mibu, a rural area surrounded by farmland. They lodged at Shintokuji and other nearby temples and private homes. Most of the rōshi were destitute and shabbily dressed. Some did not display their family crests on their clothes, but instead wore striped cotton peasant jackets. But for the two swords at their left hip, they would not have been recognizable as samurai. The local townspeople, wary of the motley corps, as-

---

* The Rōshi Corps arrived in Kyōto on February 23 on the Chinese calendar, April 10 on the Gregorian calendar.
† The Ashikaga Bakufu ruled from 1338 to 1573.

signed to them the unflattering epithet "Mibu Rōshi." When some among the corps extorted money from wealthy merchants and otherwise intimidated or violated the local people, the more derogatory "Mibu Wolves" was applied.

No sooner had they arrived at Mibu than Kiyokawa assembled all 250 men into the cramped confines of the main building at their temple headquarters. The men seated themselves on the tatami-covered floor before the Buddhist altar, swords placed at their sides. Kiyokawa stood at the altar facing the assembly. Suddenly and in no uncertain terms he declared, eyes flashing, that men of high purpose must place their true loyalty with the emperor and not with the Tokugawa. The corps had been recruited for their loyalty and patriotism, he reminded them. Their actual purpose for coming to Kyōto had not been to protect the shōgun, but rather to help Iémochi fulfill his promise to expel the foreigners. Kiyokawa now presented his men with a letter addressed to the Imperial Court, expressing these views and offering up the "loyal and patriotic" corps as an army of Sonnō-Jōi. Every man signed the letter, because they did not have the will to oppose their self-imposed leader.

On the following day Kiyokawa submitted the letter to the court. It was well received by the radicals surrounding the emperor. The Tokugawa authorities were disturbed, to say the least. There were some among them who proposed assassinating Kiyokawa. But the possibility of repercussions among the court, renegade Loyalists, and even the Rōshi Corps persuaded the authorities to consider a less dangerous solution to the problem.

A less dangerous solution availed itself in connection with recent developments in Edo. During the previous August, a British subject had been cut down in cold blood by samurai of the Satsuma clan. The murdered man and three of his countrymen had unintentionally interrupted the entourage of the Lord of Satsuma as it passed through the small village of Namamugi near Edo.*

---

* For a detailed account of the Namamugi Incident, also known as the Richardson Affair, see *Samurai Tales*.

The British demanded reparations from Edo. The British fleet was now at Yokohama to await the outcome of talks between the two governments. Should the talks collapse, the British threatened to attack.

Kiyokawa proposed that his Rōshi Corps be allowed to return immediately to Edo to help expel the foreigners. The Tokugawa authorities accepted the proposal, but with an ulterior motive. The shōgun had been intentionally vague in his promise of Jōi. He would not be bound by an imperial edict that he knew he could not obey. But the Edo regime was no stranger to deceit. The Bakufu arranged for an order to be issued by an imperial advisor for the corps to return to Edo under the pretext that, in case of war, they would finally have their chance to fight the foreigners. But the true motive of the Tokugawa authorities was, of course, to rein in Kiyokawa and his followers before they could do any serious damage.

The imperial order notwithstanding, a small number of the corps defected and remained in Kyōto. Thirteen of these defectors, most of whom hailed from either Mito Han or the province of Musashi near Edo, bore a special loyalty to the shōgun. They had come to Kyōto under orders from the Bakufu, for the dual purpose of guarding the shōgun and expelling the foreigners. They would not obey an order to retreat issued by an imperial advisor who was swayed by a self-professed enemy of the Tokugawa. Rather, they resolved to quit the Rōshi Corps in order to achieve their "loyal and patriotic" objective under the authority of the shōgun. The thirteen defectors petitioned the protector of Kyōto for official permission to remain in the Imperial Capital to "guard the shōgun until he returns to Edo." Their petition was readily accepted. These thirteen comprised the original membership of the dreaded Shinsengumi.

Kiyokawa Hachirō did not abandon his dissentious designs. Soon after returning to Edo he devised a plot to attack the foreign settlement at Yokohama. He recruited five hundred men to participate in the uprising, including Yamaoka Tetsutarō, who had returned with him. They intended to burn the town, and in the ensuing chaos slaughter as many foreigners as possible. They would set fire to the foreign ships that lay in port, plunder the coffers at the foreign government offices, march some ninety miles west of Edo to the domain of Kōfu, and capture that castle as a military base from which to finally wage war against the foreigners. When the Bakufu received word of the plot, the order for Kiyokawa's assassination was issued.

One morning in mid-April, two days before the planned uprising, Kiyokawa brushed off admonishments by friends that his life was in danger. He had an important appointment to keep at the home of a friend whom he intended to recruit for the Yokohama attack. But this friend turned out to be a traitor who had informed the Bakufu of the plan. The traitor made sure that Kiyokawa was treated to a generous amount of saké. When his intoxicated guest stood up to leave in the late afternoon, the host insisted on accompanying him along the way, citing the danger to his life.

Kiyokawa was ambushed shortly afterward by six swordsmen of the Tokugawa camp. He screamed, perhaps the name of one of his assailants, Sasaki Tadasaburō, whom he recognized as a fencing instructor at the Bakufu's Military Academy.* Before Kiyokawa could draw his sword, he was cut from behind. Blood sprayed from his body as he collapsed on the street.

With Kiyokawa's death, the planned attack on Yokohama was foiled. When word of the assassination reached a fellow conspirator, he became worried. Kiyokawa had been carrying a list of the five hundred men involved in the plot. If this list were to fall into the hands of the Edo authorities, all five hundred would be implicated, including the fellow conspirator. He rushed to the scene of the assassination. He found the body of his friend sprawled on the cruel ground. The swords were still in their scabbards. The body was dressed in wide trousers of gray stripes, and a black coat lined with silk. On the right side of the corpse was the severed head, the black hair still tied in a topknot. Nearby was a military helmet made of black lacquered cypress. The backside of the body was sliced open horizontally. A deep gash on the left shoulder was visible, and the right side was cut open cleanly to the nape of the neck. The right arm

---

* Sasaki's name would live in infamy, not as an assassin of Kiyokawa Hachirō, but as one of the alleged murderers of Sakamoto Ryōma.

extended outward. Next to the right hand was an iron-ribbed fan, as if Kiyokawa had been holding it when attacked.

The fellow conspirator immediately searched through the pockets. To his great relief, he found the list. Wary of being discovered, he was eager to vacate the scene. But he felt obligated to at least give the head a proper burial. He removed the black coat. He wrapped the head in the coat, and carried the grim package to Yamaoka's house. Yamaoka preserved the head in sugar. He hid it in the closet, but after a few days the stench became unbearable. Soon a local police officer cast a suspicious eye. To avoid detection, Yamaoka hid the head in a garbage bin, but the stench remained. When he attempted to grasp the head by the hair to remove it from the bin, the strands came out and he lost his grip. But he managed to bring the head to the adjacent training hall, where he removed one of the wooden planks and buried it under the floor. Now the smell permeated the training hall, so that he was compelled to bury it beneath a large silverberry tree behind his house. Yamaoka eventually secured a gravesite at nearby Denzūin Temple, from where Kiyokawa Hachirō and his "loyal and patriotic" corps had set out for Kyōto two months earlier.

Newly Selected Corps

Shinsengumi—literally Newly Selected Corps. Certainly the thirteen men who comprised the original membership were select. Under the supervision of the protector of Kyōto, the men of the Shinsengumi were commissioned to patrol the city day and night. They were not yet officially empowered with the authority to kill. But they shared a tacit understanding with their master that, added to their original purposes of expelling the barbarians and protecting the shōgun, was their more immediate task of restoring law and order by destroying the enemies of the Tokugawa.

The Shinsengumi was led by two extraordinarily strong-willed men. Kondō Isami and Serizawa Kamo were bitter rivals. Both had been chief instructors of their respective fencing schools, and both had brought with them into the corps their top swordsmen. Kondō Isami, born October 9, 1834, was the third and youngest son of a wealthy peasant family from the village of Kami'ishihara in the Tama region of the province of Musashi, a partial day's journey westward from Edo along the Kōshū-kaidō Road. Cutting wide and deep through this fertile farm region of gentle hills flowed the Tamagawa River, a constant source of inner strength to the young men whose martial spirit flourished along its banks. Rising high above the mountains to the southwest of Tama was the ever-looming, sometimes snow-covered, always enigmatic conical symbol of Japan, Fujisan, chameleonic with the changing seasons.

Shinsengumi Commander Kondō Isami was a peasant by birth, a warrior by nature. He was a man of traditional values and a martial mind-set, whose black training robe was embroidered in white on the back with the image of a large human skull—a symbol of his resolve to die in battle whenever he entered the dōjō. He had enlisted in the Rōshi Corps with aspirations of becoming a samurai in the service of the shōgun. As leader of the shōgun's most dreaded samurai corps, he secured a vehicle into the top strata of the Tokugawa hierarchy and indeed historic immortality.

While the entire face radiates raw power, the stern, penetrating eyes, complemented by the firm mouth and square, heavy jaw, are most striking. In his photograph, probably taken in February 1868, the then sole-surviving commander of the Shinsengumi is seated in the formal position, hands placed lightly on his thighs, prepared for battle at a moment's warning. Behind him, within arm's reach, is his long, lethal sword; and one wonders how many men he had cut down with its razor-sharp blade.

Kondō Isami's name at birth was Miyagawa Katsugorō. He was a child of Tenpō—the era of Heaven's Protection (1830–43)—certainly a misnomer, at least for the rural villages of eastern Japan, which were terrorized by marauding swordsmen during those years. The Tama region was a domain of the Tokugawa. The local people prided themselves as farmers of the shōgun. While peasants were generally forbidden by law to bear arms, the people of Tama were inclined toward the martial and literary arts. Their martial traditions dated back to the twelfth century, from the samurai who had served the military regime at Kamakura.* After the arrival of the foreigners in 1853, the martial arts again flourished in Tama.

Tama was an expansive region. The Tokugawa magistrates in charge of policing Tama did not have the resources to patrol the entire area, or to protect it against the marauding swordsmen. Village leaders were appointed by the magistrates to police their respective

---

* The Kamakura Bakufu ruled from 1192 to 1333.

villages. The peasants working under the village leaders were required to study martial arts—partly to protect themselves against the marauders. Some of the wealthy peasants built training halls at their homes and hired local fencing masters to instruct them. Among these wealthy peasants was Katsugorō's father, Miyagawa Hisajirō.

Katsugorō's mother died while he was a young boy. His father was an avid reader of history. On rainy days Katsugorō's father would call his three sons to the family hearth, where he would read to them chronicles of heroic deeds. From an early age the future Shinsengumi commander was taught an appreciation of literature and martial arts and participated in the training sessions at his family's home dojō. When Katsugorō was fourteen, his father hired a local fencing instructor to teach his three sons. The instructor's name was Kondō Shūsuké. He was the master of the Shieikan, a minor fencing school in Edo. Master Shūsuké taught the Tennen Rishin style. Katsugorō proved himself naturally inclined toward rigorous kenjutsu training. In the following year he was awarded *mokuroku*, the second of five ranks in the Tennen Rishin style.* Master Shūsuké was impressed with the boy's ferocity, both on and off the practice floor. One night when their father was away on business, Katsugorō and his two brothers were awoken by the sound of robbers breaking into their house. Far from being frightened, the brothers saw this as a perfect chance to test the fencing techniques they had studied. The robbers were armed with knives. The brothers pursued them with drawn swords. The robbers attempted to flee with stolen property in their arms. Katsugorō yelled the word "stop!" with an ear-piercing guttural wail such as he had learned from his master. The robbers threw down their booty and fled for their lives.

Kondō Shūsuké was getting along in years. Perhaps it was Katsugorō's innate courage that now convinced the master to petition Miyagawa Hisajirō for permission to adopt his fifteen-year-old son as

---

* Rank in the Tennen Rishin style was awarded students in the following order of graduating proficiency: *kirikami*, mokuroku, *chūgokui mokuroku*, *menkyo* (a license to serve as assistant instructor) and *shinan menkyo* (a license to open a dōjō and teach one's own students). It normally took a student five years of dedicated and rigorous training to attain the rank of menkyo.

his heir. Permission was presently granted, and soon it was determined that Katsugorō would become the fourth generational head of
the Tennen Rishin style. The peasant's son now became a samurai.
He left his native village to live in Edo at the home of his fencing master, where he continued to devote himself to the study of kenjutsu.

Kondō was married in his twenty-sixth year. Otsuné was three
years younger than he was. Unlike her husband, she had been born
into the warrior class. Her father was a retainer of the Shimizu family, a Tokugawa Branch House. Otsuné was homely and apparently
had a harelip. But she was wellborn, well-bred, well-educated, and,
perhaps most important, endowed with measures of propriety and
pluck more prevalent in the daughter of a samurai than in a woman
of the common classes. The sword master's heir had encountered
many other prospective brides, each more physically attractive than
Otsuné. When asked why he had chosen Otsuné for his wife, he is
said to have replied, "I had interviews with beautiful women. They
were conceited about their good looks. But Otsuné was much more
humble in her manner and very polite." Perhaps this is indicative of
a certain humanity in the future Shinsengumi commander, and certainly it had something to do with his immovable determination to
adhere to the stoic mores of his adopted social class. They were married at the end of March
1860, as the capital reeled
from the shock of Regent Ii
Naosuké's assassination.
Soon after their marriage,
Otsuné embroidered the
likeness of a skull on the
back of Kondō's training
robe—a token of her appreciation for her warrior-hus-
band's resolve to die.

*Kondō Isami's black training robe
(original; courtesy of Masataka Kojima)*

In the following year the
sword master's heir was
awarded shinan menkyo, the
highest rank in the Tennen

Rishin style. Kondō Shūsuké now retired, and his adopted son became the fourth master of that style. The Shieikan flourished under the young master. The names on the student roster exceeded three hundred, mostly men of peasant households in Tama. The young master traveled around the region to teach at local training halls. He was a large, muscular man. His feet were so big that the maid employed at the home of a friend was "stunned by the unusually large size of his wooden clogs," which he removed before entering the house. So large was his mouth that he could fit his entire fist inside— an antic that drew hysterical laughter at drinking bouts during the bloody and tumultuous years he ruled the dangerous streets of the Imperial Capital. It was also around his twenty-seventh year that the peasant-turned-swordmaster changed his name to Kondō Isami*— an appellation that would arouse feelings of derision, fear, and hate among his enemies; pride and love among the good people of his native Tama; gratitude and hope among the embattled powers that were in Edo; and awed respect among them all.

Kondō practiced the Tennen Rishin style for more than fourteen years. When the opportunity was presented him at age twenty- nine to put his sword to practical use, it was with his great courage, a burning desire to "vent [his] long-held indignation" toward the foreign intruders, and a determination to make a name for himself as a samurai in the service of the shōgun that he closed the doors of the Shieikan and, with seven of his top swordsmen, enlisted in the Rōshi Corps.

The Shinsengumi originally had three commanders. Ranking beside Kondō and Serizawa was a close ally of the latter named Shinmi Nishiki. But Shinmi was a nominal rather than actual commander. Exceedingly more important to this historical narrative, and to the history of Japan, was Hijikata Toshizō, one of two vice commanders of the Shinsengumi, whose warrior's nature earned him the epithet "Demon Commander." Hijikata was Kondō's closest friend and confidant. Like Kondō, he was also the youngest son of a wealthy Tama

---

* *Isami* is written with one Chinese character, which, quite appropriately, means "courage."

peasant. He was a handsome man just over five feet seven inches tall.*
He had a light complexion and almost classical features, which made
him stand out among his countrymen. His photograph, taken after
the fall of the Bakufu, at the end of 1868, shows Vice Commander of
the Army Hijikata Toshizō seated on a wooden chair in Western-style
clothing with knee-high military boots and a sword at his left side.
The cropped black hair, no longer in a topknot, is combed straight
back. Most striking are the eyes, betraying an unyielding yet calm
resolve to die—almost a longing for death—which he would bring
with him to his last battle.

Hijikata was one year younger than Kondō. Having lost both parents by the time he was five years old, Hijikata was raised by his elder
brother and sister-in-law at his family's home in Ishida Village, beneath the shadow of the ancient and solemn Takahata Fudō Temple.
At eleven he was briefly apprenticed at the giant mercantile enterprise
Matsuzaka'ya in Edo. Upon returning to his native countryside, the
boy divided his time between his family's home and the nearby residence of his elder sister and her husband at Hino, a post town along
the Kōshū-kaidō. When Hijikata was sixteen, he planted arrow bamboo behind his house and vowed to himself, as preposterously as
prophetically, "to become a samurai." Arrow bamboo consists of
short, straight shafts no thicker than a person's finger—ideal for making arrows. Planting arrow bamboo was considered an act of discretion—preparation for war becoming of a samurai. Similarly
samurai-like were the manly arts of calligraphy and poetry (both
Chinese and Japanese), which Hijikata pursued with a passion. He
was particularly fond of haiku. Under the pen name Hōgyoku, he left
behind in Hino a collection of haiku before setting out for Kyōto.

Hijikata's brother-in-law, Satō Hikogorō, earned menkyo rank
under Kondō Shūsuké, entitling him to teach the Tennen Rishin style.
Before that, Satō had inherited from his father an expansive and gated
country estate and a lofty position as official leader of Hino Village.
Although he belonged to the peasant class, Satō would be more aptly
called a country squire than a farmer. Shortly before Hijikata's pro-

---

* This was taller than average during mid-nineteenth-century Japan.

phetic vow, Satō had built a kenjutsu dōjō at his home, where Master Shūsuké and his heir occasionally taught. In addition to Satō, Kondō and Hijikata also maintained close relations with another member of the local squirearchy who shared their passion for kenjutsu. This was Kojima Shikanosuké, the leader of Onoji Village. Satō was six years older than Kondō; Kojima was three years Kondō's senior. The two older men tutored their fencing master in literature, while Kondō taught kenjutsu at the private dōjō of Satō and in the front garden of the Kojima estate.

Master Shūsuké and son were beholden to their wealthy students. Kojima and Satō provided an important source of financial support to the humble Kondō household. The two village leaders continued this support after Kondō and Hijikata enlisted in the Rōshi Corps. In their fencing master's absence, Satō taught the Tennen Rishin style at Hino, while Kojima performed this duty at Onoji. Both men sent provisions, including much-needed armor, to Kondō and Hijikata during the bloody years in Kyōto, and during the New Year holidays Kojima collected money from local kenjutsu students to send to their master in the west.

Satō's private training hall proved a propitious venue to this history. It was at the Hino Dōjō that the future vice commander of the Shinsengumi honed his genius with an unsheathed sword in hand and where he befriended Kondō Isami. "He [Hijikata] was graceful in appearance and contemplative by nature, which compensated for the straightforwardness of Kondō," wrote Michio Hirao,* to explain why the two men were "as close to one another as brothers." To support himself while practicing kenjutsu, Hijikata traveled through the local countryside peddling a special herbal medicine produced by his family. This medicine healed a variety of ailments, including contusions

---

* Meiji Restoration historian Michio Hirao's groundbreaking *Shinsengumi Shiroku* (literally, *Historical Record of the Shinsengumi*) was first published in 1928, under the original title *Shinsengumishi* (literally, *History of the Shinsengumi*). Hirao was first and foremost an historian, more widely known for his writings about Sakamoto Ryōma than about the Shinsengumi. Shortly before completing the Shinsengumi manuscript, in 1928 Hirao interviewed Kondō Isami's heir, Kondō Yūgorō (seventy-six years old at the time), at the latter's home at Kami'ishihara, in the Tama region of Tōkyō. Others interviewed by Hirao include members of the Miyagawa family.

such as those left by a hard wooden practice sword. So great was Hijikata's passion for fencing that, along with his black wicker medicine chest, he always carried his fencing equipment, "stopping along the way," wrote Kan Shimosawa, "at any dōjō of merit to politely request instruction. But back then he had a gentle face like a woman's. Although in the future his attitude would become self-important, since he was still cleverly charming, everyone treated him with kindness."*

"He had the slight air of a merchant," recalled a fellow swordsman who occasionally practiced at the Shieikan. "He had drooping shoulders but was tall and slender, and one of the best-looking men of the bunch [at the Shieikan]. He was shrewd in his dealings with people, and what's more he was a clever man. He tended to be a little disagreeable, and … there were quite a few people whom he disliked. When sitting opposite someone, he would first of all look that person over slowly, from his knees up to his face. Then he would quietly begin speaking."

Hijikata Toshizō did not officially enroll at Kondō's dōjō until the spring of 1859, a number of years after the two had met. At the Shieikan, Hijikata wore his face guard tied with a pretty red cord, earning the quiet ridicule of certain of his fellow swordsmen—and the coveted menkyo rank. Several years later, people in Hijikata's native village could hardly believe reports of the bloodletting in Kyōto at the hands of the vice commander of the Shinsengumi, because "he was such a gentle person." But as Shimosawa aptly points out, "Toshizō was a different man with a drawn sword in hand." Once when Hijikata returned home on a brief interlude from his duties in Kyōto, he

---

* Kan Shimosawa's *Shinsengumi Shimatsuki* (literally, *Narrative of the Shinsengumi*) has long been considered the definitive history of the Shinsengumi. Published in 1928 just before Hirao's book, Shimosawa's narrative is partially based on interviews with former corpsmen and other people who had direct contact with the Shinsengumi. Shimosawa, however, was primarily a novelist. He began the preface of his book by stating, "It is not my intention to write history." Some of his information has been repudiated by more recent studies, whose authors have enjoyed the benefit of over three-quarters of a century of subsequent scholarship unavailable to Shimosawa. Accordingly, like other early historical narratives of the Shinsengumi, Shimosawa's work is best taken for what it's worth, and relished for its portrayal of the spirit of the men of Shinsengumi rather than as a faithful history. Nevertheless, as certain of his descriptions capture the essence of this spirit, I feel that they demand an English rendering in this narrative.

reportedly told a gathering of family and friends that the steel blade of one of his swords had rotted from overexposure to human blood.

Kondō Isami and Hijikata Toshizō left their homes in the east driven by an unyielding will to power. They saw the great turmoil in the west as a once-in-a-lifetime opportunity to put their formidable fencing skills to the fight, to rise through the ranks of the Tokugawa hierarchy. That these sons of peasants could even dream of such accomplishments, unprecedented during Tokugawa history, was certainly due to their extraordinary sense of self-importance.

Accompanying them were six particularly skilled swordsmen, each of whom would be among the original Shinsengumi members. Child prodigy Okita Sōji was the eldest son of a samurai of Shirakawa Han, whose daimyō was a direct retainer of the shōgun. According to Okita family records, Okita was born at the Shirakawa residence in Edo in 1844. Having lost both parents as a young boy, at nine he was apprenticed at the Shieikan, where he grew up looking to Kondō Isami as an elder brother. At twelve, Okita was matched against the fencing instructor of the Lord of Shirakawa, and was victorious. By age fifteen, he was serving as assistant instructor of the Shieikan, teaching at the main dōjō in Edo and at villages around the local countryside. There were some who claimed that not even Kondō could beat Okita in a match. Naturally Okita received menkyo rank. When Kondō Isami became master of the Shieikan, Okita was appointed as head of the dōjō.

Nagakura Shinpachi idolized Kondō Isami, who was five years his senior. He was a rōnin of Matsumae Han, whose daimyō was an outside lord. Nagakura was born at the Matsumae residence in Edo in 1839, the only son of a well-situated samurai of that clan. The Nagakura family was related by marriage to the Lord of Matsumae. For generations the family patriarch had been permanently stationed in Edo as a liaison officer for the Matsumae domain, located on the island of Ezo in the far north. Nagakura began his kenjutsu career as a young boy. He originally studied under his father's instructor, an acclaimed master of the Shintō Munen style. As one of the master's top students, he achieved the level of mokuroku at the young age of seventeen. In his early twenties he put his fencing skills to the test, touring schools of other styles in the vicinity of the capital. After returning to Edo, he served as assistant instructor to a master of the prestigious Hokushin Ittō style. It was around this time that he began frequenting Kondō Isami's dōjō. Although he never became an official member of the Shieikan, according to Nagakura's oral recollections, it was he who urged Kondō and the others to enlist in the Rōshi Corps.

Yamanami Keisuké, one year older than Kondō Isami, was born in 1833. He was the second son of the chief fencing instructor of Sendai Han in northern Japan, also ruled by an outside lord. When Yamanami came to the Shieikan, he held menkyo rank in the Hokushin Ittō style. He challenged the sword master's heir to a match. After Kondō defeated him, Yamanami joined the Shieikan as one of its most skilled swordsmen. He subsequently served with Hijikata and Okita as assistant instructor.

Inoué Genzaburō was born in Hino in 1829, the fourth son of a Tokugawa samurai. He was the eldest of the eight Shieikan swordsmen who enlisted in the Rōshi Corps. Genzaburō's father, who served the shōgun as a petty police official, encouraged his sons to practice the martial arts. Genzaburō began practicing at the dōjō of Satō Hikogorō at a young age. Both he and his older brother, Matsugorō, received menkyo rank from Kondō Shūsuké.

Tōdō Heisuké was born in 1844. He claimed to be the illegitimate son of the outside Lord of Tsu Han, whose family name was Tōdō. The obscurity of his background notwithstanding, it is certain that Tōdō Heisuké was a rōnin when he earned mokuroku rank in the Hokushin Ittō style at the famed Chiba Dōjō. He was subsequently apprenticed at the Shieikan. Tōdō was the same age as Okita Sōji, just nineteen, when he enlisted in the Rōshi Corps.

Harada Sanosuké was born in Matsuyama Han in 1840. The Matsuyama daimyō ranked among the twenty Related Houses. His domain was located in the province of Iyo on Shikoku, the smallest of the four main Japanese islands. When Harada began frequenting Kondō's dōjō, he brought with him his expertise in *yarijutsu*, the art of the spear. A failed attempt to commit suicide by his own sword left him with a scar on his abdomen—a single horizontal line. He adopted the mark as part of his family crest—a single horizontal line in a circle.

A seventh Shinsengumi corpsman with a particularly close connection to the Shieikan was Saitō Hajimé. The same age as Okita and Tōdō, Saitō, unusually tall at five feet eleven inches, shared with these two men the distinction of being the youngest of Kondō's group and among its most gifted swordsmen. Saitō was born and raised in Edo as the son of a retainer of the Matsudaira of Akashi Han, also a Related House. Saitō had neither enlisted in Kiyokawa's Rōshi Corps nor traveled to Kyōto with the others. He had reportedly killed a samurai of the shōgun's camp in Edo shortly before fleeing to Kyōto and joining his friends.

Serizawa Kamo was born in the first year of Tenpō—1830—four years before his rival Kondō Isami. He was the pampered youngest son of a wealthy, low-ranking samurai family of Mito Han. An expert swordsman of the Shintō Munen style, he stood tall and erect—an excessively proud man, well built and endowed with extraordinary physical strength. As if to flaunt his strength, he carried a heavy iron-ribbed fan, with which he threatened to pummel men who got in his way. Engraved on his weapon-fan were eight Chinese characters which read, "Serizawa Kamo, loyal and patriotic samurai."

The "loyal and patriotic samurai" was a handsome man, with a light complexion and small dark eyes that penetrated the defenses of his many adversaries. He was as gallant as he was brutal, as courageous as cruel. He was a reckless man of fine breeding, a pathological drinker who, when in his cups, was known to draw his sword upon the slightest provocation. Before joining the Rōshi Corps, he had served as a captain in the rabidly xenophobic and pro-imperial Tengu Party in Mito Han, the birthplace of Sonnō-Jōi. Serizawa was in command of some three hundred men of the Tengu Party. It was rumored that he had punished several wrongdoers among them by severing their fingers, hands, noses, or ears. He was eventually imprisoned and sentenced to death in Edo for the cold-blooded murder of three subordinates who had aroused his ire over some petty offense. In jail he refused food. The leaden winter sky, barely visible through the small window of his cold, dank cell, recalled to him the snowy landscape outside. He likened his lot to that of the snow-laden plum blossom. He bit open his small finger, and with the blood composed his intended death poem.

Amidst the desolation of snow and frost,
the plum is the first to bloom in brilliant color.
The blossoms keep their fragrance,
even after they have scattered.

Before his execution could be carried out, he was released in the general amnesty proclaimed by the Bakufu to recruit men for the Rōshi Corps. Now, in the spring of 1863, he was in command of not a rebel group but a legitimate corps of swordsmen in the service of the shōgun.

Serizawa's notoriety preceded him to the Imperial Capital. When the Rōshi Corps reached Kyōto in February, it is said that the townspeople shook with fear of the "demon Serizawa." A dominating personality with a voracious sexual appetite, the "demon" was reputed to have his way with other men's wives. In his youth he had reportedly raped and impregnated three maids at his family's home. As commander of the Shinsengumi, it was his duty to protect the Imperial Court. But this did not deter him from making advances upon the lover of Anénokoji Kintomo, a court noble and leader of the Sonnō-Jōi faction surrounding the emperor. When the matter was brought to the attention of the protector of Kyōto, he ordered Serizawa, in no uncertain terms, to cease his transgressions among the court nobles.

Serizawa had allegedly raped the wife of a wealthy merchant in his native Mito. The wife was subsequently enraptured and begged Serizawa to keep her with him. It has been suggested that Serizawa's pathological behavior was a result of syphilis, and that he had contracted the dread disease from this woman, a former geisha. Perhaps it was a combination of the disease and his anger at having been infected that incited a fit of violence toward the woman, during which he cut her body in two and hurled it into a nearby river.

"Officer Serizawa Kamo's egoism along the way [to Kyōto from

Edo] defied description," wrote Shimosawa. While Kondō and Hijikata had joined the Rōshi Corps as mere rank and filers, Serizawa, a
samurai by birth, demanded special treatment from the start. He had
been recruited as one of twenty-three officers overseeing the corps.
Meanwhile, Kondō had been assigned the indecorous duty of traveling just ahead of the others to arrange lodgings for the officers and
men at stations along the way. On one occasion he forgot to procure
a room for Serizawa, for which he apologized profusely. But Serizawa
did not take the offense lightly, nor did he accept the apology. He
nevertheless assured his fellow officers, in a tone of irony laden with
malcontent, that he would make do without lodgings for the night.
He would light a fire to keep himself warm, he told them. "But," he
added glibly, "don't be too surprised if the fire is a trifle large." He
gathered firewood and stacked it near the center of the town, where
he lit a huge bonfire after the sun went down. The flames rose high
into the night sky, raining sparks upon the surrounding wooden
buildings. People bearing buckets of water climbed to the rooftops
to put out the fire, but the burning resentment that engulfed Serizawa's soul would not so easily be extinguished.

At Kyōto, Serizawa gloried in his newfound power. When it was
rumored that a tiger at a local circus was actually a man dressed in a
tiger skin, Serizawa thought he would expose the imposter. The
swordsman proceeded to the building where the tiger was kept. He
swaggered directly up to the cage, drew his short sword, and thrust
the blade between the bars. As the crowd around him held their
breath, the supposed imposter released an earsplitting roar, glaring
sharply into the dark eyes of the Shinsengumi commander. Serizawa
now resheathed his sword and with a sardonic smile announced, "It's
a real tiger."

* * * * *

The corps split into two factions, rallying around Serizawa and
Kondō, respectively. Of the thirteen original members, eight belonged to Kondō's faction, the others to Serizawa's. They recruited
more men. Soon their membership exceeded one hundred. The lead-

ers initiated a system of command to facilitate control over the rank and file. Beneath Commanders Serizawa Kamo and Kondō Isami, nominal Commander Shinmi Nishiki, and Vice Commanders Hijikata Toshizō and Yamanami Keisuké were fourteen assistant vice commanders. These included Okita Sōji, Nagakura Shinpachi, Harada Sanosuké, Tōdō Heisuké, Saitō Hajimé, and a new recruit named Yamazaki Susumu. (Yamazaki, a rōnin from Ōsaka, was an expert with a hard wooden staff.) These six assistants, with Hijikata and Yamanami, formed a tight-knit group around Commander Kondō. Other assistant vice commanders included Hirayama Gorō and Hirama Jūsuké, both loyal to Commander Serizawa. Beneath these officers were three "observers," including the giant Shimada Kai. Shimada was a rōnin from the pro-Tokugawa Ōgaki Han in the province of Mino. He had practiced the Shinkeitō style of kenjutsu at Edo, where he befriended Nagakura. At 330 pounds and nearly six feet tall, Shimada was by far the largest man in the Shinsengumi.

Most of the officers lived at the Yagi residence, one of numerous houses along the narrow roads and byways of Mibu Village. The master of the Yagi residence, Yagi Gennojō, a petty samurai, was the tenth generational patriarch of his family and a leader of Mibu Village. The imposing black-tiled roofs of the dark wooden front gate and two-storied main house, the quaint latticed windows, the sliding doors of the wide entranceway, the interior tatami-matted rooms overlooking the rear garden through a long wooden corridor—this house, and these rooms and this garden, so immaculately and meticulously kept, were now occupied by the leaders of the most notorious band of killers in Japanese history. Across the narrow street was the single-storied house of the Maekawa family, where the corps set up headquarters. Both houses, scenes of bloodshed to come, would serve the Shinsengumi well.

From his Mibu headquarters, Kondō Isami wrote letters to Satō and Kojima in Tama, requesting them to forward training equipment, for himself and the other men from the Shieikan. Both Kondō and Hijikata expected to see bloodshed soon. In separate letters they asked their friends to send along shirts of chain mail, in preparation for battle.

A uniform was adopted—a flashy light blue linen jacket with pointed white stripes at the base of the sleeves. The corps took as their symbol the Chinese character for "sincerity"—for their loyalty to the Tokugawa. Pronounced *makoto*, the Shinsengumi symbol was emblazoned on the corps' banner, white against a red background. According to Shimosawa, the banner was approximately five feet long, nearly four feet wide. The corpsmen carried their distinguishing banner and wore their distinguishing uniforms on their daily patrols of the city. They questioned or arrested wayward rōnin, vagrants, and otherwise suspicious men in and around the Imperial Capital. Their fearsome spectacle on the streets of Kyōto became an everyday phenomenon. According to the reminiscences of a ranking retainer of the Lord of Aizu, "the men of the Shinsengumi tied their topknots into great clumps of hair. When they walked against the wind the bushy ends would flare out wider, evoking an even more imposing spectacle." Before long there were few, if any, in Kyōto, the nearby mercantile center of Ōsaka, or the surrounding areas who did not readily recognize them as the Tokugawa's select and terrible band of swordsmen.

* * * * *

There had always been rōnin throughout the Tokugawa era. Formerly rōnin were men of the samurai class who had, for one reason or another, intentionally or not, become separated from liege lord and clan. In short, they were "lordless samurai." But the rōnin of the turbulent final years of Tokugawa rule—the biggest turning point in Japanese history—were a different breed altogether. They were far greater in number than their predecessors. And they did not necessarily derive from the samurai class. Many came from peasant households. Kondō Isami and Hijikata Toshizō are two of history's most celebrated examples of peasants-turned-rōnin. The great majority of these latter-day rōnin, however, hailed from the lowest samurai ranks of their respective clans—most notably Mito in the east, Chōshū and Tosa in the west, and Satsuma and Kumamoto in the south. During an age when the entire nation faced unprecedented dangerous straits, most of these lower samurai were prohibited from participating in government or even voicing their opinions in official matters. Depending on their han, they were nominal samurai—permitted to wear the two swords and take family crests and names, but otherwise treated as commoners. Serizawa Kamo is a famous example of a nominal samurai who became a rōnin. Another is Sakamoto Ryōma, who came from a wealthy merchant-samurai family in Tosa.* These rōnin, in essence, quit the service of their daimyō, forfeiting the financial security and physical protection provided by their feudal lords for the freedom to participate in the dangerous national movement, often at the cost of their own lives. Like the leaders of the Rōshi Corps, most, if not all, of them were ardent xenophobes, raring to fight the foreigners.

The rōnin phenomenon of this era has been likened to a movement for social equality in a suppressive society. Many rōnin had been motivated more by a desire to wear the two swords and *look like samurai* than by lofty political aspirations. They fulfilled this desire by becoming rōnin under the false pretext of "loyalty."

* * * * *

As swordsmen, Kondō Isami and Hijikata Toshizō were perhaps technically inferior to certain of their subordinates in the corps— most notably the fencing genius Okita Sōji. But what they lacked in technical finesse they compensated for with strength of mind, courage, and an unyielding will to power. Their will to power, certainly their most formidable weapon, would time and again prove indomitable on the bloody streets of Kyōto.

For all its worth, however, when the will to power is combined with the germ of self-importance—the conviction that one is of greater worth than his fellow human beings—it tends to transform into the stuff of tragedy, often lethal to the host. Although not a pathogen in the biological sense, self-importance is a germ nonetheless; throughout the history of mankind it has been commonly carried by unscrupulous men, more often than not possessed of an

---

* See Appendix I (3).

unyielding will to power. Among them have been dictators, despots, conquerors, gang bosses, mass murderers, cult leaders—tyrants, criminals, and thugs, one and all—with a propensity to kill unrivaled by the mass majority whose unfortunate lot it has been to share with them the same time and space of their brief existence on this earth. What distinguishes Kondō, Hijikata, and certain other of their countrymen, friends and foes alike, and even including scoundrels such as Serizawa, from the unscrupulous club of murderous villains who have been bound neither by national border, historical era, nor social nor ethical mores is the stringent and unwritten Code of the Samurai, *Bushidō*, which they valued above all, including life itself, and by which they faithfully lived and died—although their interpretation of the code occasionally differed. But these men of the sword in the mid-nineteenth century, both the good and the bad, were heir to a rapidly changing society, when the age of the samurai and their noble code were fast declining, only to be replaced by the modern materialism of the encroaching West.

* * * * *

In the spring of the third year of Bunkyū, 1863, the shōgun issued his long-awaited promise to the emperor to expel the foreigners by May 10. In April he traveled from Kyōto to Ōsaka, to board the Tokugawa warship *Jundō Maru*, commanded by Katsu Kaishū. It was Iémochi's purpose to observe Ōsaka Bay from shipboard, with an eye to fortifying the coastal defenses in that vital region, so close to the sacred Imperial Capital. The Shinsengumi proceeded to Ōsaka to guard the shōgun.On May 9, the day before the promised deadline, Tokugawa authorities yielded to the demands of Great Britain for reparations to the victims of the Satsuma samurai at Namamugi. This, of course, gave the radicals at court and their samurai allies a perfect excuse to strike out against the Bakufu. The authorities, in turn, called for the shōgun to return to his capital in the east, not for their falsely expressed purpose of expelling the foreigners there, which was nothing but a ploy to appease the radicals in Kyōto, including the Son of Heaven himself, but to get Iémochi away from the dangerous situation in the west.

On May 10, to demonstrate their perfect loyalty to the emperor, and in preparation for the coming war against the Tokugawa, the Loyalists in Chōshū, that most radical of samurai clans, gathered at Shimonoseki, the southwesternmost point of their domain. The Strait of Shimonoseki separated the island of Kyūshū from the main island of Honshū. Foreign ships passed through this vital strait to travel from Yokohama to Nagasaki and on to Shanghai. On the evening of the tenth, two Chōshū warships fired upon an unsuspecting American merchant vessel in the strait. On the twenty-third of the same month, the Chōshū men shot at a French dispatch boat from their batteries along the Shimonoseki coast. Three days later they opened fire on a Dutch corvette in the same waters. While the Americans and the French had avoided casualties, the Dutch suffered four dead and five severely wounded.

Chōshū had taken it upon itself to enforce the shōgun's xenophobic, and impossible, promise. By so doing, it usurped influence over the Imperial Court at the expense of Satsuma—and as a result further diminished Tokugawa authority in Kyōto. But retaliation was hard and fast. On June 1, an American warship out of Yokohama sank two Chōshū ships at Shimonoseki, damaged a third, and shelled a battery along the coast. Four days later two French warships entered the strait and destroyed several more batteries. To add insult to injury, some 250 French troops landed at Shimonoseki and temporarily occupied two of the remaining batteries. They destroyed more of the Chōshū guns, threw stores of gunpowder into the ocean, and looted swords, armor, helmets, and muskets, before reboarding their ships and departing the same day.

The swift and one-sided retaliation had taught the Chōshū men a hard lesson. Like samurai throughout Japan, they had always been confident that when it came to actual combat, the foreigners would be no match for their superior fighting spirit. This myth had been shattered in just five days by the superior military force of three foreign warships. These champions of Expel the Barbarians had once and for all realized that until they could eliminate the immense technological gap between themselves and the great foreign powers, their slogan was a pipe dream.

Serizawa and Kondō felt certain that they understood the situation in the Imperial Capital better than the authorities three hundred miles away at Edo Castle. On May 25, they petitioned the Bakufu to keep the shōgun in Kyōto. Their purpose was to avoid giving the radicals an excuse to attack the Bakufu as punishment for the shōgun's returning to Edo without fulfilling his promise. But Serizawa and Kondō were mere war dogs of the Bakufu. Consequently, their petition was ignored. In mid-June, the shōgun sailed for Edo aboard the *Jundō Maru*.

It is an irony of history that the Shinsengumi and the Chōshū-led Loyalists shared the same great objective: expelling the foreigners for the sake of the emperor. However, the means by which they would achieve this objective made them bitter enemies. The Shinsengumi intended to fight the foreigners under the military authority of the Tokugawa Shōgun. The Chōshū-led Loyalists meant to destroy the Tokugawa Bakufu as the most dangerous impediment to their objective. After the Edo authorities agreed to pay reparations to Great Britain, Kondō Isami realized that the Bakufu was not yet ready to implement Jōi. Although he intended to eventually return to the east to wage war against the foreigners there, he nevertheless determined that his corps, the avowed protector of the shōgun, must for the time being remain in the turbulent west, even in Iémochi's absence. His corps must suppress the anti-Tokugawa radicals who would use the shōgun's inability to expel the foreigners as an excuse to strike out against him. For Kondō Isami, protecting the Tokugawa Shōgun now took precedence over everything.

The Shinsengumi's mortal enemies basked in imperial grace during the sweltering and frenetic summer of the third year of Bunkyū. In Kyōto, the Chōshū Loyalists enjoyed the support of the extremists surrounding the emperor, led by court noble Sanjō Sanétomi. But Chōshū's glory in Kyōto was as short-lived as its triumph at Shimonoseki had been. In mid-August, Aizu and Satsuma formed a military alliance, tipping the balance of power at the Imperial Court back into the hands of the Tokugawa. On August 18, under the cover of night, heavily armed Satsuma and Aizu troops seized the Nine Forbidden

Gates of the palace, barring entrance by the Chōshū men. Fourteen hundred armed Loyalists, including one thousand rōnin, assembled at Sakaimachi Gate, which thus far had been Chōshū's to guard. The tense scene was described by a chief vassal of the outside Lord of Yonézawa, in a letter to his son:

> The two sides faced each other, their cannon and rifles ready to fire.... Each man wore armor, and I wish you could have seen the imposing spectacle. Chōshū Han showed no fear in the face of [the dangerous situation]. Among their samurai were youths who looked to be around fifteen or sixteen years old. They wore white crepe jackets and white headbands, carried Western rifles in their hands and thought nothing of the huge army confronting them. Rather, they advanced to the front of the line, eager for the enemy to attack.

Their brave determination notwithstanding, the Chōshū warriors were no match for their heavily armed Satsuma and Aizu foes. Betrayed by the Imperial Court, these champions of Imperial Loyalism aimed their guns at the palace. But now they were presented with an imperial order to retreat immediately or be branded an "Imperial Enemy." They had no choice but to obey. Chōshū was banished from Kyōto, along with seven radical court nobles led by Sanjō Sanétomi. Satsuma and Aizu were aided in the fight by men of the Shinsengumi, including Hijikata Toshizō. The Demon Commander's valor was evident in the two enemy sword marks left on the iron head guard he wore at his forehead. He sent this head guard to his brother-in-law, Satō Hikogorō, in Hino. Accompanying the package was a letter, in which Hijikata glibly remarked, "In Kyōto, I have not yet been killed."

The so-called Coup of 8/18 exacerbated the turmoil in the city. Chōshū samurai and their rōnin allies who managed to remain in Kyōto went into hiding. They renewed their vows of Heaven's Revenge, and there were rumors that Chōshū was planning a counter-coup in Kyōto. Panic spread through the general populace and the court. In the aftermath of the coup, the Shinsengumi received official orders from the protector of Kyōto to "patrol the city day and night."

The Shinsengumi did their job well. The extraordinary sense of self-importance and the unyielding will to power of their leaders interacted with each other, and reacted with the unique historical era they had inherited, to produce in these particularly skilled swordsmen a propensity to kill unsurpassed even in these bloodiest of times. Soon a semblance of order was restored to the city. In the following month the Imperial Court rewarded each corpsmen with one gold *ryō*.*

The protector of Kyōto was similarly happy with his Newly Selected Corps, which, in fact, were becoming his most powerful security force. The corps' unprecedented strength was bolstered by their severe code of conduct, devised by Kondō and Hijikata. That both leaders hailed from peasant households certainly steeled their resolve to conduct themselves and their corps according to the most stoic traditions of the warrior class. Strictly prohibited were "violating the Code of the Samurai," "quitting the corps," "raising money for selfish purposes," "taking it upon oneself to make accusations," and "fighting for personal reasons." Violation of any of these prohibitions was punishable by *seppuku*.† Not all violators, however, were given the honor of dying like samurai. The less worthy ones were beheaded. Attached to the prohibitions was a particularly severe regulation that perhaps more than anything else accounted for the lethality of the Shinsengumi: "In case of a fight, if you do not kill your opponent you will be ordered to commit *seppuku*, just as if you had been wounded from behind."‡

This sanguine code of conduct was, in fact, strictly enforced—although it would not be established as the official code of the Shinsengumi for nearly two years.§ The number of corpsmen forced to commit seppuku, or who were beheaded or otherwise murdered, has been lost to history, though several incidents have been recorded. Ta'uchi Tomo of the province of Musashi made an unexpected visit to the home of his mistress in the southern outskirts of Kyōto. The

---

* See Appendix I (4).

† See Appendix I (5).

‡ See Appendix I (6).

§ It is believed to have been established as the official code around the end of May 1865.

table had been set with saké and some food, which aroused his suspicion. As he questioned the woman, he was suddenly attacked from behind by her secret lover. A fellow corpsman discovered Ta'uchi bleeding from his wounds. He helped him back to headquarters, where Kondō and Hijikata ordered him to commit seppuku—a propensity to kill. Another man was similarly punished for having an affair with a married woman—a propensity to kill. A fencing instructor in the corps who espoused radical Loyalist views was condemned to seppuku for "disrupting order in the corps"—a propensity to kill. One of the earliest members deserted after seeing fellow corpsmen condemned to death and countless of the enemy butchered in the streets of Kyōto. Having been with the corps for a long time, he was privy to confidential information, the divulgence of which was not to be tolerated. He was hunted down, captured, and hacked to death by several of his former comrades—a propensity to kill. Another corpsman was beheaded for attempting to extort money from a wealthy merchant—a propensity to kill. Two others, one of whom had been expelled from the Shinsengumi for cowardice, were murdered on the streets of Kyōto for attempting to use the corps' name for their own profit—a propensity to kill. A man in charge of accounting for the Shinsengumi was ordered by Hijikata to commit seppuku for "the crime of miscalculation"—a propensity to kill.

Although quitting the corps was certainly a capital offense, it was by no means easy to apprehend a deserter. Tracking down a deserter could be a drawn-out and complicated process, as was the case for one Shibata Hikosaburō. Shibata enlisted in 1864. About a year and a half later, in June 1866, he deserted after extorting money for personal use. When Hijikata received word of Shibata's whereabouts in Izushi Han, northwest of Kyōto, he sent four men after him. The pursuers carried a detailed description of Shibata, including his features, age, dress, alias, and the fact that he spoke with a Musashi dialect. He was handed over to his pursuers by Izushi officials, brought back to Shinsengumi headquarters in Kyōto, and forced to commit seppuku as an example to would-be deserters—a propensity to kill.

The most infamous instance of harshness by the Shinsengumi to one of their own is the unfortunate, if historically blurred, case of Vice

Commander Yamanami Keisuké. According to Nagakura Shinpachi, Yamanami, "vehement in his Imperial Loyalism, was every bit as great as Kiyokawa Hachirō, Serizawa Kamo and Kondō Isami." Even the protector of Kyōto was counted among Yamanami's admirers. When Yamanami's sword was severed in a battle in which he had killed a rōnin, the Aizu daimyō rewarded him with a new sword and eight ryō.

The trouble with Yamanami seems to have originated over a disagreement in philosophy, though Shimosawa also cites a bitter rivalry with the other vice commander, Hijikata Toshizō. Yamanami was apparently vexed over the lately inflated self-importance of Kondō and Hijikata. He felt that they had forgotten the original purpose for which the members of the Shieikan had enlisted in the "loyal and patriotic" corps. The unyielding will to power that had lately consumed his erstwhile friends had diminished their former patriotic ideals. According to most sources, Yamanami's vexation was exacerbated sometime in early 1865, when Kondō and Hijikata, unhappy with their cramped headquarters at Mibu, decided to move to a more spacious location at Nishihonganji Temple in the southwest of the city. The temple priests were perplexed over the decision. Their attempts to rebuff the Shinsengumi were ignored by Kondō and Hijikata. Yamanami objected to what he considered coercion of Buddhist priests. "Certainly there are many other suitable places," he admonished Kondō, and suggested that his commander reconsider. But his commander would not reconsider, and Yamanami resolved to pay the ultimate price. He composed a farewell letter explaining the reasons he could no longer, in good conscience, risk his life under Kondō 's command. Then he defected.*

Yamanami fled to the town of Ōtsu, about seven miles east of Kyōto on Lake Biwa. Although sources differ in the details of subsequent events, according to both Nagakura and Shimosawa, Kondō sent Okita to retrieve Yamanami. This was no easy task. For all of Okita's skill with a sword, Yamanami himself was an expert in the Hokushin Ittō style. He was also proficient in *jūjutsu*. That Okita ap-

---

* It has been suggested that the Shinsengumi did not start talking to the temple priests until after Yamanami's death. If this is true, then the matter of Nishihonganji was unrelated to Yamanami's desertion.

prehended him without a struggle seems to indicate that Yamanami was resigned to his fate. Upon his return to Mibu, he was summoned to an assembly of Shinsengumi leaders in the Maekawa house.

"Desertion," Kondō said, breaking an austere silence, "is prohibited by Shinsengumi regulations." Kondō spoke solemnly as he ordered Yamanami to commit seppuku—a propensity to kill. Yamanami calmly expressed his appreciation and happiness at being called upon to perform this most honorable task for a samurai. He then excused himself momentarily. When he returned to the room he had changed into formal attire. He placed a mat over the clean tatami floor so as not to soil it with his blood. He sat on the mat, assumed the formal position, and placed his short sword in front of himself. He thanked all present for their long-lasting fellowship. He exchanged ceremonious farewell cups of water with them and courteously delivered his farewell speech. He asked Okita Sōji to serve as his second, instructing the genius swordsman not to "lower your sword until I give the word." Then he gently took up his short sword and plunged it into his lower abdomen. After slicing the blade across in one straight line, he fell forward with a final thrust of energy, earning, according to Nagakura, "Kondō's praise for the splendidness" by which he performed this ultimate task.

The number of rank and filers who suffered a similar fate is unknown. The officers were no exception. Of the twenty-two most noted officers, only three survived those bloody times. At least six were assassinated, three committed seppuku, and two were executed. In 1876, eight years after the death of Kondō Isami and the final collapse of the Tokugawa Bakufu, in the Itabashi district of Tōkyō—the new Eastern Capital—at a spot on the earth just a stone's throw from the execution grounds where Kondō had been beheaded, Nagakura erected a stone monument for the repose of the souls of his comrades who did not survive the revolution. Their names are engraved on the stone. Thirty-nine are listed as having died in battle, and seventy-one having met their end by disease, accident, seppuku, or execution.

The most severe treatment fell upon traitors and spies. Immediately following the coup in August, all Chōshū men and their rōnin allies were officially banned from the Imperial Capital. Some of them, how-ever, managed to remain in the city for reconnaissance purposes, disguised as merchants or beggars. These outlaws were hunted by men of the Tokugawa camp, including Aizu and the Shinsengumi.

"The Shinsengumi became the object of hatred among shishi from Chōshū," Nagakura recalled. "They concluded that as long as Kondō and his men dominated the Kyōto scene, it would be difficult for them to effect [another] uprising. And so Katsura Kogorō* chose four of his comrades … as assassins" to infiltrate the Shinsengumi. On August 25, one week after the coup, several Chōshū men sud-denly showed up at Mibu headquarters. They claimed to have left the service of their han due to a falling-out with their clansmen. They requested permission to join the Shinsengumi. Kondō accepted them into the corps, intending to use them as spies to "find and kill the malcontents from Chōshū hiding in Kyōto." He ordered his new re-cruits to stay at the Maekawa residence, and gave them 100 ryō to pay for uniforms and other expenses. Having concluded his meeting with the four Chōshū men, "Kondō [had] a strange flicker in his eyes … and after some time summoned Nagakura† and three others" and told them to "be on guard" regarding the four new recruits.

Near the end of September, Kondō discovered the truth about his four new recruits. "We can't let them get away," Kondō said, and or-dered Nagakura, Okita, and others to "kill them immediately." Naga-kura and two others found two of the Chōshū men sunning themselves on the long wooden veranda at the Maekawa residence. With their swords they swiftly killed both men, stabbing them through from behind. Meanwhile, Okita and his fellow assistant vice commander, Tōdō Heisuké, burst into another room of the house in pursuit of two more of the enemy, who escaped through a window. An additional two corpsmen, also uncovered as Chōshū spies, at-tempted to flee. One was captured. The other escaped after being cut from behind. "We tried to bring the captured man … to Commander Kondō [for questioning]," Nagakura recalled. When he refused to

---

* A leader of the Chōshū Loyalists.
† In his oral recollections, dictated to a newspaper journalist over a two-year period be-ginning in 1911, Nagakura is referred to by name.

cooperate, Harada Sanosuké, known for his short temper, drew his long sword, and with one swift stroke beheaded him. "Not only were we commissioned to round up the vagrants who swaggered through the streets of Kyōto, but [now] we were also invested with the authority to kill them. Shishi hiding in Kyōto and Ōsaka feared the commander of the Shinsengumi as if he were a demon."

OF INSULT AND
RETRIBUTION

Under Tokugawa law, it was an inalienable right of the men of the warrior class to inflict capital and swift retribution for an insult perpetrated by a commoner. "The samurai held strength and courage as the ultimate forms of male virtue, while cowardice and meanness represented the basest immorality," wrote an acclaimed chronicler of samurai history and lore. "In the face of disrespect or contempt, the only way for a man to preserve his dignity as a samurai was to strike down the perpetrator immediately."*

As the tension mounted in Kyōto between Chōshū on one side, and Satsuma and Aizu on the other, Loyalist rōnin from various clans rushed to the scene of the impending war. To avoid trouble with the Tokugawa forces in Kyōto, including the Shinsengumi, most of the rebels stayed in nearby Ōsaka to await the outbreak of fighting. So great were their numbers, however, that the Tokugawa magistrates in Ōsaka were compelled to request aid from the protector of Kyōto, who dispatched a contingent of men, led by Kondō Isami and Serizawa Kamo, to arrest or kill the rebels.

---

* Although the writer referred specifically to the samurai of Satsuma, certainly these qualities were not limited to the Satsuma clan.

The fifteenth of July was scorching. Serizawa, Yamanami, Okita, Nagakura, Saitō, Hirayama, and two others left the Kyō'ya inn to cool off aboard a pleasure boat on the Yodogawa River. (The Kyō'ya, located in the southeast section of the city, on the western bank of the Yodogawa, just south of Tenmanbashi Bridge, served as temporary headquarters for the Shinsengumi in Ōsaka.) On the riverboat they drank saké and, after disembarking, decided to spend the evening at a nearby pleasure quarter. Due to the intense heat, most of them were dressed simply in robes and trousers of the kind usually worn in the kenjutsu training hall. They carried only their short swords because their long swords would have been cumbersome on a riverboat.

Near a small bridge by the riverside they encountered a heavyset man steadily approaching from the opposite direction. By his great bulk, thin cotton robe, and topknot, they readily recognized him as a sumo wrestler. Unfortunately for the wrestler, however, he did not recognize the crudely attired men swaggering toward him. And to make matters worse, this particular sumo man belonged to a stable of wrestlers who tended to look down upon men of the samurai class. "Of this Serizawa was aware," Nagakura recalled. And Serizawa was not one to tolerate any form of insult, least of all from a commoner.

"Move to the side of the road," Serizawa demanded. The wrestler glared. Serizawa drew his short sword. In the same motion, he sliced open the wrestler's chest, killing him instantly. Without further ado, the Shinsengumi men proceeded on their way.

The trouble came later that night as the eight swordsmen cavorted with as many young harlots in a banquet room at a pleasure house known as the Sumiyoshi. Suddenly a ruckus was heard from the street. Serizawa looked out the second-story window. In the light of the full moon he saw a group of some twenty wrestlers wielding heavy wooden clubs. Serizawa jumped down to the ground below, drawing his short sword. His seven comrades followed, and in the moonlight outside the house of pleasure pandemonium ensued. One of the wrestlers knocked Nagakura's sword out of his hands. As Nagakura retrieved his sword, he noticed that the blade was damaged. Meanwhile, another man charged him. Nagakura dropped this assailant with a deep cut to the shoulder. "Hirayama received a blow to the chest, but after a desperate fight killed his opponent. Okita was struck on the side of the head. But ignoring the gushing blood, he brandished his sword like a windmill…. Yamanami chased down a fleeing man and sliced open his back, killing him instantly." The sumo wrestlers had no idea that they had challenged the notorious Mibu Wolves. The survivors who fled the scene were nevertheless aware that these were particularly tough opponents, and that five of their stablemates lay dead in as many pools of blood, while several others had been badly wounded.

The Shinsengumi reported the incident to the Ōsaka magistrate. They denied any knowledge of who had attacked them, or their motive. They claimed to have fought back in self-defense, killing a number of their assailants. "Be informed in advance," the Shinsengumi warned, "that if they should attack us again, we will kill every last one of them."

Meanwhile, representatives of the sumo stable demanded that the Ōsaka magistrate "find and kill whoever those rōshi were who cut down [our wrestlers]." The magistrate's reply was as curt as it was severe: "The rōshi whom the wrestlers attacked were men of the Shinsengumi. There can be no greater insult than starting a fight with samurai. It was perfectly reasonable for those samurai to seek retribution for such an insult." The matter was finally settled when the sumo men, to avoid further trouble, apologized to Kondō and Serizawa and presented them with a cask of saké and fifty ryō.

For all his murderous intolerance, Serizawa Kamo, upon occasion, presented a leniency that at once amused and bemused his fellow corpsmen.

In August the Shinsengumi was again dispatched to patrol Ōsaka. One evening Serizawa and Nagakura kept watch at the Kyō'ya, drinking saké while the others were out on patrol. To brighten the atmosphere, Serizawa sent for two young girls whom he had previously seen at a local pleasure house called the Yoshida'ya. Soon the girls arrived. They poured saké and probably sang and danced. Serizawa joked and flirted, and after a while both he and Nagakura were quite drunk. When Nagakura suggested they call it a night, Serizawa glibly asked one of the girls to spend the night with him. When the girl re-fused, Serizawa flew into a rage and ordered both to leave.

The following day Serizawa was still angry with the women for the slight of the previous night. Bent on retribution, he pressed Naga-kura to accompany him to the Yoshida'ya. "There was a dog sleeping near the front gate of the Yoshida'ya," Nagakura recalled. "When Ser-izawa saw this, he unfolded his big iron-ribbed fan, and with it struck the dog dead." When the two samurai entered the house, Serizawa was seething with anger. In the front hallway, they were respectfully greeted by ten women kneeling in two straight lines. "Without saying a word, Serizawa looked around at everyone. Suddenly, he struck one of the women with his iron-ribbed fan, rendering her unconscious," before ascending the wooden staircase to the second story.

They were joined in an upstairs room by Hijikata, Saitō, and Hi-rayama, whom Nagakura had previously asked to "just kind of show up" in order to help humor Serizawa. But Serizawa would not be hu-mored just yet. "I was worried that the two women might be killed over such a trifling thing, and that [as a result] the Shinsengumi's reputation would be tainted." Nagakura had ample cause to worry. Serizawa ordered the steward of the house to bring the two women, insisting that "their insult to a samurai was inexcusable," and that he would now settle the matter. The steward was perplexed, but dared not refuse. He went downstairs to retrieve the women. "The way he's acting now, he might cut off your heads," he warned them. The women began crying hysterically, because they apparently knew of Serizawa's reputation. "You must come," the steward told them. He suggested that they sit on either side of him, "docilely, with your hands on your laps." If Serizawa should appear hostile, "as if he is going to cut you, then I will put my arms around your necks and tell him that if he is going to kill you, he should kill me first. But I don't think he'd kill me. So don't worry about it, and come with me to the room."

Soon they joined Serizawa and the four other corpsmen. "I should kill both of them for their insult," Serizawa told the steward, who lis-tened passively, the girls on either side of him. "But since they're women, I'm going to pardon them."

Serizawa must certainly have been enjoying the mental torture he was inflicting upon the two women, because no sooner had he spoken than he placed his hand on the hilt of his short sword and said, "Instead, I'll cut off their hair." He looked hard at the woman who had refused him the night before, and Hijikata now insisted that he should be the one to do the cutting—a precaution so that Serizawa would not get carried away with a drawn sword in hand. As Hijikata spoke both women gasped, the steward winced, and the vice commander drew his short sword. With one clean slice, he severed the woman's long black hair. Taking Hijikata's lead, Hirayama made short work of the other woman's hair, and Serizawa's rage was abated.

THE PURGE

When men of overbearing personalities clash, the result is often violent. If these men are infected with the germ of self-importance, grave danger may loom. If the clash is intensified by unyielding will to power, the situation may turn deadly. But if even one among them is possessed of an unflinching propensity to kill, the inevitable outcome must be cold-blooded murder.

Invested as they were with an official sanction to kill, the Shinsengumi swaggered through the streets of Kyōto and Ōsaka. As the authority of the corps grew, Commander Serizawa Kamo took advantage of his waxing power. Easily provoked, he terrified those who dared arouse his anger and, according to Nagakura Shinpachi, "his extreme violence perplexed even the corpsmen." Once when Serizawa and some of his men were on an outing at the Katsuragawa River in the west of Kyōto, a hapless boatman accidentally brushed his boat line against Serizawa. Had the line touched any of the others, the trivial incident would have probably gone unnoticed, and certainly unrecorded in the annals of Japanese history. But Serizawa flew into a rage, cut the line, tied up the terrified boatman, and was pacified only by the profuse apologies of a samurai who happened to be riding on the boat.

It wasn't long before the Tokugawa magistrates in charge of keeping the peace in Kyōto and Ōsaka became vexed at the unruly behavior of Commander Serizawa. At the end of June 1863, a certain official of Minakuchi Han, whose daimyō was a direct retainer of the shōgun, issued an official complaint about Serizawa to Aizu Han. When Serizawa heard about it, he immediately sent four of his top swordsmen, including Nagakura, Harada and Inoué, to the Minakuchi estate in Kyōto to apprehend the official. "But," as Nagakura recalled, "the official suspected that if he came to [our] headquarters, his head would roll." The official apologized profusely. At Nagakura's suggestion, he composed a letter of apology addressed to the Shinsengumi. The letter was soon delivered to Serizawa, who, placated by the apology, showed it to the other corpsmen, "roaring with laughter." It seemed as if the problem had been settled without further incident, until the next day when a friend of the Minakuchi official showed up at Mibu headquarters. He had come to retrieve the letter because "if the Lord of Minakuchi should hear about this, my friend will be ordered to commit seppuku." Since the letter was addressed to the Shinsengumi as a whole, a decision to return it required the assent of all the corpsmen. On the next day a gathering of more than one hundred men of the Shinsengumi was held in a spacious banquet room at the Sumi'ya, a veritable pleasure palace in the Shimabara quarter of western Kyōto, to decide on the Minakuchi man's fate. "Nobody objected to returning the letter of apology," recalled Nagakura, and the matter was finally settled.

Presently some of the men removed themselves to a smaller room more conducive to the planned festivities. On the tatami-matted floor were low wooden tables set with fine porcelain and lacquerware, on which were served delicacies to complement superb Kyōto saké. In a wooden alcove built into one of the walls was a splendid ceramic vase. Adorning the sliding screen doors were ornate landscape paintings, including, perhaps, a masterpiece of the Kanō style. "We've been invited here today by the Lord of Minakuchi," Serizawa addressed the gathering, certainly pleased with himself and his own importance. Young women of the pleasure quarter had been called in to entertain the men—to dance, sing, play on the three-stringed *shamisen*, and keep saké cups full. After a short time Serizawa became drunk and, as usual, easily provoked. He drained his saké cup and suddenly slammed it on the table. "With his eyes fixed," Nagakura recalled, "he glared at everyone with that sullen look of his," apparently slighted that his cup had not been immediately refilled. Now he took up his heavy iron-ribbed fan and smashed the table, shattering the porcelain and lacquerware. The women were frightened. When they attempted to leave the room, Serizawa stood up and knocked down several of them; others wept hysterically. After similarly clearing the other tables, he went to the alcove and smashed the ceramic vase. He staggered into an adjacent corridor. He went to the staircase and, with a loud roar, ripped out the heavy wooden handrail. He carried the handrail downstairs, where casks of saké were stored. These he smashed with the handrail, so that a liquid of a slightly golden hue gushed out onto the polished wooden floor. Next he went to the kitchen and smashed every dish in sight. By now the proprietor of the Sumi'ya, his staff, and the young women had fled the house. Most of the corpsmen, probably disgusted with and certainly ashamed of their commander's behavior, had also left. Only Nagakura, Hijikata, and an old man employed by the Sumi'ya remained with Serizawa. "Tell the proprietor," Serizawa slurred, looking hard at the old man, "that Serizawa Kamo of the Shinsengumi hereby orders him to spend seven days under house confinement for his insolent behavior." When Hijikata reported the tirade to Kondō at Mibu headquarters, the commander, Nagakura reported, "just folded his arms and released a heavy sigh."

For all his unruliness, Serizawa was a man of breeding and not without a certain sensitivity. He wielded this certain sensitivity to his benefit, particularly with a certain type of woman. He was a stylish dresser and ruggedly handsome. As commander of the Shinsengumi, he believed that he was above the rule of law— extraordinary self-importance! He had no qualms about accepting merchandise on credit from shops in town—without any intention of paying his debts. Was it not true, he reasoned, that he risked his life daily to protect the populace of Kyōto? Were not law and order invaluable commodities that the merchants needed for their very survival? He even rationalized that the merchants, including the proprietor of a certain kimono shop, and his attractive wife, were indebted to him. This was why Serizawa did not pay for the exquisite kimono he ordered from the shop, although the proprietor attempted to collect the debt on numerous occasions. Finally, the proprietor committed a fatal blunder by sending his wife, O'umé, to collect, naively assuming that Serizawa could be charmed into paying.

Unbeknownst to the proprietor, Serizawa had already been charmed on several occasions at the shop. When O'umé paid him a visit at the Yagi residence, Serizawa was only too happy to invite her into his room. He indulged her entreaty to pay his debt. Then after she finished speaking, he raped her. But Serizawa's virulence and brute strength, combined with that certain sensitivity, enraptured O'umé, who left her husband to become the mistress of the Shinsengumi commander.

In July, while the Shinsengumi was in Ōsaka, a group of anti-Tokugawa rebels abducted a wealthy merchant from his home in Kyōto. They murdered him and left his severed head skewered on a bamboo stake stuck in the mud along the river near Sanjō Bridge. They claimed Heaven's Revenge for the merchant's "crime of engaging in commerce with filthy barbarians." Another motive was extortion. The rebels needed to raise money to fund a planned uprising. Near the head, they placed a leaflet naming the wealthy proprietor of a silk wholesaler known as the Yamato'ya. They threatened the silk merchant with the same fate, if he should commit a "similar crime." Tacitly implied was that the Yamato'ya's proprietor could redeem himself by contributing money to the Loyalists' cause, which he readily did.

But the problem would not end so easily. The incident soon came to the attention of Serizawa Kamo. Five days before the coup in August he told his men, "If the Yamato'ya is funding renegades who are causing so much trouble in Kyōto, then they had better give us some money also." Serizawa and several others paid a sudden visit to the Yamato'ya. "Law and order are not free of charge," they threatened. When their demand for money was flatly refused, Serizawa took drastic measures.

The Shinsengumi commander led his men back to Mibu head-

quarters. They returned to the house of the silk wholesaler that evening armed with guns, including a cannon. They loaded the cannon
with gunpowder-laden balls, and aimed it at the Yamato'ya's storehouse. "Burn it to the ground," Serizawa roared, then stood by and
watched as his men fired round after round at the storehouse. Sparks
and burning cinders flew into the air. Nearby buildings caught fire.
The bell sounded in the fire tower, and soon the fire brigade arrived
at the scene. Serizawa, wearing a mask to conceal his identity, ordered
his men to train their rifles on the brigade and threatened to shoot if
the firemen attempted to extinguish the blaze. Serizawa climbed to
the rooftop of a nearby building, where he laughed hysterically over
the havoc he and his men had caused. They continued the uproar
throughout the night and into the following day, until the storehouse
was completely destroyed. Serizawa did not return to Mibu headquarters until four in the afternoon, drunk with the ecstasy of his
power and repeatedly shouting, "How delightful! How delightful!"*

The protector of Kyōto was extremely disturbed. His Newly Selected
Corps had been established to preserve law and order. He could no
longer indulge behavior contrary to that purpose. Kondō and Hijikata shared Lord Katamori's indignation, albeit for different reasons.
Unlike Serizawa Kamo, who was the son of a samurai, Kondō and
Hijikata hailed from peasant households. The role of a samurai was
to wage war, and he was rewarded accordingly with a stipend. He did
not engage in moneymaking affairs, which were left to the merchants
and peasants. This was certainly how Serizawa thought. But not so
Kondō Isami, nor Hijikata Toshizō. As long as they were rōshi, they
were compelled to work, and had to earn their living by their own
hands. They earned their living by killing, and they were not adverse
to killing one of their own to protect their livelihood. That these former peasants now headed a Tokugawa police force was nothing short
of miraculous, and they were poignantly aware that their rise to
power was made possible only by the bloody times it had been theirs
to inherit. Serizawa's behavior jeopardized the very existence of their

---

* Once source argues that Serizawa and his men did not use a cannon to ignite the fire.

corps, which had become their raison d'être. Over the past several months the two had been waiting for an opportunity to purge the Serizawa faction from the corps. Lord Katamori would provide them with that opportunity. But they would have to wait for the right time. That time would come during the short period of relative calm immediately following the August coup.

If Serizawa's fellow corpsmen were perplexed by his tirades, they could not but admire his physical courage. Just before the coup, as tension mounted around the Imperial Palace, the Shinsengumi received orders to report to Hamaguri Gate of the palace to assist the Aizu and Satsuma forces against Chōshū. Eighty corpsmen marched in two columns under the command of Kondō and Serizawa. Their distinguishing light blue uniforms and red and white "makoto" banner notwithstanding, the armor-clad Aizu men, preoccupied as they were with the impending battle, did not readily recognize them. The guards at the gate were armed with sharp spears. They demanded in no uncertain terms that the Shinsengumi identify themselves, pointing their spears at the oncoming columns. The Shinsengumi procession halted. The men were confused. They had expected to be welcomed as comrades-in-arms, but instead were treated with suspicion. While Kondō paused at the unexpected circumstances, Serizawa defiantly swaggered up to the gate. One of the guards thrust the blade of his spear just six inches from Serizawa's face. "We are the Shinsengumi," Serizawa announced, "under the authority of the Lord of Aizu. We have received orders to protect the palace and will now enter." He laughed derisively at the sudden perplexity of the Aizu men. He drew the heavy iron-ribbed fan from his sash. With a single motion he opened the fan, displaying the patriotic inscription and knocking the guard's blade aside. The Aizu men realized their blunder. "Please excuse our impertinence," they said. Serizawa closed his fan, replaced it in his sash as if it were a small sword, and proceeded with his men through the gate.

Serizawa Kamo's right-hand man, Shinmi Nishiki, shared his leader's disdain for the merchant class and his conviction that the Shinsengumi commanders were above the rule of law. (Shinmi had been demoted from his original position as one of the three commanders to vice commander. The other two vice commanders were Hijikata and Yamanami.) This disdain, founded on arrogance, and this conviction, founded on distortion, would prove fatal to Shinmi, but only after Kondō and Hijikata had received orders from the protector of Kyōto to eliminate Serizawa.

Like Serizawa, Shinmi held menkyo rank in the Shintō Munen style. His superior swordsmanship notwithstanding, he had repeatedly violated Shinsengumi regulations. Not only did Shinmi spend more time at the pleasure quarters than on his official duties, but on a number of occasions he had extorted large sums of money from private individuals under the false pretense that these funds would be appropriated to the corps. Around the beginning of September Shinmi was confronted with these charges by a group of Kondō's men at a brothel in the Gion district of Kyōto. He was pressed to commit seppuku on the spot. Shinmi knew that if he refused, he would be subject to beheading, according to corps regulations. Left with no alternative, and in the face of his scowling adversaries, Vice Commander Shinmi vindicated his tainted honor by his own sword. "Having lost his right-hand man," Nagakura recalled, "Serizawa became more and more agitated. He now engaged in misconduct day and night according to his whims and without any regard for the corps." With Shinmi's death, only four of the Serizawa faction remained to be eliminated.

According to Nagakura, Kondō was a "courageous man who did not take delight in brandishing his sword." He would draw his blade only when necessary, and would kill only when the need presented itself. That need, however, presented itself often, one of the most significant occasions being one rainy night in September.*

For some time Serizawa and his men had been wary of Kondō and Hijikata, suspecting that the two were up to no good. Their suspicion had been exacerbated several days earlier by the forced sep-

---

* Discrepancy exists as to the actual date of Serizawa's assassination. Some sources indicate September 16, others September 18.

puku of Shinmi. But when Kondō and Hijikata held a party at the Sumi'ya, the remnants of the Serizawa faction attended. Accompanying Serizawa were Hirayama Gorō and Hirama Jūsuké, both assistant vice commanders. Hirayama held menkyo rank in the Shintō Munen style. Hirama, who was Serizawa's fencing student, held the rank of mokuroku.

Kondō could not do enough to please his three guests. He saw to it that large quantities of saké were served them by several pretty young women whom he had hired for the occasion. "There was a sumptuous feast and the place shook with song," Nagakura re-called. The hour was late when Serizawa and the two others took their leave. Staggering from too much drink, they hired a palanquin to carry them through the pouring rain to Mibu. O'umé was waiting for Serizawa at the Yagi residence. Hirayama and Hirama each called for girls from the pleasure quarter. The party resumed in Serizawa's room. According to Nagakura, Hijikata joined Serizawa's party to make sure that the three men were completely inebriated. "After they were too drunk to even sit up, they went to bed."

Serizawa's room overlooked the rear garden through the long wooden corridor, which led to adjacent rooms. As the hard rain pelted the tiled roof, four men stole into the room from the garden. Serizawa was sound asleep with O'umé, his short sword within arm's reach. Also asleep in this room were the other two men with their harlots. Sleeping in the next room were the wife and two young sons of Yagi Gennojō, the master of the house. One of the harlots got up to use the latrine. As she opened the sliding screen door of the sleeping quarters, she was confronted in the darkness by two men with drawn swords. "Save yourself and get out of here," one of them whispered.

Serizawa awoke from his stupor. He grabbed his sword. He managed to stand up. He struggled to defend himself. But Hijikata and Okita cut him badly. He tried to escape through the wooden corridor. He ran to the adjacent room where the woman and children were asleep. As he entered the room, one of his assassins delivered the coup de grâce from behind. He collapsed atop the sleeping children, the younger of whom was accidentally cut on the right leg. With Serizawa's bloodied corpse sprawled across the bed, the older brother,

Tamésaburō, noticed Hirama, his sword drawn, running frantically through the house. Tamésaburō went to the next room. He saw a woman's naked corpse and a man's dead body, the severed head nearby. Meanwhile, Hirama and the other harlot had managed to escape with their lives, their whereabouts unknown. Out of pure fear, the woman and children who witnessed the murders would never reveal to the authorities the identity of the assassins.

The next day Kondō issued an official report to Lord Matsudaira Katamori, stating that Serizawa and Hirayama had been killed in their sleep by unknown assassins. Their funeral at Mibu Temple, near the Yagi residence, was a solemn occasion befitting their positions in the Shinsengumi. The coffins of the two men were laid side by side. Their wounds were wrapped with white cotton cloth. Their wooden practice swords were placed at their sides. The corpses were formally dressed in wide trousers and jackets adorned with their respective family crests. In attendance were all of the corpsmen, including Kondō and the four assassins.

No such pomp was reserved for Serizawa's mistress. O'umé's corpse was never claimed. Her cremation and funeral in a cemetery for the forlorn were arranged by the master of the Maekawa residence. With all but one Mito man eliminated from the corps, the Serizawa faction ceased to exist. Kondō and Hijikata now gained uncontested control of the Shinsengumi.

A Propensity to Kill

"I despise killing and have never killed a man," Katsu Kaishū once said. "Take my sword, for example. I used to keep it tied so tightly to the sword guard, that I couldn't draw the blade even if I had wanted to. I've always been resolved not to cut a person even if that person should cut me. I look at such a person as no more than a flea. If one lands on your shoulder, all it can do is bite a little. This causes nothing more than an itch, and has nothing to do with life." Sakamoto Ryōma, also noted for his abhorrence of bloodshed, killed a man only once—in self-defense. Both Ryōma and his mentor Kaishū were expert swordsmen whose respect for life was founded on strength. Similarly, the cherished slogan of Saigō the Great, quintessential samurai and military leader of Satsuma, was "Love mankind, revere heaven." Certainly it was the conviction of these three warriors, among the most lauded in Japanese history, that killing in any situation but a last resort was a gross violation of Bushidō. Not so the men of the Shinsengumi, whose propensity to kill, bolstered by their own stringent and sanguine code, was unsurpassed during those extraordinarily bloody times.

The Shinsengumi's loyalty to the Tokugawa Bakufu was unquestionable. They nevertheless embraced the same rigid antiforeignism and Imperial Loyalism espoused by the anti-Tokugawa radicals whom they were commissioned to destroy. In October 1863, two months after Chōshū had been expelled from Kyōto and one month after the assassination of Serizawa Kamo, Kondō Isami attended a gathering of representatives of various han, including Satsuma, Aizu, and Tosa, who supported a Union of Court and Camp. The men consumed large quantities of saké and talked a great deal. Little was said, however, about the myriad problems confronting Japan, the most pressing of which regarded foreign relations, the punishment of Chōshū, and a union between the emperor and shōgun to solve these problems through a national consensus. Kondō, stern as always and probably annoyed at the mute silence regarding these critical matters, was urged by Aizu and Satsuma men to present his political views. "Both Satsuma and Chōshū have attempted to expel the barbarians," he said, referring to the former's sea battle against the British in the previous July* and the latter's attack on foreign ships in May. "But both were attempts by only one han. Still we have not come together as a whole nation to act against the barbarians. Through a Union of Court and Camp we must embrace the Imperial Court, aid the Bakufu, arrive at a [consensus in] national sentiment through cooperation between those in high positions and those below [them], and by so doing expel the barbarians."

With the exception of Chōshū and the radical elements of Tosa and Satsuma who were not represented at the gathering, Kondō's political stance was common among samurai throughout Japan. Even the most radical of the anti-Tokugawa men would have agreed with Kondō, had he not called for Kyōto to unite with Edo and for the feudal lords to aid the Tokugawa. While Kondō and most, if not all, of the men under his command fully intended to expel the foreigners, they would do so under the legal authority of the Tokugawa Shōgun and not under the renegade Chōshū domain. This had been their primary motive for breaking ranks with Kiyokawa Hachirō, when the latter returned to Edo in obedience of an imperial order. The Bakufu, of course, had no intention of expelling the foreigners. Edo's immediate concern was to suppress the Loyalists in Kyōto, to which end it worked to form an alliance with the Imperial Court. The Imperial

---

* See Appendix I (7).

Court, however, refused to relinquish its xenophobic stance, while the Bakufu, which had monopolistic control of international trade, favored intercourse with foreign nations. Further complicating the situation were certain powerful feudal lords who, jealous of Edo's trade monopoly, supported a Union of Court and Camp even as they vied among one another to gain political ground on the Bakufu. The most prominent of these lords were the so-called Four Brilliant Lords of these very troubled times: Shimazu Hisamitsu of Satsuma, Yamanouchi Yōdō of Tosa, Daté Munénari of Uwajima, and Matsudaira Shungaku of Fukui. The former three were outside lords, the latter a close relative of the shōgun.

As sole commander of the Shinsengumi, then, Kondō Isami's two immediate objectives were to suppress the enemies of the Tokugawa and to expel the foreigners. Needless to say, the Edo authorities were pleased with this powerful security force under the protector of Kyōto. In October, in recognition of their loyalty, the rōshi of the Shinsengumi were invited to officially join the ranks of the *hatamoto*, the so-called Eighty Thousand Knights of the Tokugawa Shōgun.* A generous monthly stipend was attached. Although the entire corps, from Kondō and Hijikata on down, undoubtedly and indisputably coveted official ranking within the Tokugawa hierarchy, Kondō refused the offer. As long as the foreigners remained in Japan, he felt that his corps had fulfilled only one of its objectives. Until the foreigners could be expelled, he did not feel deserving of official rank. Kondō did, however, accept the stipend, which he badly needed. He now received fifty ryō per month, Hijikata forty ryō. Lesser officers received thirty ryō, and the rank and file ten ryō each.†

---

* The hatamoto were direct retainers of the shōgun, whose annual rice revenue of less than 10,000 koku did not qualify them as daimyō. (The qualification of daimyō was the possession of lands with a rice yield exceeding 10,000 koku.) The actual number of hatamoto was much fewer than 80,000. According to Katsu Kaishū, the hatamoto numbered slightly more than 33,000.

† Considering that the annual rice yields of the smallest feudal domains were valued at only 10,000 ryō, these were substantial sums of money. Kondō's monthly pay of fifty ryō in the Kyōto of the 1860s would be approximately equal to $10,000 in the United States at the beginning of the twenty-first century.

* * * * *

During the two and a half centuries of Pax Tokugawa, many in the samurai class, particularly those in the service of the Bakufu, had lost interest in the martial arts. Their swords had become symbols of their social status rather than weapons of war. These samurai had become administrators and government officials instead of warriors. Katsu Kaishū, always critical of his fellow Tokugawa samurai, had the following to say about the situation:

> Originally many hatamoto of the Tokugawa ... had fortitude
> and invincibility. But during the more than two hundred years
> of peace they indulged in luxury, lapsed into idleness, and
> eventually became pulpy. Long ago they lost the hereditary
> customs of their ancestors. And so, in the face of the great dif-
> ficulties of the final years of the Bakufu, all they could do was
> get excited and make a lot of noise, as if someone had turned
> over their toy boxes. They were completely useless.

The decadence of samurai in Edo notwithstanding, the threat of foreign aggression served as a great awakening to those in other parts of Japan. There was a renaissance in the martial arts. Many among the warrior class rediscovered the original purpose of their swords, and practiced kenjutsu with a renewed passion. Even men of the peasant class dressed themselves as samurai, armed themselves with two swords, and took up the study of kenjutsu. The latter phenomenon, of course, was prevalent in the native countryside of the master of the Shieikan. Kondō Isami held to the common belief that rigorous martial arts training was essential for cultivating courage, martial spirit, and fighting technique. With Hijikata, he established a mandatory curriculum based on this belief. Included in the corps' curriculum were kenjutsu, jūjutsu, yarijutsu, artillery, and horsemanship. It was not tolerated for any member to miss even one training session. Members were also required to study the manly art of literature. Kondō himself practiced calligraphy with near-religious fervor for two hours each night—rarely, if ever, missing a session. He was determined to take his place among the great men of his time, most of whom excelled in both poetry and martial arts. He took the pseudonym Tōshū, literally Eastern Province, from his belief in the warlike superiority of the samurai of the east over their counterparts in the west.

To further prepare the rank and file for the myriad and unknown dangers of street fighting and actual warfare, special practice sessions were held in the dark of night, using real swords instead of the bamboo or wooden practice weapons of the training hall. Upon occasion the men were aroused from sleep by a fellow corpsman brandishing a drawn blade. The result could be bloody, if not fatal. (Since the men slept in barracks, it is not inconceivable that even a man who successfully defended himself from a surprise attack might have ultimately been ordered to commit seppuku. In such a scenario, the defender, after disposing of his assailant, might have been cut from behind by a man near him who had been aroused from sleep by the sudden disturbance. It was, after all, a violation of Bushidō to be attacked from behind, and it was against Shinsengumi regulations to violate the Code of the Samurai.) To hone their ability to cut through human flesh, the men of the Shinsengumi were subjected to performing executions, or serving as seconds for fellow corpsmen who had been condemned to commit seppuku. It was the obligation of the second to decapitate the condemned man only after the latter had duly sliced open his belly—or if the condemned man was not up to the task, to push him over the brink with one clean stroke of the sword.

Every day the men would go out and cross swords with the enemy. One corpsman claimed that the blood of the man he had killed today splattered on the ridge of the adjacent house. Another said that the blood [of his victim] hadn't splattered beyond the white paneled wall. Still another boasted that the blood of the man he had cut down had reached the roof of the house.

This passage from Shimosawa's narrative suggests, at the very least, that more men were killed by the Shinsengumi than can be accounted for. Killing had become a daily occupation for the corpsmen, whose very livelihood now depended on terror and bloodshed. Perhaps the most brutal killer in the corps was the commander. "He was fearsome even when drinking," Kondō Isami's former mistress, who had been employed as a courtesan in Kyōto, reminisced nearly half a century later. "People would talk about whom they had killed today, and whom they were going to kill tomorrow. It was all so frightful. According to what I had heard, by that time Kondō had killed fifty or sixty men."

While the men of the Shinsengumi were possessed of superior martial spirit, fighting technique, and an unflinching propensity to kill, not even these attributes necessarily distinguished them from others of their countrymen, including their enemies. Takéchi Hanpeita, the leader of the radical Tosa Loyalist Party, wielded a hit squad to terrorize the streets of Kyōto in the early 1860s. Hanpeita's notorious hit men, Okada Izō and Tanaka Shinbé, both of whom used the nom de guerre *Hito-kiri* (literally, Person Cutter), had cut down numerous men during Hanpeita's reign of terror. There were many such professional killers as Okada and Tanaka on both sides of the revolution. What distinguished the Shinsengumi, then, from other terrorists and assassins was the advantage they held in their official sanction to kill. For better or for worse, their martial spirit, fighting technique, and propensity to kill were bolstered by the support they received by the central government in Edo.

But perhaps most significantly, the superior force of the Shinsengumi was tempered by their stringent code and by a strict screening process by which Kondō and Hijikata recruited the rank and file. Before a candidate would be accepted as a "regular corpsman," he had to prove himself worthy, demonstrating the proper degrees of courage, martial sprit, fighting technique, and propensity to kill. A candidate might be tested in the training hall, through a bout with real swords. He might be required to perform an execution or assist as a second in a seppuku. If a candidate even grimaced or turned the slightest bit pale at the sight of the gore, he would fail the test. Even if he passed the test, he might still receive only "temporary" status. Before being made a full-fledged member, he might be required to prove his worthiness through actual battle in the streets. If he demonstrated the proper skill, courage, and propensity to kill in real combat, he would become a regular. If not, he might be killed by the enemy or executed for violating the code. The following noted example of this requirement of success in combat is that of a man named Hashimoto Kaisuké.

In July 1864, in a failed attempt to regain the favor of the Imperial Court, Chōshū fired upon its Satsuma and Aizu foes, who defended the palace gates.* In the following month the Bakufu issued a decree for the great feudal domains to prepare their armies for a military expedition against Chōshū.† Edo's widely maligned intent, which would ultimately fail, was to punish Chōshū while regaining its absolute authority of the past. In efforts to check rampant rumors in Kyōto regarding the expedition, to gain popular support, and to assure the people that Pax Tokugawa reigned now that Chōshū had been suppressed, the Bakufu posted bulletin boards along roadsides and bridges around the city. These bulletin boards defamed Chōshū for its "unequivocal treason." But the Bakufu would not gain the support of the people in Kyōto; and its ill-advised public relations ploy only further antagonized Chōshū and its supporters, including the numerous rōnin hiding in the Imperial Capital. It was generally believed that the Shinsengumi and their Aizu allies resorted to extortion, intimidation, and violence. The Shinsengumi and Aizu were, to say the least, unpopular among the local people, who were sympathetic, if not boldly supportive, of the Chōshū Loyalists and their rōnin allies.

The Bakufu continued to post the defamatory bulletin boards for two years, until they became an eyesore to the Loyalists. Finally, in August 1866, under the cover of night, a group of rōnin smeared black ink on a bulletin board at the western approach of Sanjō Large Bridge.‡ When the authorities discovered the vandalism the next morning, they erected a new bulletin board. When this and subse-

---

* See pages 119–23.
† See pages 133-34, 139-40.
‡ Sanjō-dōri, a main thoroughfare running east-west through the center of Kyōto, spanned the Takaségawa Canal and the Kamogawa River on the eastern side of the city. The smaller span, over the canal, was Sanjō Small Bridge. The larger one, over the river, was Sanjō Large Bridge.

quent bulletin boards were similarly defaced, the Shinsengumi was called in.

On the night of September 12, Vice Commander Hijikata Toshizō dispatched thirty-four men to suppress the vandalism. The men divided into three groups on the eastern, western, and southern sides of the bridge. Two corpsmen, dressed like beggars in straw overcoats and armed with guns, waited for the vandals beneath the bridge.*

If anyone suspicious should approach, these spies would fire their guns to warn the others, who would rush to the bridge to apprehend the vandals. One of the spies was the candidate Hashimoto Kaisuké.

At around midnight Hashimoto spotted eight Tosa men approaching northward along the riverbed. In the bright silver light of a full autumn moon he could clearly see their long swords at their sides, and he could hear them singing as they walked deliberately over the rocky beach. As soon as it became apparent that they were headed straight for the bulletin board at the approach to the bridge, Hashimoto fired a warning shot.

Pandemonium ensued atop the bridge when the Tosa men threw two bulletin boards into the river below. The samurai fought beneath the moonlight, their swords clanging and flashing amid their battle cries. The Tosa men were outnumbered and outexperienced. They fled to a nearby street, where Hashimoto killed one of the enemy with his sword. Harada killed another; they captured a third, alive but badly wounded. The other five Tosa men escaped. Hashimoto and a few others of the Shinsengumi were slightly wounded. Soon they returned to headquarters to report the incident to Hijikata. Hashimoto passed the test, was awarded fifteen ryō for his valor, and became a full-fledged member of the Shinsengumi.

The grim propensity and formidable skills of the tried-and-true killers of the Shinsengumi were repeatedly wielded by their commander. As previously noted, Kondō Isami was possessed of an unyielding

---

* The area beneath Sanjō Large Bridge was a traditional gathering place for beggars and other vagrants. It was also a favorite location among rōnin, disguised as beggars, to carry out their insurgent activities. It was therefore an ideal spot for the Shinsengumi spies, who correctly surmised that they would not attract attention to themselves.

will to power, intensified by the germ of self-importance. It was this selfsame will to power that had been the demise of Serizawa Kamo, whom Kondō had purged from his corps. And certainly it was Serizawa's extraordinary sense of self-importance that in the previous summer had led him to cut down the lone sumo wrestler in Ōsaka, which, in turn, incited the attempted revenge by the wrestler's stablemates. Kondō had immediately reported the incident to a Tokugawa magistrate in Ōsaka. "We killed them because they insulted us," he said, fully expecting his statement to settle the matter. But there was an official at the magistrate's office, named Uchiyama Hikojirō, who did not approve of the Shinsengumi's strong-arm methods of procuring money. What's more, he was known for his unwillingness to look the other way. He prodded Kondō regarding the details of the alleged insult. Kondō strongly objected on the grounds that since his corps had acted under the authority of the protector of Kyōto, the matter was beyond the jurisdiction of an Ōsaka magistrate. Although Uchiyama was forced to drop the investigation, he would one day pay the ultimate price for challenging Commander Kondō's authority.

That day came in the following May (1864). Kondō, accompanied by Okita, Harada, Nagakura, and Inoué, made a special trip to Ōsaka. They learned that Uchiyama worked until around ten o'clock each night, and that he employed a palanquin to take him from his office to his home. They knew that his palanquin must cross a certain bridge, and that the immediate vicinity would be desolate at that late hour. Kondō and his men waited in the darkness at the approach to the bridge.

Uchiyama's palanquin was accompanied by a bodyguard. But to no avail. With the sudden appearance of five men in the darkness, each brandishing a drawn sword, the bodyguard and palanquin bearers fled for their lives. Okita thrust his sword through the thin paper wall of the palanquin, stabbing Uchiyama. They pulled the wounded man onto the street and beheaded him. They skewered the bloody head onto a bamboo stake. They stuck the stake into the soft ground near the bridge. They left behind a placard to falsely announce to the world that Uchiyama had been punished with Heaven's Revenge for crimes against the people. Their plan, of course, was to make it appear as if still another Tokugawa official had been killed by rōnin. Their plan was successful. The Shinsengumi would not be implicated in Uchiyama's assassination for more than a quarter century later, long after all of the men involved, with the exception of Nagakura, had died.

SLAUGHTER
AT THE IKÉDA'YA

On a windy night in June the rebels would set fire to the Imperial Palace and in the ensuing uproar kidnap the emperor. They would wait in hiding for the protector of Kyōto to rush to the scene, as he inevitably would, and cut him down on the spot. They would kill any other feudal lords who opposed them, and remove the emperor to Chōshū. They would then request the Son of Heaven to issue an imperial decree to attack the Bakufu and have the court appoint the Lord of Chōshū as protector of Kyōto.

That this plot was ill-timed, ill-devised, and ill-fated and that it would ultimately bring about the end of the movement to expel the foreigners did not diminish the far-reaching effect of the turning point in the revolution that was its natural result. Meanwhile, the propensity to kill that was the trademark of the Shinsengumi became most blatant at the bloody and infamous nexus of that turning point—the slaughter at the Ikéda'ya.

In the fifth month of the first and only year of the era of Genji—May 1864—at the approach of yet another frenetic and even bloodier summer in the Imperial Capital, Commander Kondō Isami had second thoughts about his role as chief policeman in Kyōto, and considered disbanding the Shinsengumi. In the previous January, Shōgun Tokugawa Iémochi had visited Kyōto for a second time to shore up consensus among the leading proponents of a Union of Court and Camp, who had regained political control after the August coup. Talks were held between January and March at both the Imperial Court and Nijō Castle, the Tokugawa stronghold in Kyōto. In attendance were six powerful feudal lords who supported a union. Included were Hitotsubashi Yoshinobu, and the Lords of Aizu, Fukui, Tosa, Satsuma, and Uwajima.* Two main issues were discussed. The first concerned closing the eastern port at Yokohama to foreigners, which would restrict foreign trade to Nagasaki in the southwest and Hokodaté in the far north. The Tokugawa side argued that Yokohama should be closed to demonstrate to the Imperial Court Iémochi's good intentions of fulfilling his promise to expel the foreigners. But the Bakufu was bluffing. It had no intention of closing Yokohama or expelling the foreigners. Its ulterior motive remained constant: appeasing the xenophobic emperor in order to regain the political upper hand from the powerful feudal domains. The other feudal lords in attendance, most notably Shimazu Hisamitsu of Satsuma, opposed the Tokugawa side, arguing that reneging on the commercial treaties might incite a war with the foreigners. The other issue regarded treatment of the renegade Chōshū domain. Yoshinobu led the Tokugawa side in calling for harsh treatment of this avowed enemy of the Bakufu, including a possible military expedition to punish Chōshū. The other lords argued for leniency. Consensus could not be reached, and the talks broke down in March. Meanwhile, the shōgun was presented with an imperial mandate to expel the foreigners.

But expelling the foreigners by military force was no more possible then than it had been in the previous year, when Chōshū had fired on foreign ships at Shimonoseki. When it came to Kondō's attention that the shōgun would again leave Kyōto without a definite plan for

---

* At that time Lord Yoshinobu was the official guardian of the shōgun. In March he was appointed as the Tokugawa's inspector-general of the forces protecting the emperor. Before becoming the last shōgun in December 1866, he would resume the Tokugawa family name of his birth.

Jōi, he promptly submitted a letter to Aizu Han, requesting permission to disband the Shinsengumi. He reminded the authorities that he and his men had originally enlisted in the Rōshi Corps not only to protect the shōgun, which entailed rounding up and killing enemies of the Tokugawa, but also to fight in Kyōto at the vanguard of the movement to Expel the Barbarians. As if to appease Kondō, the authorities again offered him and his men official ranking within the Tokugawa hierarchy. They also assured Kondō, tongue in cheek, that the shōgun would close Yokohama and that the Shinsengumi would eventually return to Edo to help him expel the foreigners from Japan. Kondō expressed his inclination to accept this second offer to join the Tokugawa ranks, probably because he was beginning to realize that the Bakufu would not start a war with foreign powers. Kondō was absolutely correct—and it is an irony of history that despite his misgivings, just one month after he had submitted the letter to Aizu, an event occurred at an inn in Kyōto that firmly established the Shinsengumi as the Bakufu's most formidable force in rounding up and killing enemies of the Tokugawa.

* * * * *

Since the Coup of 8/18, it had been rumored that troops in Chōshū were planning an attack on the Imperial Capital. Imperial Loyalists continued to wreak Heaven's Revenge upon the Tokugawa and their supporters in Kyōto and Ōsaka. Chōshū was naturally suspected of the crimes. In April the Shinsengumi arrested a Chōshū man for arson. Under the pain of torture he divulged that some 250 Chōshū samurai were hiding in Kyōto. On June 1 the Shinsengumi arrested two suspicious men on the east bank of the Kamogawa. Also under the pain of torture, they divulged that Chōshū forces planned to assassinate the protector of Kyōto and burn the Imperial Palace. Previously, at the end of May, the Shinsengumi had learned that samurai of Chōshū, banned from Kyōto, and renegade rōnin had been coming and going from the Ikéda'ya inn. The Ikéda'ya was located in the Kawaramachi district, on the west side of the Kamogawa River, just north of Sanjō Small Bridge—in close proximity to the headquarters of feudal lords and the Imperial Palace, the nerve center of the city. It was known that the Ikéda'ya inn was frequented by Chōshū samurai, and that the proprietor was a Loyalist sympathizer who was only too happy to provide his house to the rebels for the cause of the revolution. Kondō Isami assigned four corpsmen to investigate the potentially dangerous situation. Among them were Yamazaki Susumu and Shimada Kai.

Kondō's spies implicated a man named Furudaka Shuntarō.* Furudaka was a rōnin from the province of Ōmi, near Kyōto. Two years earlier he had inherited a shop called the Masu'ya, which he operated under the alias Kiémon.† It did not escape the Shinsengumi command that the Masu'ya was located near the Ikéda'ya and the headquarters of both Chōshū and Tosa. But they did not know that since the August coup, Furudaka's house had served as a place of refuge for dissident Loyalists, including men from those two clans, who plotted the overthrow of the government.

Among these dissidents was Miyabé Teizō, a rōnin of Kumamoto Han. The kingpin of the planned uprising, Miyabé had previously served the powerful outside Lord of Kumamoto as chief instructor of military science. He was now counted among the national leaders of the anti-Tokugawa, antiforeign Loyalist movement. At age forty-four, he was one of the oldest, and most respected, Imperial Loyalists in Kyōto, the majority of whom were in their twenties or thirties. After the August coup, Miyabé had served as staff officer of the imperial guard, accompanying Sanjō Sanétomi during his flight to Chōshū.‡ Miyabé returned to Kyōto undercover in May.

An indiscretion on the part of Miyabé provided the Shinsengumi with a concrete lead to the Masu'ya. On June 1 he sent his elderly

---

* The name is also pronounced "Furutaka" and "Kotaka."

† It is not clear what type of merchandise the Masu'ya handled. According to Shimosawa, the shop dealt in saddlery and secondhand articles. Both Nagakura's oral account and his memoirs indicate only saddlery. In the explanatory notes to Nagakura's memoirs, historian Sachihiko Kimura conjectures from the Masu'ya's location amid lumber merchants along the Takaségawa Canal that the shop dealt in firewood and charcoal. Michio Hirao mentions only secondhand articles. Another source writes that the Masu'ya dealt in arms.

‡ Sanjō Sanétomi was the leader of the Seven Banished Nobles. In 1869 he would serve as minister of the right, the most senior post in the new Meiji government.

manservant, Chūzō, on an errand in town. Recognized by the Shinsengumi, Chūzō was apprehended near a Buddhist temple and interrogated as to the whereabouts of his master. When the old man refused to speak, they tied him to the main temple gate and left him there until such time as he would cooperate. When the proprietress of a nearby inn saw the old man, she set him free. The Shinsengumi was watching. They followed Chūzō to the Masu'ya. By the time they arrived, Miyabé had left the Masu'ya for the safe confines of the Chōshū estate but the samurai who called himself Kiémon, master of the Masu'ya, suffered dire consequences.

At dawn on June 5, more than twenty of the Shinsengumi, including Nagakura, Okita, Harada, Inoué, and a recruit of the previous October named Takéda Kanryūsai, raided the Masu'ya. They were looking for Miyabé, who, of course, was nowhere to be found. Instead, they discovered Furudaka, whom they promptly arrested. Upon searching the house, they located a cache of guns and ammunition, along with incriminating documents exchanged among the plotters, hidden in a secret compartment in a closet wall. Through these documents the Shinsengumi confirmed the veracity of what they had heard from the two men they had recently arrested on the east bank of the Kamogawa. The rebels indeed planned to burn the palace and assassinate the protector of Kyōto. Equally startling, and certainly no less disturbing, was that the rebels also intended to kidnap the emperor. The Shinsengumi now confirmed that Furudaka was deeply involved in the plot, serving as procurer of weapons—although the details required to squelch the uprising, including the when, the where, and the how of it, eluded them.

They brought Furudaka to Mibu headquarters. He was placed in the dank and dim confines of a two-storied storeroom at the Maekawa residence, where he was interrogated by Kondō and Hijikata. Furudaka refused to speak. According to Nagakura, "Furudaka had come to Kyōto resolved to die and wouldn't say a word." He was whipped until the skin on his back was shredded. He "closed his eyes, clenched his teeth, and passed out, but would not open his mouth." Finally Hijikata ran out of patience. He tied Furudaka's hands from behind, and hung him upside down with a heavy rope suspended from a wooden rafter. He drove wooden spikes through the soles of Furu-daka's feet. He attached large candles to the spikes and lit the wicks. A steady stream of molten wax flowed down Furudaka's legs. The pain was excruciating. After suffering for nearly half an hour, he fi-nally broke down. Not only did he confirm the plan for a coup d'état, as had been previously indicated in the documents discovered at his home, but he also made it known that his comrades, including men from Chōshū, were hiding at private residences and inns around Kawaramachi.

The unexpected implications of Furudaka's confession at once alarmed and enraged Kondō and Hijikata—and stimulated their pro-pensity to kill. No less alarmed and enraged were the rebels when they learned of Furudaka's arrest and the discovery of the incrimi-nating letters and weapons cache. Most of the rebels were from Chōshū, Tosa, or Kumamoto. While they did not believe that Furu-daka would willfully divulge their plans to the enemy, the notorious reputation of the Shinsengumi was enough to incite their worst fears. The more levelheaded among them, assuming that Furudaka had been killed and their plot discovered, proposed returning to their respective domains and devising a counterplan to strike at a more opportune time. But certain hotheaded men argued to raid Shinseng-umi headquarters without delay, kill any of the enemy inside, rescue Furudaka if he was alive, and proceed with their original plan. The rebels called a meeting that night to decide which course to take. The meeting place was the Ikéda'ya inn in Kawaramachi.

On the same evening, samurai of five pro-Tokugawa clans, in-cluding Aizu, Hikoné, and Kuwana,* along with the Shinsengumi and other forces, performed security checks at inns, teahouses, restaurants, and headquarters of feudal domains in and around Kawaramachi. The number of men in the Shinsengumi had dwindled to forty. Some of them were ill, leaving just thirty-four men available for service on that evening. Kondō took nine of these men to search the west side of the river. Among them were Nagakura, Okita, and

---

* Kuwana ranked among the twenty Related Houses. The Lord of Kuwana, Matsudaira Sada'aki, was the younger brother of the Lord of Aizu. He occupied the powerful post of inspector of the Imperial Court and nobles.

Tōdō—three of the corps' best swordsmen. Hijikata led some twenty men, including Harada, Inoué, and Saitō, to the east side.[*]

June 5 was the eve of the great Gion Festival in Kyōto, which attracted sightseers from all over Japan. It was a hot summer night. The vicinity of Sanjō Small Bridge, alight with a fete of red and white lanterns, was crowded with people seeking relief in the cool breeze blowing from the Kamogawa. As Nagakura would recall nearly five decades later, certainly none among the crowd suspected, even in their wildest imagination, that one of the bloodiest fights and most significant incidents of the sanguine final years of the Tokugawa Bakufu was about to unfold in their midst. Nor did Kondō's men, even as they reached the front gate of the Ikéda'ya at around ten o'clock, suspect that they were about to cross swords with numerous of the enemy upstairs.[†]

The rebels upstairs, meanwhile, had no inkling that ten expert swordsman, as resolved to die to protect the Bakufu as they themselves were to destroy it, now passed through the front gate of the inn. Kondō's men wore shirts of chain mail and iron helmets with flowing mail hoods and gloves, such as those Kondō had received from his friends in Tama.[‡] The rebels had no such protection. They were crowded into one room, dressed lightly for the hot night. They drank saké, and fervently discussed their war plans. The more they drank, the greater their excitement; the greater their excitement, the more they drank. The ten men downstairs must have heard the ruckus upstairs. Kondō entered first, followed by Nagakura, Okita, and Tōdō. The others remained outside to prevent escape. As the four swordsmen entered, they found guns and spears. They tied these weapons together so that they could not be readily used. Kondō called for the proprietor, who came quickly from the next room.

---

[*] Kondō assigned more men to Hijikata's group than to his own because more of the enemy were expected to be found on the east side than on the west.

[†] The number of rebels reported to be upstairs at the Ikéda'ya depends on the source. Shimosawa (p. 129) indicates fifteen or sixteen; *Shinsengumi Nisshi* 1 (p. 191), twenty; Nagakura (*Shinsengumi Tenmatsuki*, p. 89), more than twenty; history writer Hiroshi Tominari (*Shinsengumi: Ikéda'ya Jiken Tenmatsuki*, p. 193), more than thirty. Kondō himself reported that eleven were killed and twenty-three captured.

[‡] Kondō's chain-mail shirt weighed over thirteen pounds.

"Who's there?" the proprietor asked.

"Shinsengumi!" Kondō roared. "We've come to search the place."

The proprietor panicked. He ran up the rear staircase. The four swordsmen followed him. Upstairs they encountered some twenty men, their swords drawn. "We've come to investigate," Kondō announced. "If you resist, we'll kill you without mercy." According to Nagakura's memoirs, "All of them trembled with fear and moved back. Just then, one of the rebels, a particularly brave man, suddenly attacked with his sword. Okita killed him with one stroke. Others fled downstairs.... Kondō instructed us to follow them."

Downstairs Okita began coughing up blood, incapacitated by a fit of the tuberculosis that would eventually kill him. Kondō guarded the rear of the house. Nagakura covered the area near the front door. Tōdō watched the garden. Soon Hijikata and his men arrived at the scene. As one of the rebels tried to escape through the front door, Tani Sanjurō, of Hijikata's group, stabbed him with a spear. Nagakura followed, delivering the coup de grâce to the man's shoulder. Now another man tried to flee through the front door. Nagakura sliced open his upper body, from the shoulder to the opposite side. "When I went to the garden, there was one man hiding in the latrine. I stabbed him through. He tried to draw his sword, but was so weak that he collapsed. I immediately cut him again on the body."

Soon samurai of Aizu and other clans surrounded the Ikéda'ya. The rebels "came at us like cornered rats, brandishing their swords fiercely above their heads," Nagakura recalled. "Tōdō's helmet was knocked off by an enemy sword," Kondō wrote to his family and friends in the east. "Tōdō was cut at the center of his forehead," Nagakura wrote. "The blood ran into his eyes, making it difficult for him to fight." The man who had cut Tōdō came after Nagakura. A desperate fight ensued, during which the tip of the enemy's blade caught Nagakura about the chest, "not exactly wounding me but ripping my clothes to shreds." Nagakura blocked another attack to his wrist and immediately delivered a counterattack, cutting the man from the left side of the face to the neck. "Blood sprayed as he fell." Meanwhile, Nagakura "noticed that my right hand was sticky. Looking closer, I saw that the flesh had been torn away at the base of my thumb." Kondō fought furiously against four or five of the enemy. "He was nearly cut three different times." When Harada, Inoué, and Takéda burst into the house, four of the rebels threw down their swords and allowed themselves to be captured. Just then, several more corpsmen who had been guarding the front entrance rushed inside. Suddenly one of the rebels upstairs fell through the ceiling. "Takéda Kanryūsai cut him," and Shimada Kai delivered the death-blow with his sword.

"We fought against a large number of rebels," Kondō wrote. "The sparks flew [from our swords]. After we had fought for a couple of hours, Nagakura's sword had been broken in two, Okita's sword had been broken off at the tip, the blade of Tōdō's sword had been cut up like a bamboo whisk.... My sword, perhaps because it is the prize sword *Kotetsu*, was unscathed.... Although I have been in frequent battles ... our opponents were many and all courageous fighters, so that I nearly lost my life."

By the time the fighting ended, thousands of samurai of the Tokugawa camp had been deployed to the area surrounding the Ikéda'ya. According to Kondō's letter, seven rebels were killed during the fighting, four subsequently died from their wounds, and twenty-three were captured. A number of rebels committed suicide after being severely wounded, both inside and outside the Ikéda'ya.

The rebel leader Miyabé Teizō had put up a fierce fight but was no match for Kondō, Okita, Nagakura et al. Miyabé received multiple wounds to the body. Rather than be taken alive, he committed seppuku at the base of the stairs. Miyabé had been particularly close to two late Loyalist leaders—Yoshida Shōin and Kiyokawa Hachirō. The former was the archetype of Japanese revolutionaries and beloved teacher of the Imperial Loyalists of the Chōshū clan. He preached the doctrines of Imperial Reverence and Expel the Barbarians. Shōin was beheaded during Ii Naosuké's purge. Miyabé, Kiyokawa, and Shōin had all been eliminated. That the Shinsengumi was directly responsible for the demise of the first, had opposed the second, and killed disciples of the third certainly did not escape the appreciation of the protector of Kyōto or the authorities in Edo.

Among Shōin's disciples killed at the Ikéda'ya was Yoshida Toshimaro of Chōshū. Before his death, Shōin had expressed his expectation that Toshimaro would play a vital role in the revolution. Toshimaro was only eighteen years old when Shōin was executed in Edo in 1859. Five years later in Kyōto, he and Miyabé planned the foiled uprising. After receiving a minor shoulder wound, Toshimaro escaped from the Ikéda'ya to call for reinforcements at the nearby Chōshū estate. The circumstances of his death are unclear. According to Shimosawa, after arming himself with a spear, he ran back to the Ikéda'ya to continue fighting. In the garden at the rear of the house, he encountered Okita, who killed him without a contest.*

Mochizuki Kaméyata, a Tosa rōnin, close friend of Sakamoto Ryōma, and student of Katsu Kaishū, also died in the fighting. Although he had managed to escape from the Ikéda'ya, the dragnet on the streets outside was tight. When some Aizu men tried to arrest him, he abruptly hacked off one of their arms. With a second stroke he split open the face of another. He ran toward the safe confines of the Chōshū estate. But he was badly wounded, and his energy drained fast. Rather than allow himself to be captured, he kneeled down, drew his short sword, and plunged the blade into his lower abdomen.

Of the scores of Chōshū samurai hiding in Kyōto, few would survive the revolution. Among the survivors was Katsura Kogorō, a founding father of modern Japan.† A brilliant scholar under Yoshida Shōin, expert swordsman, behind-the-scenes manipulator who was never in the wrong place at the wrong time, cagey negotiator of the future Satsuma-Chōshū Alliance that would ultimately topple the Tokugawa, Katsura, age thirty-one, was the political leader of the Chōshū revolutionaries. He had left Hagi, one of the two political centers of Chōshū, the previous January. He arrived in Kyōto the same month, used an alias, and hid at the Kyōto estate of Tsushima Han.

While the radicals in Kyōto were raring to attack the Tokugawa side, the cool, calculating Chōshū leader opposed them. After the

---

* Another source indicates that Yoshida Toshimaro's bloody corpse was discovered the next morning near the Chōshū estate.

† Katsura Kogorō later changed his name to Kido Takayoshi.

breakdown of the talks among the leading feudal lords, Katsura surmised that Chōshū was on the verge of regaining the political edge
in Kyōto, and he wanted to postpone an uprising until that political
edge could be secured. To this end, he negotiated undercover in
Kyōto to gain support among the revolutionaries of certain powerful
clans, including Tottori, Chikuzen, Bizen and Tsushima—all ruled
by outside lords. He temporarily succeeded in persuading his comrades-in-arms in Chōshū to delay their war plans. After the Ikéda'ya
Incident, however, they would no longer be pacified. His whereabouts during the attack are a mystery of history. Having been requested by Miyabé and the others to attend the meeting, he had gone
to the Ikéda'ya about one hour before the attack. Katsura mentioned
in his autobiography that "since nobody had yet arrived, I went to the
nearby Tsushima estate."

The proprietor of the Ikéda'ya fled with his wife and children.
"His hands had not been tied," Nagakura recalled. After the fighting
inside, the proprietor had "untied the ropes binding some of the
Chōshū rebels, allowing them to escape. When Harada Sanosuké
noticed this, he pursued and killed them." On the following day, the
proprietor was arrested, interrogated, and thrown in jail, where he
"died from severe torture."

The aftermath of the "unparalleled tragedy," as described by
Nagakura, was telltale of the extraordinary violence of the battle:

> Not one of the paper screen doors was left intact, all of them
> having been smashed to pieces. The wooden boards of the
> ceiling were also torn apart when men who had been hiding
> above the boards were stabbed with spears from below. The
> tatami mats in a number of rooms, both upstairs and down-
> stairs, were spotted with fresh blood. Particularly pitiful were
> the arms and feet, and pieces of facial skin with the hair still
> attached, scattered about.

The scene outside was similarly "pitiful." According to one eyewitness, the corpses of men who had committed seppuku remained
on the streets for hours, which, in the intense summer heat, must

have presented a ghastly spectacle.* Another eyewitness reported vast amounts of blood in front of the nearby estates of the Chōshū and Kaga domains and in the garden of a merchant house also in close proximity to the Ikéda'ya.

Only three of the men gathered at the Ikéda'ya inn on the night of June 5, 1864, would survive the revolution. The casualties suffered by the Loyalists, both at the Ikéda'ya and in the retaliatory attack by Chōshū in the following month,† were devastating. Through their raid on the Ikéda'ya, the Shinsengumi are credited with having de-layed the Meiji Restoration by a full year. "Had the Shinsengumi not achieved a great victory by attacking the Ikéda'ya," Nagakura claimed, "the life of the Tokugawa Bakufu would have been that much shorter." But the outrage ignited among the Chōshū samurai served to shore up previously lacking consensus in their clan for an all-out war against the Tokugawa, marking a turning point in the revolution. And it is this fact that gives pause to the widespread notion that the Ikéda'ya Incident delayed the Meiji Restoration and rather lends sup-port to the argument that the slaughter actually hastened the final collapse of the Bakufu.

Unarguable is that at the Ikéda'ya the Shinsengumi cut their way into the very psyche of these bloody times, becoming the most feared police force in Japanese history. The men gloried in their victory. As Kondō and his men marched back to their headquarters the next morning, "a crowd of tens of thousands [watched us] from the road-side." They marched in double file. Some carried their drawn swords in hand—because their blades of tempered steel, bent or broken, could not be resheathed. Okita, having recovered from his coughing fit, walked of his own accord. Tōdō, covered with blood, had to be carried on a stretcher. Nagakura was also bloodied. According to Shimosawa, Kondō and Hijikata led the way, smiling at every step. Certainly the two Shinsengumi leaders were elated. They had wielded their propensity to kill to exercise their will to power and now walked

---

* Many of the dead referred to here had most likely been killed after fleeing their respec-tive places of hiding, and were not among those who had gathered at the Ikéda'ya.
† See pages 119–23.

away victorious, demonstrating to themselves and to the world their extraordinary importance. Merely suppressing rōnin was a thing of the past; killing the enemies of the Tokugawa Shogunate was now their raison d'être. In their victory, they were unfazed by the fact that they had butchered some of the finest men of their generation. Kondō and Hijikata "were so composed," wrote Shimosawa, "that one would never have thought they had just fought such a fierce battle."

Only one corpsman was killed during the fighting. Four others were wounded, two fatally. Two days after the Ikéda'ya Incident, Aizu Han rewarded the Shinsengumi with six hundred ryō, among other gifts. Of this, Commander Kondō received thirty ryō, a new sword, and a cask of saké. Vice Commander Hijikata was awarded twenty-three ryō. Okita, Nagakura, Tōdō, Takéda, and two others each received twenty ryō. Eleven corpsmen, including Inoué, Harada, Saitō, and Shimada, were awarded seventeen ryō each. Twelve corpsmen received fifteen ryō each. The families of the three men who had been killed were each awarded twenty ryō.*

---

* Given that one ryō was worth approximately $200 in U.S. currency in 2004, the Shinsengumi as a whole received the equivalent of about $120,000.

A Tale of Bushidō

To bear the full and final burden of responsibility for one's actions was a fundamental requirement of Bushidō. The Code of the Samurai was given precedence over personal rights and wrongs in any given situation, just as it superseded family, clan, and liege lord. And it was by this unyielding and noble code that the samurai preserved their ancient and unchallenged honor, even as their social and political systems crumbled around them.

After the Ikéda'ya Incident, the authorities ordered the Shinsengumi and other security forces to patrol the city day and night in search of Chōshū samurai or their accomplices who might still be lurking in Kyōto. The Shinsengumi performed their job well. "Their surveillance at night brought them from rooftop to rooftop," wrote one contemporary. "If they discovered rōnin, they'd kick down the doors to arrest every last one of them, even thirty or forty at a time." According to Shimada Kai, Kondō went out on patrol astride a white horse and was always accompanied by five or six men wearing white headbands and carrying spears.

On the night of June 10, just five days after the Ikéda'ya Incident, the Shinsengumi learned that Chōshū men had assembled at a restaurant, the Akébono-tei, in the Higashiyama hills on the east side of the city. Several of the Shinsengumi proceeded to the Akébono-tei, accompanied by Aizu men. Upon arriving, instead of Chōshū men, they found one lone samurai of the Tosa clan. The man's name was Asada Tokitarō. He served as an official at Tosa headquarters in Kawaramachi. When accosted, Asada attempted to flee. One of the Aizu samurai, Shiba Tsukasa, assumed that Asada was from Chōshū. Shiba pursued Asada, and when he caught up to him, stabbed him on his side. The wound was not fatal but certainly debilitating. Asada now identified himself and demanded the reason for the Aizu man's actions. Shiba, of course, was perplexed by his blunder. After administering first aid to Asada, the Aizu men brought him to Tosa headquarters. Meanwhile, Shiba returned to Aizu headquarters to inform his lord of the mishap.

The Tosa men in Kyōto did not accept the affront lightly. One hundred of them gathered at the Akébono-tei to plan a retaliatory attack on Shinsengumi and Aizu headquarters. Meanwhile, the Aizu daimyō dispatched several men to the restaurant to apologize. But the Tosa men would not accept their apology. According to certain sources, an Aizu samurai, one Chiba Jirō, took matters into his own hands. He proceeded directly to Tosa headquarters, where he disemboweled himself. The Tosa men were finally appeased, but the incident at the Akébono-tei would not be settled so easily.

Although the Tosa daimyō was an outside lord and his domain a hotbed of anti-Tokugawa sentiment, it was a well-known fact that Yamanouchi Yōdō himself was loyal to the Tokugawa. Tosa was one of the most powerful clans in Japan, and Lord Yōdō one of the Four Brilliant Lords. The Lord of Aizu worried that the incident might adversely affect relations between Aizu and Tosa and, as a result, between Tosa and Edo. On the following day, he sent one of his samurai, accompanied by a physician, to Tosa headquarters. They brought gifts and offered to administer medical care to the wounded man. The Tosa officials refused their offer with the telling explanation that "the customs of our han do not permit a samurai to regret [the loss of his] life after allowing himself to be recklessly wounded." The Aizu representatives, of course, did not need to be reminded that the whole incident had been a violation of Bushidō.

Nor did Shiba. Regretting that his actions "might not only damage relations between Aizu and Tosa, but that [as a result] they might cause harm to the entire nation," he determined that "regardless of right or wrong, I have no alternative but suicide."* On the day after the incident, he prepared himself accordingly. After shaving the crown of his head and neatly arranging his topknot, he dressed himself in white and quietly sat down to die. He exchanged parting cups of saké with his two brothers and others of his comrades, then uttered his final word: "Farewell." He unsheathed his short sword and plunged the blade into his lower abdomen. That instant one of his brothers drew his long sword and decapitated him with one clean stroke. Shiba Tsukasa was twenty-one years old.

While the Lord of Aizu was distraught at the loss of this loyal vassal, he immediately sent a messenger to Tosa headquarters to inform them of Shiba's atonement and to request that a Tosa representative inspect the corpse. Meanwhile, Asada's own gross violation of Bushidō had not escaped him. Asada was shamed for having attempted to flee the initial danger. But even more disgraceful was that he had returned to Tosa headquarters without fighting the men who had wounded him. When the Aizu messenger reached Tosa headquarters, he was duly informed that Asada had similarly taken his own life.

* * * * *

A question comes to mind: Has Bushidō survived the social and political systems of the samurai? Three decades after the end of feudalism in Japan, this question was put to no less a spokesman of the samurai class than Katsu Kaishū, at the close of the nineteenth century, shortly before his death in 1899.

> The samurai spirit must in time disappear. Although it is certainly unfortunate, it does not surprise me at all. I have long known that this would happen once the feudal system was eliminated.

---

* From a signed statement by Shiba, quoted in *Shinsengumi Shiroku*, p. 96.

But even now, if I were extremely wealthy, I'm sure that I would be able to restore that spirit within four or five years. The reason for this is simple. During the feudal era the samurai had to neither till the fields nor sell things. They had the farmers and the merchants do those things [for them], while they received stipends from their feudal lords. They could idle away their time from morning until night without worrying about not having enough to eat. And so all they had to do … was to read books and make a fuss about such things as loyalty and honor.

Once the feudal system was eliminated and the samurai lost their stipends, it was only natural for the samurai spirit to gradually decline…. If you were now to give them money and let them take things easy like they did in the old days, I am certain that Bushidō could be restored.

Battle at the Forbidden Gates

Chōshū had thrown restraint to the wind. As a means for revolution, it was determined to regain the imperial grace it had lost in the Coup of 8/18. The Tokugawa regime must be destroyed, the Chōshū men declared, and they would stop at nothing to realize this great objective. They would capture the emperor as they would a king in a game of chess—because the side in control of the Son of Heaven ruled the nation. But first they must attack their archenemies. Chōshū blamed the Lord of Aizu, master of the Shinsengumi, for the Ikéda'ya slaughter. It rightly surmised that Satsuma's alliance with Aizu was one of expedience, which the former would terminate when the time was ripe. Since its banishment from Kyōto, Chōshū had been convinced of Satsuma's treachery. It suspected Satsuma of plotting to overthrow the Tokugawa Bakufu at Edo only to establish a Shimazu Bakufu at Kagoshima.* The Chōshū men would do everything and anything within their power to prevent this. They would even lay down their lives and incur the stigma of "Imperial Enemy" in the Battle at the Forbidden Gates.

---

* Kagoshima was the castle town and political center of Satsuma. Shimazu, of course, was the name of the ruling family of Satsuma.

News of the slaughter at the Ikéda'ya reached Chōshū Han four days after the incident. The Chōshū samurai were outraged. The entire domain was up in arms. Seven days later they dispatched troops to retaliate. Until the Ikéda'ya, Chōshū policy had been divided between conservatives who advocated restraint in the face of Tokugawa authority and radicals who screamed for war. But their mutual outrage now united the two sides, who called for full-fledged war against the Tokugawa regime.*

By the end of June, more than two thousand Chōshū-led Loyalists, including some three hundred rōnin who had been hiding at the Chōshū estate in Kyōto, were raring to fight. They divided into four divisions at as many locations outside the city—Saga in the northwest, Fushimi and Yamazaki in the south, and Yawata in the southwest. They communicated to the Imperial Court their complete devotion to the emperor; they defended the innocence of the Lord of Chōshū and the court nobles who had been banished after the coup. They informed the court of their intention to remain in Kyōto to investigate those responsible for the Ikéda'ya slaughter. If their appeal was not accepted, they would attack the troops surrounding the Imperial Palace and retake the court by force, although they were outnumbered more than ten to one. Once in control of the Imperial Court, the Loyalists would reinstall the banished nobles for the dual of purpose of restoring Chōshū to imperial grace in order to finally topple the Bakufu, and revenging the slaughter of their comrades at the Ikéda'ya.

Neither the Tokugawa nor the Imperial Court would accept Chōshū's demands, which they correctly interpreted as a threat rather than a peaceful entreaty. The Bakufu placed fifty thousand troops on high alert throughout the city. Among them were samurai under the command of the protector of Kyōto, defending the Nine Forbidden Gates of the Imperial Palace. The court issued an edict stating that the Aizu-Satsuma coup of the previous summer was in complete harmony with the emperor's will, and that Chōshū must withdraw from

---

* The two leading Chōshū revolutionaries, Katsura Kogorō and Takasugi Shinsaku, even now opposed an attack on Kyōto as dangerously reckless. They called for restraint until they could better prepare for war.

Kyōto immediately. When the edict reached the Chōshū commanders at their camps surrounding the city, they rejected it as having been arranged by the Bakufu and Satsuma. The Bakufu now set July 19 as the deadline by which Chōshū must withdraw its troops.*

In the face of impending war, Kondō Isami, clad in chain mail and helmet, two swords at his side, now issued his nine *Martial Prohibitions*, which he read in a loud, clear voice laced with austerity and conviction, to an assembly of his entire corps at the black-tiled front gate of Shinsengumi headquarters. Standing at his side was Hijikata Toshizō, also in chain mail and helmet, observing his troops through piercing dark eyes, his overpowering presence a constant reminder to the rank and file of the mortal allegiance they had pledged when joining the corps. One hundred warriors stood at perfect attention in so many well-formed lines, beneath the red and white banner of "sincerity," each with two swords at his left hip, many bearing lethal spears, some wearing iron helmets, all clad in the light blue jackets with the pointed white stripes on the sleeves. The *Martial Prohibitions* were explicit instructions that each man must strictly obey his duties and follow the orders of his squad captain; never comment on the power of an enemy or ally, or start false rumors; abstain from eating delicacies; never become agitated in an emergency situation, but rather calmly await orders; abstain from fighting or quarreling with others, regardless of personal grudges; check his food and weapons before leaving for battle; fight to the death if his squad captain should fall in battle, and kill any cowards or those who try to flee; during a fierce battle, never remove the body of a fallen comrade other than the squad captain, and never flee; never loot or plunder after victory, but obey the law.

In preparation for the war, the Shinsengumi was stationed with the Mimawarigumi (literally, Patrolling Corps), a separate security corps supervised by the protector of Kyōto, to defend the Kujō-Kawaramachi area in the south of the city. The warriors of the Shinsengumi must have been a particularly impressive sight, because

---

* See Appendix I (8).

the townspeople flocked to get a glimpse of them at their encampment in Kujō-Kawaramachi.

On the sweltering night of July 18, one day before the announced deadline for Chōshū's withdrawal, the warriors of that clan began their nightlong march toward the Imperial Palace at the deep, dark toll of the eight o'clock bell. The fighting broke out at dawn the next morning. The Chōshū samurai, completely outnumbered, were armed with swords, spears, and guns. They attacked Aizu and Kuwana near Hamaguri Gate, one of the Nine Forbidden Gates of the Imperial Palace. The Chōshū men fought fiercely, and for a while it seemed they would win the fight. But Satsuma suddenly joined in, firing upon Chōshū's flank with four field guns.

Kondō, Hijikata, and their entire corps were certainly eager for battle. It is doubtful, however, that they actually had the chance to fight. All they could do, Hirao wrote, "was listen to the roar of gunfire coming from the direction of the Imperial Palace, with the knowledge that a fierce battle had begun." Meanwhile, no less a loyal retainer of the Tokugawa Shōgun than Katsu Kaishū, deeply troubled by the fighting in Kyōto, wondered about the outcome from his naval academy in nearby Kōbé—where he imparted his extensive knowledge of naval science to allies of Chōshū, most notably Sakamoto Ryōma. "At night the sky over Kyōto was bright red," Kaishū recalled of his view of the distant flames that destroyed much of the city. After the fighting he proceeded to Kyōto. He traveled on foot along the Yodogawa River. On the way he encountered a boat carrying three samurai heading away from Kyōto. The three samurai disembarked when they saw the elite Tokugawa official. At first Kaishū thought they intended to kill him, until "two of them suddenly stabbed each other to death, while the other one stabbed himself through the throat. It was only then that I realized that [these were Chōshū samurai and that] Chōshū had lost the war."

Indeed, before the end of the day all four Chōshū divisions had been defeated in the Battle at the Forbidden Gates. More than one hundred Loyalists perished. Forced to retreat once again, the rebels returned to Chōshū in disgrace. Chōshū was declared an "Imperial Enemy" for firing upon the palace. The Loyalists' second defeat in less than a year was the deathblow to the movement of Imperial Reverence and Expel the Barbarians, as the Tokugawa Bakufu, and its most dreaded security force, reigned supreme.

The Shinsengumi had brought their captives from the Ikéda'ya to Mibu headquarters for questioning. Shortly after, these men were transferred to Rokkaku Jail, in western Kyōto, just north of Mibu. Among the prisoners were numerous rōnin from various domains, including Furudaka Shuntarō, and the proprietor of the Ikéda'ya. When Furudaka saw his fellow Loyalists brought into the jail, wrote Shimosawa, "so ashamed was he for giving them away that he was unable even to exchange words with them. [Rather] he prayed silently that his day of execution would come soon." Furudaka's prayers were answered on July 20, the day after the Battle at the Forbidden Gates.

The flames of war fast approached the jail. The jailers worried that the prisoners might escape. The magistrate of the jail panicked. He took drastic measures. The following is an eyewitness's account of the ensuing bloodbath:

> The fire had started in the east on the morning of July 19. The roar of guns thundered in the sky and the cries of war pierced my ears. Two or three hundred Bakufu troops suddenly came to guard the jail. After a while the flames in the east died down, but [another] fire started near the Imperial Palace. The flames were spreading southward, explosions shook the earth and the report of guns rang out even more violently. I thought that Chōshū must have finally attacked Kyōto, as they had previously intended, but that it was disquieting that they would bring the fire to the palace gates....

> ... That night I found out that Chōshū had been defeated.... From the window I could see that Kyōto was engulfed in flames, gleaming brilliantly and colorfully in the night.

> I spent a sleepless night. The fire had swept through the lower part of Kyōto ... and [from the smoke] the sun was the color

of copper. But the fire still burned. Suddenly there was a great uproar outside. The jailers rang the alarm bell to call the troops. "The enemy is approaching the jail," they said. They told them to load their guns, and ran around with their un-sheathed swords in hand. But they soon realized that what they had feared was only a [Bakufu] artillery corps patrolling Kyōto... .

At around noontime I heard a voice saying that since the flames had reached Horikawa,* the prisoners should be moved elsewhere because of the danger. In the afternoon a number of officers carrying spears were coming and going outside my cell, preceded by the jailers.

Thirty-three men, including Furudaka, were now taken from their cells. The author of the account above remained alive in his cell to hear "the sound of swords severing heads," until all thirty-three of them were finally executed before nightfall. When the massacre was brought to the attention of the Lord of Aizu, even he was disturbed. He is said to have immediately summoned the magistrate and cen-sured him harshly.

* * * * *

Chōshū continued to bring disaster upon itself. After the thrashing they had incurred by the American and French warships at Shimono-seki in the previous summer, the Chōshū men realized that expelling the foreigners by military force was impossible. They nevertheless continued to menace foreign ships passing through Shimonoseki Strait. "The [Chōshū] batteries had been destroyed," wrote Sir Ernest Satow, then-interpreter to the British minister in Japan, "but as soon as the foreign men-of-war quitted [sic] the scene, the Chōshū men set to work to rebuild forts, to construct others, and to mount all the guns they could bring together. So the hornet's nest was after no long

---

* Horikawa was the castle moat, just west of the jail.

interval in good repair again, and more formidable for attack and defence than before." Chōshū's show of antiforeignism was actually a ploy to stir up indignation throughout Japan, particularly in Kyōto, against the Bakufu for failing to expel the foreigners.

The foreign legations at Yokohama would not suffer Chōshū's political charades. Of this the Bakufu was well aware, just as it secretly welcomed the foreigners' ultimatum for Chōshū to allow their ships peaceful passage through Shimonoseki Strait. Chōshū ignored the ultimatum, much to the satisfaction of the Bakufu. Edo, in fact, fully expected the foreigners to punish the renegade han. These expectations were realized on August 5, when an allied squadron of seventeen warships of Great Britain, France, the United States, and Holland, carrying 288 cannon and more than five thousand troops, pounded the Shimonoseki coastline. In one day the foreigners destroyed nearly all of Chōshū's forts at Shimonoseki, and easily overran the hundreds of samurai defending the coast.* "The Japanese could not stand our advance, the sharp musketry fire threw them into disorder, and they had to run for it," wrote Satow, who had landed with the troops. "In only one case was an attempt made to come to close quarters. One fellow had concealed himself behind a door with uplifted sword in both hands ready to cut down a man just about to enter. But contrary to his expectation, his intended victim gave him a prod in the belly which laid him on his back and spoilt his little game."

Nine days later a peace treaty was concluded between Chōshū and the four foreign nations. The leaders of the movement to Expel the Barbarians finally abandoned their xenophobic policy—this time both in name and in practice and, as a matter of course, forfeited their claim that they alone were the true champions of the Imperial Court. For the next three and a half years, Chōshū would instead focus its energies on its one great objective—toppling the Tokugawa Shogunate.

---

* According to initial estimates by the British, the Chōshū troops numbered six hundred. Satow notes, however, that he later heard "from a Chōshū man who was present that their force was only half of that."

Return of a Hero

His indomitable will to power notwithstanding, the commander was endowed with a certain purity inherent in his humble background and refined through years of training with the sword. In the Imperial Capital his corps had metamorphosed from a vehicle of "loyalty and patriotism" into an instrument of cold-blooded murder; but he had nevertheless retained in his heart the essence of that purity. And while that essential purity was indeed diminished by fleeting wealth, rank, and distinction, which with a poet's brush he claimed never to have desired, it was embellished by a permanent and historical heroism that would accompany him in death.

After the Ikéda'ya Incident there was not a soul in Kyōto who did not recognize the name Kondō Isami or who did not know of the lethal corps of swordsmen he commanded. This is not to say that the Shinsengumi had gained the favor of the good people of the Imperial Capital, whose sympathy still rested with the Loyalists. The mere mention of Kondō's corps evoked hatred among the Loyalists, whose comrades they had slaughtered; fear among those whom they now hunted; gratitude and praise among the protector of Kyōto and Bakufu elite; awed reverence and even adoration among the people of Musashi province and the shōgun's capital three hundred miles to the east.

At the end of August 1864, the Shinsengumi commander was a different man from the reserved and stoic fencing instructor who, with seven of his top swordsmen, had left Edo in February of the previous year to join the disorderly ranks of the Rōshi Corps, and different even from the co-commander who less than one year before had eliminated his only rival. The germ of self-importance in Kondō, nurtured by his unyielding will to power, had, according to Nagakura, degenerated into "reckless ... and egotistic behavior." Kondō had ruled the Shinsengumi like a tyrant since Serizawa's assassination. "He treated our comrades at Mibu headquarters as if they were his vassals. If they did not listen to him, he would resort to the sword." Many of the corpsmen, including Nagakura, had become disillusioned with the corps and even indignant at their commander. They contemplated quitting the Shinsengumi, which, of course, was a capital offense. "There were signs that the corps would break apart." Six ranking corpsmen, including Nagakura, Harada, Saitō, and Shimada, submitted to the Lord of Aizu an appeal expressing their grievances. They probably expected to be ordered by Kondō to commit seppuku for the violation of protocol. But the Lord of Aizu was neither about to let these six tried-and-true warriors die nor his crack security force break up, which, as protector of Kyōto and master of the Shinsengumi, he worried "would be attributed to my lack of insight." He would not inform the commander of his meeting with the six corpsmen or of their appeal. Instead, he called together the seven of them, including Kondō, to settle the matter over amicable cups of saké.

* * * * *

Perhaps it was the combination of the uncertainty of life, the constant threat of imminent death, and the virulence of youth that encouraged unbridled profligacy among samurai on both sides of the revolution. There is a saying: a hero is fond of the sensual pleasures. Katsura Kogorō of Chōshū was certainly a hero. His visits to the Yoshida'ya inn, in the Sanbongi pleasure quarter near the western bank of the Kamogawa, are the stuff of both history and legend. Katsura gleaned valuable information through his lover-spy and future wife, the *geigi*

Ikumatsu, who entertained patrons from Aizu and Kuwana, the Shin-sengumi, and others of the Tokugawa camp.* Ikumatsu saved Katsu-ra's life in the dangerous aftermath of the Battle at the Forbidden Gates. After his comrades retreated to Chōshū, he remained in Kyōto undercover to gather information. He was the most hunted survivor of the Ikéda'ya Incident. The Shinsengumi and Aizu samurai scoured the city in his pursuit. Disguised as a beggar, he hid for five days and nights under the bridges of the Kamogawa, among the throngs left homeless from the conflagration of war. Each night Ikumatsu braved the dangerous streets to bring him cooked rice as sustenance from starvation. She was later arrested and interrogated as to his where-abouts, but to no avail. Katsura eventually escaped to Tajima prov-ince, leaving Ikumatsu behind in the safe confines of Tsushima's Kyōto estate.

It has been suggested that Katsu Kaishū had numerous mistresses only because he was a hero. As the great man began to rise through the ranks of the Tokugawa hierarchy, he purchased a sizable house in Edo's Akasaka district, suitable for a man of his station. Young live-in maids came to serve at the Katsu residence, and the master had his way with each of them. They remained in his home with the children they bore him, under the same roof as his wife and other children. Kaishū's wife, Tamiko, was a former geisha. She was very much the madam of the household, whom the servants at once re-spected and feared. In 1887 Kaishū was created a count by the Impe-rial Court. The former geisha was now a countess and the wife of one of the most illustrious men in Japan. Her servants displayed their reverence to their mistress each morning. They sat formally in a row at the entrance to her room. They greeted their mistress with a si-multaneous bow. Kaishū, in his own way, also respected his wife: "Had Tamiko been born a man, she would have certainly made a great statesman. It is much to her credit that she never quarreled with any of the women I bedded." Kaishū had the following to say about the carnal desire of great men:

---

* Neither the geigi of Kyōto nor the geisha of Edo were harlots. Rather, they were enter-tainers accomplished in the arts of song and dance and highly refined in the complex etiquette demanded by their profession.

Try as he might, carnal desire is not something that a young man can easily suppress. On the other hand, the most vigorous [driving force] in a young man is the ambition to achieve greatness. It is extremely admirable if he can use the fire of his ambition to burn up his carnal desire. It is a true hero who can calm himself when his passion is aroused. Before he knows it, he will gradually be driven by his ambition to achieve great things ... no longer thinking of anything else.

If Katsu Kaishū analyzed the hero's carnal desire, his teacher, Sakuma Shōzan, encouraged prurience among great men. During the Tokugawa era, unless the patriarch of a samurai household produced a male heir, his family line was in danger of being discontinued. Sakuma was as concerned with the dire necessity of producing a son as he was convinced of his own historical greatness. He professed that a woman's sole purpose was to procreate, and that a great man should sire children with as many women as possible for the sake of society. Since a woman was merely a vehicle of procreation, her sexual appeal was secondary to her robust ability to bear healthy children. In addition to his wife, Junko, who was Kaishū's younger sister, Sakuma kept at least two mistresses-—one of whom bore his only son. In September 1864, two months after Sakuma was assassinated in Kyōto* and while Kondō Isami was in Edo, Hijikata Toshizō sent a letter to Kaishū informing him that his "nephew," Sakuma Kakujirō, had joined the Shinsengumi to avenge his father's murder.†

Despite his unquestionable ambition, Kondō Isami, who had left his wife and child at his home in Edo, would never "burn up his carnal desire" in Kyōto. Ruggedly handsome, the notorious swordsman certainly struck a dashing figure in the pleasure quarters. According to Shimada Kai, Kondō was accustomed to dressing formally in wide riding trousers of fine silk, patterned with thin dark stripes, with a black crepe jacket, so that he looked more like a feudal lord than a lordless samurai. His clothes were adorned with the Kondō family

---

* See Appendix I (8).
† Sakuma Shōzan's wife was Katsu Kaishū's sister.

crest—three horizontal bars in a circle. He often wore his full head of thick black hair tied in a bushy topknot, his large mouth closed in firm resolution. On his feet he wore wooden clogs. The two swords at his left hip were of a modest makeup, with black hilts and wax-colored scabbards. His "reckless and egotistic behavior" notwithstanding, the Shinsengumi commander exercised due discretion so as not to be recognized coming and going on his frequent visits to the Kyōto pleasure quarters. As Shimada recalled, "He always kept the curtain of his palanquin tightly drawn and covered his face with a hood."

During the nearly five years Kondō Isami spent in Kyōto, he enjoyed the favor of numerous women. One of them, a courtesan named Miyuki, he kept in a house in the southwestern part of the city. According to Shimosawa, she was "a tall and slender beauty, twenty-three or twenty-four years old." A half century later, in 1911, Miyuki recalled her first meeting with Kondō. "I was being kept [by another man at a house] near the Ikéda'ya, where all that commotion had occurred. The Shinsengumi suddenly raided the house, saying they suspected that a rōnin by the name of so-and-so was hiding there. They searched the entire house most violently. I was frightened because during those days the Shinsengumi derived pleasure from killing people. While I was shaking with fear, a person who seemed like the commander came and quieted everyone down... . That was the first time I ever saw Kondō." Soon after the incident, Miyuki received a station at the Kitsu'ya, a house in the Shimabara pleasure quarter. Kondō apparently expected to find her at the Kitsu'ya, because he "came the first day I was there." Miyuki had a younger sister. Her name was Otaka. "He took care of us both," Miyuki said. Otaka was eighteen years old and, Shimosawa wrote, "no less a beauty than her older sister."

"I had rheumatism," Miyuki recalled. "While I was away receiving treatment at a physician's house in Fushimi, Kondō flirted with Otaka over drinks. They eventually became close with each other. Since she had worked at a teahouse in Ōsaka, I wouldn't exactly say that she was respectable, but my little sister had not intended to steal him from me, either." Otaka had Kondō's child—a girl she named Oyū. The name was written with the Chinese character for courage. That the name well suited the father is a fact of history. That the child was deserving of her father's namesake is attested to by her aunt. "They were like two peas in a pod," Miyuki said.

Kondō sired a baby boy with a woman named Komano, who worked the Sanbongi pleasure quarter. Like Ikumatsu, who entertained men of the enemy side to provide Katsura Kogorō with information vital to Chōshū, Komano spied for the Shinsengumi. Miyuki was "determined not to lose out to her. There were a number of times when I sent someone to get Kondō away from her and bring him back to the Kitsu'ya." Kondō enjoyed the pleasures of another geigi named Uéno, who, Shimosawa was quick to mention, "was no beauty." He was also intimate with a courtesan named Kin, one of Miyuki's rivals at the Kitsu'ya. At age twenty-three, Kin "was one of the most beautiful women in all of Kyōto," wrote Shimosawa, "with the refined elegance of trickling water." Kondō also spent a good deal of time at the Ōgaki'ya house in the Nijō district just north of Mibu. Another one of Kondō's favorite haunts was the Yamaginu teahouse in the Gion district, which, Miyuki said, "was the Shinsengumi's gathering place. When they got money for entertainment after the uproar at the Ikéda'ya, they were always telling us to drink and dance [with them], day and night."

Their exorbitance required money. Unlike many of the renegades they hunted, the men of the Shinsengumi received steady pay. As Miyuki pointed out, "they had no shortage of money.… . No matter where they went, they were well received by the women."

Hijikata was also a famous carouser. "Kondō often brought Hijikata Toshizō with him," said Miyuki. "He was intimate with a courtesan named Shinonomé." And he liked to make his escapades known. In a letter to Kojima, Hijikata boasted of intimate relationships with twelve women in Ōsaka and Kyōto. Once he sent a package from Kyōto to his fencing friends at the Hino Dōjō. Accompanying the package was a short note, indicating "something precious inside for you all." Hijikata's friends eagerly opened the package. Inside they found numerous and passionate love letters to Hijikata from women of the pleasure quarters. The Hino men just laughed at Hijikata's antic, saying: "It looks like Toshizō has scored another point on us."

* * * * *

In July the Imperial Court issued an edict (arranged by Edo) ordering the Bakufu to punish Chōshū for its crime of attacking the Imperial Palace. On August 13, the Bakufu, in turn, issued orders for twenty-one feudal domains to prepare their armies for a military expedition against Chōshū. Edo expected to take advantage of Chōshū's misfortunes to restore its own authority, which had been on the decline since the assassination of Ii Naosuké four years earlier, and had been seriously challenged by Chōshū until the coup in Kyōto the previous year. But the days of the shōgun's absolute rule were over—although neither his ministers at Edo, nor his allies at the Imperial Court, nor his deputies in Kyōto, nor the leaders of his most dreaded security force, would recognize this bitter fact. A lack of consensus between the ministers in Edo and Lord Yoshinobu, who in March had been appointed inspector-general of the forces protecting the emperor in Kyōto, and who two years hence would become the fifteenth and last Tokugawa Shōgun, delayed the expedition. Furthermore, among those daimyō who had been ordered to provide troops for the expedition were sympathizers of Chōshū. Even the feudal lords who ostensibly supported the Bakufu were not eager to bolster Tokugawa prestige at their own monetary and human expense. Further complicating the situation, the shōgun remained at Edo Castle—although he was expected to lead the expeditionary forces westward to Chōshū.

Aside from the tense political situation, the Shinsengumi commander was concerned about the failing health of his adoptive father. Kondō Isami had been in Kyōto for a year and a half. He had not been home during that time. He greatly wanted to return to Edo to see Kondō Shūsuké, and to visit his wife, Otsuné, and their two-year-old daughter, Tamako. The dire situation in Kyōto, however, had not permitted him the luxury of absence to attend to personal affairs. But Chōshū had been subdued, if only temporarily. Furthermore, Kondō worried that the Loyalists would use Iémochi's lack of resolution to launch the expedition as an excuse to stir up anti-Tokugawa sentiment at the Imperial Court, under the pretext that the shōgun was neglecting the imperial edict. Since his great victory at the Ikéda'ya, Kondō's political views had become respected by men at the highest levels of government. He now petitioned the Lord of Aizu for permission to travel to Edo to urge the shōgun's senior council to send Iémochi to Kyōto for an audience with the emperor as an indication of his good intentions to honor the edict. Official permission was granted Kondō in September.

On September 5, Kondō, Nagakura (by now the two men had mended their differences), Takéda, and a fourth corpsman hired as many express palanquins for the first leg of the three-hundred-mile journey to Edo. Soon they arrived at the domain of the Lord of Kuwana on the Bay of Isé, where rough seas threatened their crossing. Braving the storm, they hastened across the bay by ferry. Upon landing, they continued eastward, again by express palanquin. Two days later they reached the official Hakoné checkpoint, in the mountain pass some sixty miles west of the shōgun's capital. A notice posted at the guardhouse informed travelers that they must produce a passport. But Kondō Isami was not about to be imposed upon by the formalities of a guardhouse. Ordering his perplexed palanquin bearers to proceed past the armed guards, he announced loudly from the confines of his sedan, "This is Kondō Isami, commander of the Shinsengumi in Kyōto. I'm coming through on official business." Dumbfounded, the guards merely watched as the four palanquins moved unchecked through the checkpoint. Kondō's party reached Edo on September 9, after a four-day journey that normally took two weeks.

When Kondō had left his home in Edo, he was a fencing instructor with high aspirations. He now returned in glory as commander of the Bakufu's top security force and a hero among the people of the east. The hero was reunited, however fleetingly, with his adoptive father, wife, and daughter. Kondō's biological father, Miyagawa Hisajirō, declined to meet his youngest son because he did not want to "take up his precious time, when he is working so hard for the country." Kojima and Satō were of a much different sentiment. They hurried to the Shieikan to see Kondō, who boasted to them of the details of the fighting at the Ikéda'ya and the Forbidden Gates. The Shinsengumi commander also met with the Lord of Matsumae, a member of the shōgun's senior council, to press upon him the necessity of sending Iémochi to Kyōto. Kondō's appeal was rejected. As the Lord of Matsumae hinted, the Bakufu simply could not afford the great financial burden occasioned by a shogunal entourage of some three thousand men on a three-hundred-mile overland journey lasting nearly three weeks.

With the Bakufu preparing for its expedition against Chōshū, Kondō certainly expected that his corps would be called upon to fight in that war. To this end, he would need new recruits. Having hailed from eastern Japan, Kondō believed that the samurai of the east surpassed their counterparts of the west in the arts of war. Kondō, ever the warrior, took the opportunity of his return to Edo to enlist more than fifty new men. Among them was one Itō Kashitarō, who would serve as staff officer of the corps, third in command after Kondō and Hijikata. Itō was a rōnin from the province of Hitachi, northeast of Edo, and very much a part of the eastern Japan whose warriors Kondō held in such high esteem. Itō, in fact, was a famous swordsman of the Hokushin Ittō style. He was also an intellectual—a noted scholar of Japanese classical literature and poetry, with a keen sense of politics. At age twenty-eight, Itō was "slender, clear-eyed, and extremely handsome."* He shared some basic qualities with Kondō and Hijikata. He was a man of ability and courage. He was a natural leader. He advocated Expel the Barbarians. Also like Kondō, Itō had been the chief instructor at a fencing academy in Edo. More significantly and in direct contrast to both Kondō and Hijikata, Itō was a devout Imperial Loyalist. His devotion to the emperor, however, did not necessarily belie his loyalty to the Bakufu or to the Shinsengumi. Emperor Kōmei did not condone the anti-Tokugawa radicals who had wrought havoc in his once peaceful capital. In fact, he quietly detested the Chōshū-led Loyalists who revered him. The emperor would never oppose the Tokugawa, upon whom he depended to preserve the sovereignty of Japan. More than anything, the emperor desired harmony in his empire so that Japan might be strong enough to defend itself against

---

* Shinohara Tainoshin quoted by Kan Shimosawa, *Shinsengumi Shimatsuki*, p. 169.

foreign aggression. This was why in 1862 he had allowed his younger sister, Princess Kazu, to marry Shōgun Iémochi, despite bitter opposition among the Loyalists. And now that Princess Kazu was living in Edo Castle, Emperor Kōmei was deeply concerned for her safety. An attack on the Edo regime might cost the princess her life. It was with this reason in mind that in the summer of 1863 the emperor had secretly issued an imperial edict to Satsuma to restore order in his capital. Satsuma, of course, subsequently formed its alliance with Aizu to oust Chōshū from Kyōto.

Although Kondō had been unable to convince the authorities in Edo to send the shōgun to Kyōto, his success in bringing Itō into the Shinsengumi fold made his Edo trip worthwhile. Kondō had great expectations for Itō, who brought a number of his followers into the Shinsengumi, including swordsmen from his dōjō.

Perhaps Kondō Isami had begun to doubt the Bakufu's ability to expel the foreigners. Perhaps he had even come to question his own simpleminded, however widespread, belief that Japanese were superior to foreigners by virtue of samurai spirit, tradition, and culture. It was with these doubts in mind that, shortly before leaving Edo, he visited the home of physician Matsumoto Ryōjun, a scholar of Western ideas. In the previous decade Matsumoto had been among twenty-six Tokugawa samurai to join Chief Naval Cadet Katsu Kaishū at the Bakufu's naval academy in Nagasaki. Matsumoto studied medicine in Nagasaki under the Dutch naval medical officer Pompe van Meerdervoort. In 1863 Matsumoto modernized the practice of medicine at the Tokugawa medical facility in Edo, and was appointed official physician to the shōgun. This progressive Tokugawa official was impressed enough with the reactionary Shinsengumi commander to include an account of their first meeting in his autobiography, dictated some forty years later.

My family was afraid of [Kondō Isami] because he was a rōshi. (During those days rōshi used to force their way into people's houses and intimidatingly demand money. Or they would come to the homes of people who had adopted Western ideas and conducted trade with foreigners. The rōshi would use violent language and threaten them, and in extreme cases kill them if they did not abide by their demands. It was therefore not without reason that my family was afraid.) I told them there was nothing to fear. Although there are many people who say that Isami was a violent man, from his actions I could see that such was not the case.... A person [like him], who was ready to give his life for the nation, was a man of integrity and morals. I showed him to the drawing room and asked him the purpose of his visit.

Kondō told Matsumoto that he had come to hear about "foreign nations." Matsumoto replied that rōshi had been "butchering foreigners at random" and "were poorly lacking in good sense." He said that Japan must learn from the foreigners rather than despise them. He cited a Confucius saying: "A warrior must know his enemy to know himself." He warned of the militarization of the great Western powers, who vied among one another to reap the benefits of Asia. They had colonized India and China, and now they had designs on Japan. Matsumoto's words echoed the "control the barbarians through barbarian technology" slogan of Sakuma Shōzan.* He showed Kondō maps and mechanical drawings and went to great pains to explain them. And while it had been Matsumoto's intention to awaken Kondō to Japan's urgent need to adopt Western military technology, he probably only intensified the swordsman's resentment of the foreign intruders.

Three days later Kondō visited Matsumoto's home again. His second visit was for a more immediate, practical purpose. "He [Kondō] laughed, and said he was ill." Matsumoto diagnosed Kondō with a stomach ailment, caused by "bad diet." The physician gave the Shinsengumi commander medicine, arranged with him to meet again in Kyōto, and sent him on his way. Kondō left Edo the next day, October 15, and reached Kyōto twelve days later.

---

* See Appendix I (8).

ENDINGS AND TRANSFORMATIONS

The end was imminent, yet so far off. As the supreme lord weakened in the face of his enemies, his most lethal fighting force achieved its greatest moment. As war and death shook the very foundations of the military regime of his ancestors, a sincerity supported by bloodletting, a terrible propensity for the same, and a will to power that knew no bounds catapulted his fighting force into the highest order of things.

The Tokugawa Bakufu proceeded with its plan for a military expedition against Chōshū. By mid-November 1864, 150,000 troops had been amassed at the Chōshū borders—although it was becoming apparent that these troops lacked both the morale and the will to fight. Furthermore, Satsuma had recently undergone a change of heart vis-à-vis Chōshū. These two leaders in the mounting revolution were still enemies. Satsuma's military alliance with Aizu in the previous year had resulted in Chōshū's banishment from Kyōto, its fall from imperial grace, and its eventual "Imperial Enemy" stigma. But Satsuma and Chōshū shared one very significant and deep sentiment—two and a half centuries of festering resentment toward the Tokugawa.

Now that the Bakufu had lost its undisputed authority of the past,

Saigō Kichinosuké,* de facto leader of the Satsuma military and staff officer of the Tokugawa's expeditionary forces against Chōshū, concluded that it was no longer in the best interest of Satsuma to fight against Chōshū. On the contrary, it now occurred to Saigō that the mere presence of this most overt enemy of the Tokugawa served as a constant menace to Edo, further diminishing the shōgun's authority. Saigō was also aware of internal discord in Chōshū, which had recently weakened that clan in the face of the impending attack. The Chōshū domain, in fact, was on the verge of civil war. The conservatives in Chōshū, still fearful of the wrath of the Tokugawa Bakufu, reverted to their pre-Ikéda'ya espousal of allegiance to Edo. The Chōshū Loyalists, radical as ever, called for military preparation to fight the Tokugawa. But now that Imperial Reverence and Expel the Barbarians was a thing of the past, Chōshū was temporarily under the control of the conservatives.

Taking advantage of Chōshū's internal discord, Saigō presented that government with a set of conditions by which war could be avoided. The three Chōshū ministers officially responsible for the attack on the Imperial Capital would be ordered to commit seppuku and their four staff commanders executed; the Chōshū daimyō and his heir would send a letter of apology to the Bakufu for initiating the attack, and both would be placed under house arrest; Yamaguchi Castle, the secondary castle of Chōshū Han, would be demolished. Chōshū accepted the conditions, and, for the time being, war was avoided.

But the Bakufu did not benefit from Chōshū's capitulation. A vivid example of Edo's inability to regain undisputed authority was its attempt in the previous September to reinstate the centuries-old system of alternate attendance, which it had abolished two years earlier. Having crushed the Loyalists in Kyōto, the shogunate was under the false impression that it had indeed recouped its lost authority. However, its order for the wives and heirs of all the feudal lords in Japan to return to their residences in Edo, as stipulated by alternate attendance, was simply ignored.

---

* Later, Saigō Takamori.

What's more, Chōshū remained a very real threat to the Tokugawa. Although the Chōshū government had capitulated to Edo's demands, the rebels in Chōshū had not. Far from giving up the fight, the Chōshū Loyalists were as determined as ever to overthrow the Bakufu. Their determination was indicated by their new battle cry— Imperial Loyalism and Down with the Bakufu.* They were led by a particularly fiery young samurai by the name of Takasugi Shinsaku. In June 1863, only days after Chōshū had been bombarded by foreign ships at Shimonoseki, Takasugi formed Japan's first modern militia. He named this army *Kiheitai*—Extraordinary Corps. Kiheitai was extraordinary not only for its superior fighting ability but also as Japan's first fighting force in which men of the merchant and peasant classes fought alongside samurai. Until that time the military of Chōshū, like that of all feudal clans in Japan, consisted entirely of samurai, whose sole purpose for hundreds of years had been to defend their han. But after two and a half centuries of Pax Tokugawa, these samurai had forgotten how to fight. Takasugi challenged the social structure of Tokugawa feudalism by arming the commoners. And though he had ostensibly formed his corps to defend Chōshū from foreign invasion, his ultimate goal was the overthrow of the Bakufu.

In April 1865, the first year of the era of Keiō, the Bakufu issued orders for the great feudal lords to dispatch armies to western Japan in preparation for a so-called second expedition against Chōshū. Edo, of course, was unaware that at this very time Sakamoto Ryōma was arranging with Saigō for Satsuma's aid in procuring modern rifles and warships from foreign merchants in Nagasaki to arm Chōshū. In contrast, most Tokugawa troops carried old-fashioned guns. Furthermore, the Bakufu lacked the capital to wage a war and the moral support among the feudal domains, most notably Satsuma, to sustain one. Of this last point, and of Chōshū's resolve to fight, Kondō Isami was painfully aware.

In November, Kondō and eight of his corpsmen, including Itō, Takéda, and Yamazaki, accompanied Bakufu Chief Inspector Nagai

---

* With the death of the Imperial Reverence and Expel the Barbarians movement, the Loyalists adopted the more radical slogan Imperial Loyalism and Down with the Bakufu.

Naomuné on a trip to Hiroshima Han, on Chōshū's eastern border. Nagai was dispatched to question Chōshū representatives regarding their clan's intention to abide by the conditions of the peace agreement of the previous year. If they would not abide by the conditions, the Bakufu would launch an expedition against them—which, of course, was exactly what Chōshū wanted. Kondō, for his part, intended to travel undercover to Hagi Castle Town, the nerve center of the Chōshū Loyalists, to glean information. He was fully aware of the great danger to his life. Before leaving, he had entrusted the command of his corps to Hijikata, and had quietly appointed Okita as his successor as chief instructor of the Tennen Rishin style. As it turned out, Kondō's precautions, while becoming of a samurai, proved unnecessary. He was unable to gain entrance into Chōshū.

After returning to Kyōto, Kondō reported to the Lord of Aizu that Chōshū was preparing for war. He also expressed some disturbing impressions of Bakufu troops in Hiroshima: "Although the hatamoto have gradually reached Geishū province,* they display no fighting spirit whatsoever." Both Kondō and the Lord of Aizu felt that the Bakufu's long delay in initiating the fighting had diminished the will to fight among the frontline troops. Kondō was disgusted with these so-called Knights of the Tokugawa, who spent their time "getting souvenirs together" and "grew weary just waiting to return to the east." He advised that "since we cannot expect victory if war should break out," any sign of submission by Chōshū should be accepted "with leniency."

Far from showing any sign of submission, the Chōshū daimyō refused a summons to Edo. Instead, he ordered the people throughout his realm, commoners and samurai alike, to prepare for all-out war. Sakamoto Ryōma described the situation in Chōshū as he had witnessed it: "Chōshū is putting everything into the training of its troops. Since April they have been drilling from around six to ten every morning. It's the same all over Chōshū. Each of their battalions is made up of between three and four hundred men, with a general staff officer in command. The battalions in every district and every

---

* Hiroshima Han.

village drill each morning. There is nothing like it anywhere else in Japan. No matter where you go in Chōshū—the mountains, the rivers, the valleys—you are bound to come across fortifications; and there are land mines planted on most of the main roads. Chōshū is certainly at the forefront of Western artillery."

In a final effort to avoid war, the Bakufu dispatched Senior Councilor Ogasawara Nagamichi (Lord of Karatsu) to Chōshū in January 1866. Ogasawara was escorted by Nagai, who was again accompanied by the Shinsengumi commander and several of his men. Included among the Shinsengumi men were Itō and his close friend and confidant Shinohara Tainoshin. The senior councilor carried demands from Edo that the Lord of Chōshū and his heir submit to confinement at their residence, and that their domain be reduced by the enormous amount of 100,000 koku. Both demands were ignored.

✻ ✻ ✻ ✻ ✻

In May, as Shōgun Tokugawa Iémochi led his army westward from Edo to launch the expedition against Chōshū, a group of samurai of Zézé Han planned to assassinate him. The group was led by one Kawasé Dazai, the son of a hereditary councilor to the Lord of Zézé. While the Zézé daimyō was a direct retainer of the shōgun, Kawasé's group were ardent Imperial Loyalists who supported Chōshū. By assassinating Iémochi, they would dissuade the Bakufu from launching the expedition. Their plan was foiled when it came to the attention of a certain Zézé man who arranged for the information to be relayed to the protector of Kyōto. The Shinsengumi was immediately dispatched to Kawasé's house in Ōtsu, just east of Kyōto. But Kawasé had been warned, and by the time the Shinsengumi arrived, he was gone. The only one at home was Kawasé's wife. When the Shinsengumi informed her that they would take her to their headquarters for questioning, she begged for time to prepare herself. She went to a room at the rear of the house, where she quickly burned letters and other documents that implicated her husband in the assassination plot. After destroying the evidence, and without further ado, she took up a dagger and stabbed herself in the throat. She died of her wound eleven days later. Thirty samurai involved in the plot, including Kawasé, were subsequently arrested. In November, four of them were forced to commit seppuku; seven were executed. Kawasé was beheaded the following year. A samurai of the Yonézawa clan was arrested by the Shinsengumi for harboring Kagawa Keizō of Mito, one of the assassination plotters. The prisoner refused to talk under interrogation by Kondō and Hijikata. Staff Officer Itō Kashitarō was so impressed by the Yonézawa man's courage that he convinced Kondō and Hijikata to release him, citing his apparent innocence. Itō did not need mention his own Loyalist sympathies, which were growing more and more prevalent.

* * * * *

Nishihonganji Temple, a center of the Jōdo Shinshū Honganji sect, was situated on a large tract of land along Horikawa-dōri Road in the southwest of Kyōto. The priests of Nishihonganji sympathized with the Loyalists. They harbored men who fought on Chōshū's side in the Battle at the Forbidden Gates. After the battle, the priests hid several Chōshū samurai at their temple. These Chōshū samurai later fled the city, disguised as clerics. When this came to the attention of the Shinsengumi, they arrested a number of Nishihonganji priests.

The following spring Kondō and Hijikata moved their headquarters from Mibu to Nishihonganji. The expansive precincts of Nishihonganji better accommodated their increasing ranks. Furthermore, Nishihonganji was located in closer proximity to trouble spots in the city than was Mibu.* And perhaps even more significantly, the Shinsengumi suspected that the Nishihonganji priests still sided with the enemy. By moving to Nishihonganji Temple, they could keep a closer watch on the people coming and going from the compound and the doings of the priests. The good priests were perplexed when the Shinsengumi informed them of their intention. They feared the violence that would certainly accompany the corps but dared not refuse the

---

* The decision to move to Nishihonganji might have resulted in the desertion and eventual seppuku of Vice Commander Yamanami Keisuké.

request outright. In hopes of dissuading them, the priests presented the Shinsengumi with cash gifts. They wined and dined them at exquisite restaurants in the city. But Kondō and Hijikata would not be dissuaded, and the priests finally acquiesced.

On one of the temple gates the corps hung a wooden placard, boldly announcing in black Chinese ink that the great temple was now home to the Shinsengumi. They occupied three buildings at Nishihonganji, including a large meeting hall and the double-tiered drum tower. So spacious was the meeting hall that it required five hundred tatami mats to cover its floor. The Shinsengumi partitioned the building into barracks for the rank and file. Between the main temple hall and the new headquarters, they constructed a bathhouse, a jail, and execution grounds. They used the spacious precincts as training grounds. Each day the men drilled with their swords and spears and practiced firing two cannon they had acquired from the Lord of Aizu. The explosions startled worshippers and the local townspeople. Eventually the temple priests implored them to refrain from firing their guns within the precincts. At first the Shinsengumi refused, on the grounds that they were training "for the sake of the country." Kondō finally ordered his men to cease the cannon practice at the insistence of the Lord of Aizu. Even more perplexing than cannon fire to the Buddhist priests was the unholy smell of pork, which the corpsmen purchased from local vendors at the temple gates and stewed in large iron pots in their barracks.

At the end of May, soon after moving to Nishihonganji, the Shinsengumi reorganized. Ten squads were formed under Commander Kondō, Vice Commander Hijikata, and Staff Officer Itō. Each squad consisted of ten rank and filers overseen by one captain (assistant vice commander) and two corporals. The captains included Okita, Nagakura, Saitō, Takéda, Inoué, Tōdō, and Harada. Among the corporals were Shimada Kai and Hashimoto Kaisuké. Seven observers and nineteen instructors were appointed from among the officers. The observers, including Yamazaki Susumu and Shinohara Tainoshin, monitored the rank and file. The instructors taught kenjutsu, jūjutsu, yarijutsu, horsemanship, artillery, and literature. Among the kenjutsu instructors were Okita, Nagakura, and Saitō. Tani Sanjurō taught yarijutsu. Shinohara taught jūjutsu. Itō and Takéda taught literature. At the apex of their reorganization to control the rank and file, Kondō and Hijikata now declared the theretofore unofficial regulations, which had been the foundation of the corps' unprecedented strength, as the official code of conduct of the Shinsengumi.

* * * * *

Sakamoto Ryōma despised everything that the Shinsengumi repre-sented, especially the Tokugawa Bakufu. In January 1866, the second year of the era of Keiō, Ryōma sealed the fate of the Edo regime when he brokered a military alliance between Satsuma and Chōshū. Sat-suma now refused to fight against Chōshū. Aizu cried treason and threatened to attack Satsuma. Wary as ever of Satsuma's military clout and fearing that a confrontation between Aizu and Satsuma might induce the latter to enter the war on the side of Chōshū, the Bakufu commissioned Katsu Kaishū to mediate between the two adversaries. A year and a half earlier, in the fall of 1864, Kaishū had been dis-missed from his post as Tokugawa navy commissioner and placed under house arrest in Edo for aiding enemies of the Bakufu—i.e., Sakamoto Ryōma and his unruly band of rōnin. At the end of May 1866, Kaishū was summoned to Edo Castle and reinstated to his for-mer post because the shōgun himself recognized that he was the only man in Edo who commanded enough respect among Satsuma and Aizu to settle the matter. As the end of Tokugawa rule approached, Kaishū repeatedly risked his life for the sake of the Tokugawa. He was despised by men on both sides of the revolution and had nearly been assassinated on several occasions. For all his loyalty to the shōgun, however, Kaishū was a realist. He was also a visionary who several years before had already perceived the inevitability of the Bakufu's collapse. It was for this reason that, when his house arrest was immi-nent, he met with Saigō Kichinosuké of Satsuma. He told Saigō that the Bakufu was no longer capable of ruling, that the future of Japan no longer rested with the Tokugawa but rather with a unified repre-sentative Japanese government, that a federation of the feudal domains was vital to strengthen the nation and convince the foreign powers to revise the humiliating treaties Japan had been forced to sign in the previous decade, and that Satsuma and Chōshū must not fight against each other but rather unite for the sake of a stronger Japan. In short, the loyal Tokugawa retainer hinted to the leader of one of Edo's two most dangerous adversaries that because the end of two and a half centuries of Tokugawa rule was fast approaching, Satsuma and Chōshū must join forces with each other to topple the Bakufu.

In June, Kaishū wrote a short letter to the Aizu daimyō, censuring him for his reactionary antiforeignism, and for his "inability to observe the world situation" and "cope with present changes." Kaishū admonished Lord Katamori that in "suspecting Satsuma, it seems as if you hate them" and that he feared "this might cause great trouble for the nation." He ended the letter by expressing his hope that "the Bakufu will now do its utmost to sincerely and impartially perform its duties properly, irrespective of other matters." By thus admonishing the shōgun's cousin, Kaishū pressed the Bakufu to administer the government for the welfare of the entire nation, not simply for the sole benefit of the House of Tokugawa. Certainly a man of Kaishū's moral courage had little to fear from the Lord of Aizu. It seemed, in fact, that the protector of Kyōto, as if to belie the aura of dread surrounding his Mibu Wolves and the fighting spirit of his own samurai, was a weak man. Kaishū recalled his mediation between Satsuma and Aizu thirty years later: "I went immediately to Kyōto. The first person I visited was [the Lord of] Aizu. [He] was drinking saké ... with two of his women. He was in bed as if ill. It was just horrible! He told me he understood [the situation] and that he would not do such a terrible thing.* But his retainers wouldn't listen to him, so he said to me, 'Now that you're here, things will be all right. Do something to convince my retainers.' "

Kaishū successfully settled the matter between Aizu and Satsuma. Earlier in the month, however, on June 7, Edo had already opened hostilities against Chōshū. Then, on July 20 of the second year of Keiō (1866)—the second-to-last year of Tokugawa rule—as if the Sun

---

* By "terrible thing," Kaishū meant "attack Satsuma."

Goddess were intent on restoring her imperial descendant in Kyōto to his ancient seat of power, Tokugawa Iémochi, the twenty-year-old shōgun, suddenly died at Ōsaka Castle.

Needless to say, the death of the supreme leader of the hegemony in the east dealt a severe blow to his campaign in the west. The war was waged on four fronts surrounding the Chōshū domain. By the first week in August, the Tokugawa forces had been beaten on all four fronts. Faced with inevitable defeat, the Bakufu used the shōgun's death as an excuse to end hostilities. In December, five months after Iémochi's death, Tokugawa Yoshinobu, the former inspector-general of the forces protecting the emperor in Kyōto, was conferred by the emperor with the illustrious title "commander in chief of the expeditionary forces against the barbarians," thus becoming the fifteenth and last Tokugawa Shōgun.

Meanwhile, the Sun Goddess continued to torment the Bakufu, even at the expense of one of her own. On December 25, twenty days after Yoshinobu's accession, Emperor Kōmei, whose pro-Tokugawa stance had bolstered the Bakufu, suddenly died at his palace in Kyōto. Although the cause of death was attributed to smallpox, rumor had it that the emperor had been poisoned. The rumor was not far-fetched. Alive, the emperor posed a major obstacle to the anti-Tokugawa faction at court, whose return to power had been reinforced by the recent Chōshū victory. Kōmei's heir, who would be known to history as Emperor Meiji, was just fourteen years old. His maternal grandfather and official guardian, Nakayama Tadayasu, was a confidant of Iwakura Tomomi, the leader of the anti-Tokugawa faction at court. Nakayama was now in a position to aid Iwakura. At the end of 1866, as Katsu Kaishū had long foreseen, the collapse of the Tokugawa Bakufu was imminent.

* * * * *

As the Bakufu crumbled, so did the Shinsengumi. Before the final fall, however, Kondō Isami and Hijikata Toshizō were in command of a corps of about one hundred men. In June 1867, four and a half years after the formation of the Rōshi Corps, all members of the Shinsengumi were finally granted hatamoto status, ranking them among the Eighty Thousand Knights of the Tokugawa Shōgun. But only Commander Kondō was given the high honor of direct access to the shōgun. Awarded generous stipends, the Shinsengumi were no longer stigmatized as rōshi. This sudden rise to power, even for men of the samurai class, was unprecedented in Tokugawa history.

Just four days after his ascent into the upper echelons of the Tokugawa hierarchy, Kondō Isami attended an important political meeting of elite feudal lords of the Tokugawa camp. The meeting had been called in response to a memorial that was dangerously critical of the Bakufu. The memorial had been recently submitted to the Imperial Court by four influential feudal lords—Fukui, Tosa, Satsuma, and Uwajima—the latter three of whom were outside the Tokugawa camp. The lords censured the Bakufu for its "unreasonable actions" in the second expedition against Chōshū, which had been launched for "unwarranted reasons" and "caused a great national disturbance." Kondō vehemently denounced the memorial, defended the Bakufu, and strongly criticized the shōgun's most important retainers for "incomprehensibly and blindly following outside lords, when, as relatives of the shōgun, they should be defending the Bakufu, regardless of its faults." Kondō composed a letter expressing these ideas, which he intended to submit to the Imperial Court. That Kondō was in a position to even consider petitioning the court was indicative of his weighty influence in Kyōto politics, rivaling the most powerful feudal lords. The Shinsengumi were no longer simply a security force on the bloody streets of the Imperial Capital but had transformed into a political force to be reckoned with on the perilous national stage. That reckoning was soon to come.

BLOOD AT THE CROSSROADS

The corps commander was set in his ways. He would lay down his life for the shōgun. He would not hesitate to condemn a man to death who opposed his supreme lord, and would rush to kill anyone who threatened him. In contrast, the staff officer, whom the commander had brought into the corps, was analytical and flexible. He asserted his independence and his openly radical views. He attracted an independent following among the corpsmen, including, of course, those who shared his radical views. The commander felt responsible for creating this dangerous situation. The commander would no longer tolerate the errant staff officer and his independent following.

Dissent divided the Shinsengumi. As had been the case under Commander Serizawa Kamo, the corps split into two factions under the influence of Staff Officer Itō Kashitarō. Since joining the Shinsengumi in December 1864, Itō had openly espoused Imperial Loyalism. He was in cahoots with Chōshū and Satsuma and overtly critical of the Tokugawa regime and its expedition against Chōshū. When Itō accompanied Kondō during the latter's second trip to Hiroshima, the staff officer remained in the west for more than fifty days, cultivating good relations with anti-Tokugawa samurai of the Chōshū camp.

Emboldened by Chōshū's victory in August 1866, Itō and his men became so fervent in their Imperial Loyalism that they could no longer rationalize their membership in the Shinsengumi. Near the end of September, Itō and Observer Shinohara Tainoshin met with the two Shinsengumi leaders at the home of Kondō's mistress, Miyuki. Itō and Shinohara informed Kondō and Hijikata of their decision not to quit but "to secede" from the corps. "We discussed the national situation," Shinohara wrote in his memoirs. "All that either of them [Kondō and Hijikata] would do was to talk about the authority of the Tokugawa." And while Itō and Shinohara expressed their devotion to Imperial Loyalism, the two Shinsengumi leaders refused to question the "success or failures of the Tokugawa, or to understand the purport of Imperial Loyalism, but rather insisted on controlling people through military means." Itō and Shinohara lied that they had nurtured close relations with Satsuma and Chōshū only to glean secret information from them. To gain the complete trust of the enemy, they said, they must officially leave the Shinsengumi. Perhaps they wondered whether Commander Kondō was actually deceived or merely pretended to be and, giving up hope in the men of Itō's faction, accepted their plans.

But Commander Kondō was not deceived. After being informed of Itō's decision to leave the corps, Kondō ordered Number Three Squad Captain Saitō Hajimé to spy on the errant staff officer.

Saitō and Number Two Squad Captain Nagakura Shinpachi celebrated New Year's Day 1867 with Itō and six of his men at the Sumi'ya pleasure palace. The men drank heavily and relished the company of several young women. The festivities continued after nightfall, when all the men were required by Shinsengumi curfew to return to headquarters. According to Nagakura, "in order to discourage debauchery among the men, the Shinsengumi punished anyone who returned late." Wary of trouble, the rank and filers returned to headquarters before curfew that evening, while the three officers remained. They drank well into the night. When they awoke the next morning, they continued their revel, because, as Itō said, however tongue in cheek, "since we are going to have to commit seppuku anyway, we might as well drink." They finally returned to headquarters after four straight days of celebration. Nagakura mistakenly thought that "Kondō's face was filled with rage when he saw the three of us." Nagakura was apparently still unaware that Saitō had been spying on Itō and believed that Kondō was indeed angry for the violation of Shinsengumi regulations. But Kondō was not angry. The matter was settled with Itō and Saitō's being confined to headquarters for three days, and Nagakura for six. But the incident further widened the gap between Kondō and Nagakura, which had recently reemerged over the commander's "reckless ... and egotistic behavior." The relationship between the two men would continue to deteriorate during their tragic final year together.

In the following March, Kondō Isami's cousin Miyagawa Nobukichi came from Tama to enlist in the Shinsengumi. Nine years younger than Kondō, Miyagawa had studied kenjutsu at the Shieikan. During the same month that Miyagawa joined the Shinsengumi, Itō Kashitarō "seceded." Miyagawa and Itō would meet in adverse circumstances later that year.

The staff officer met with little opposition from the two Shinsengumi leaders. Itō took twelve men with him.* Among them were Number Nine Squad Captain Suzuki Mikisaburō (Itō's younger brother), Observer Shinohara Tainoshin, Number Eight Squad Captain Tōdō Heisuké, Corpsman Hashimoto Kaisuké, and Saitō. (Saitō infiltrated Itō's group as Kondō's spy.) The defection of Tōdō, formerly of the Shieikan and one of the thirteen original Shinsengumi members, was a thorn in Kondō's side. Through the good offices of a temple elder, Itō's group received imperial orders to join the special Guard of the Imperial Tomb for Emperor Kōmei. In June they set up headquarters at Gesshin'in, a subtemple of Kōdaiji, in the Higashiyama district on the eastern side of the city. Completely independent from the Shinsengumi, they now became the Kōdaiji Faction. In the face of the high moral ground connoted by the title Guard of the Imperial Tomb, Kondō and Hijikata, were, for all their outrage, unable to prevent the blatant violation of corps regulations.

---

* Three more corpsmen would subsequently join them.

Itō had left behind ten of his allies in the Shinsengumi to gather vital information and, upon occasion, stir up trouble among the rank and file. When the men of the Shinsengumi were awarded hatamoto status in June, these ten decided to quit the corps on the grounds that they had joined for the express purposes of expelling the barbarians and practicing Imperial Loyalism, and not to serve as retainers of the Tokugawa. But Itō had a previous agreement with Kondō that neither side would accept would-be defectors from the other side. Well aware of the danger in inciting the wrath of Kondō and Hijikata, Itō was not about to renege on the agreement. When the ten men came to join his Guard of the Imperial Tomb, Itō advised them to first obtain official permission from the Lord of Aizu.

The ten men proceeded to Aizu headquarters. They were told that the official in charge was out at the time. Four of them, the leaders of the group, were shown to a drawing room and cordially invited to await his return. According to Shimosawa, while the four men waited, they were treated to a noon meal and generous servings of saké. Evening came, and the official had still not returned. They grew restless. But soon the evening meal was served, accompanied by plenty of saké. After ample food and drink, they grew drowsy. Meanwhile, the Shinsengumi had been summoned to the Aizu estate. Among them were Number Six Squad Captain Inoué Genzaburō and Observer Ōishi Kuwajirō, who, Shimosawa wrote, "liked assassination more than anything." Around midnight, as the four would-be defectors sat in the gloomy drawing room, their assassins were upon them with drawn spears. Three of them were killed instantly. The fourth one, Sano Shiménosuké, was stabbed through the abdomen by Ōishi. But he managed to draw his sword and cut Ōishi before finally succumbing to his wounds. The six others were brought back to headquarters at Nishihonganji and summarily expelled from the corps.

The Shinsengumi denied that they had murdered the four men. According to their official report, the four committed seppuku at Aizu headquarters. This was a reasonable claim—they had committed a capital offense and simply chose to end their lives of their own accord rather than be ordered to plunge in the blade. As if to bolster the veracity of their report, on the following day the Shinsengumi buried the four with high honors at a nearby Buddhist temple.

Kondō and Hijikata became unsatisfied with their headquarters at Nishihonganji. A partitioned temple hall no longer served as adequate living quarters for their men. They required new accommodations more suitable for direct Tokugawa retainers. Although they lacked the funds for construction, they soon came upon a solution. They knew that the priests at Nishihonganji had ample money at their disposal. They also knew that the good priests would not long endure spectacles of bloodshed and violence. The two leaders put to use their martial ingenuity and their propensity to kill to convince the priests to pay. According to Shimosawa, in plain view of the main temple building, corpsmen who had violated the code were made to commit seppuku, while captured enemies were executed amid shrieks of agony. "The Shinsengumi conducted military drills daily," Nagakura wrote. "One day the head priest was so startled by the roar of cannon fire that he fell down backward." On another occasion the poor priest was so frightened that he "confined himself to a room [in the rear of the main temple building] and hid his head under the bedding."

The commander and vice commander of this legal terrorist organization reasoned that the priests, in all propriety, should finance the construction of their new headquarters. Didn't the men of the Shinsengumi risk their lives daily to maintain law and order? Weren't they dedicated to destroying the rebel forces who would overthrow the Tokugawa Shōgun, under whom Buddhism had flourished these past two and a half centuries? And whether or not the Shinsengumi leaders yet foresaw the imminent collapse of the Bakufu or the ramifications thereof, wouldn't the Buddhist priests suffer as a consequence of the newly revised Shintoism, which would replace Buddhism as the national religion after the fall of the Tokugawa regime?

Five days after their ascension into the Tokugawa hierarchy, the Shinsengumi moved their headquarters to a newly constructed compound at Fudō-dō Village just southeast of Nishihonganji. The new, gated headquarters were an elaborate affair, rivaling the Kyōto estates of feudal lords. They occupied ten thousand square meters of fenced land. Kondō, Hijikata, and some of the officers had their own quarters separate from the rank and file. There were guest rooms, servants' quarters, and stables. The giant bathing area accommodated thirty people at a time. Ironically, just months after Kondō had taken up residence at these headquarters, his Shieikan was sold and his wife and daughter moved to a lesser house in Edo.

Soon after moving to their new headquarters, Kondō and Hijikata again demonstrated their propensity to kill anyone who dared cross them. Takéda Kanryūsai, a rōnin from Matsué Han in Izumo province, served as Number Five Squad captain. He had been with the corps since its early days. He had helped arrest Furudaka Shuntarō, fought at the Ikéda'ya, and accompanied Kondō on his trips to Edo and western Japan. But he was generally disliked by his fellow corpsmen. He had a tendency to boast and constantly flattered the commander and vice commander. Furthermore, unlike most of his comrades, Takéda was more of a scholar than a warrior. He had been enlisted less for his martial prowess than for his extensive knowledge in the tried-and-true military tactics of the Kōshū Naganuma school. He was put in charge of military drills in the enviable position of instructor. But recently the Bakufu had begun westernizing its military under the tutelage of French officers. Takéda's instruction became outdated—a fact that did not escape his fellow corpsmen. What's more, his name did not appear on the roster of men recently granted hatamoto status by the Bakufu. He felt deceived by Commander Kondō and Vice Commander Hijikata. He unsuccessfully tried to gain the favor of Staff Officer Itō. When it came to the attention of the Shinsengumi that Takéda had secretly joined ranks with the Loyalist side and that he had even been frequenting the Satsuma estate in Fushimi, Kondō Isami acted accordingly.

The commander summoned all of his officers, including Takéda, to a certain restaurant for what he sardonically called a "farewell party" for the Number Five Squad Captain. After saké had been served, Kondō said to Takéda with a forced smile, "I hear that you will be leaving the corps to serve Satsuma." He did not need to mention that quitting the corps was a capital offense. Takéda must now have realized that his recent clandestine visits to the Satsuma estate had been discovered. He lied that he had merely considered joining the enemy to gather information. Kondō feigned approval of Takéda's alleged tactic. He clapped his large hands loudly, certainly pleased with himself, and insisted that Takéda visit the Satsuma estate that very night. Citing the danger of traveling alone at night, he ordered Number Three Squad Captain Saitō Hajimé and another man to accompany Takéda along the way. Takéda did not get along with Saitō, who had been drinking that evening and who had a reputation as a bad drunk. Takéda said that he would travel alone, fearing the worst if he accepted Kondō's offer. But the commander would hear nothing of it, and insisted that Saitō and the other man accompany him.

Soon the three men left the party. They traveled in single file along a narrow road in the darkness. Takéda walked in front, with the other two close behind. They came to a bridge near a particularly desolate stretch in the road. Just as they crossed the bridge, Saitō drew his long sword and with one swift motion sliced open Takéda's back from left hip to right shoulder. Death was instantaneous. Saitō knelt over the bloody corpse and removed both of Takéda's swords. "For all his boasting to the contrary," he reportedly said, "Takéda was an easy kill."

Itō Kashitarō advocated opening Japan to foreign trade in order to develop a "wealthy country and strong military" through taxes levied on foreigners. He espoused the employment of all classes of people, not only samurai, in the armed forces. After the shōgun would restore the political power to the emperor, the rule of the nation must never again fall into the hands of a military regime. In the future, the entire Japanese nation, including all the feudal lords, must be ruled by the Imperial Court. Since most, if not all, of the court nobles lacked administrative experience, Itō's Kōdaiji Faction and other educated men like themselves would assist the court. There was no place for the Tokugawa Bakufu or its supporters in Itō's grand scheme.

Meanwhile, most of the samurai in the Tokugawa camp, and the hereditary lords who occupied the most important posts in the Bakufu, would not step down without a fight. Prominent among them were Kondō Isami and Hijikata Toshizō. They were determined to preserve their control. The Shinsengumi commander and his vice commander were diametrically opposed to their former staff officer, both politically and ideologically.

According to Nagakura, Itō did not believe the Shinsengumi's claim that Sano and the three others had committed seppuku at Aizu headquarters. He was angered. He was indignant. He planned to assassinate Kondō and his officers and assume command of the Shinsengumi. "[Itō] intended to set fire to Shinsengumi [headquarters] ... and kill [us] as we evacuated [the building]." Having curried favor with Satsuma, Itō would use the Shinsengumi organization to fight for the imperial cause against the Tokugawa. Fortunately for Kondō and his officers, Saitō Hajimé was a good actor. Itō embraced Saitō as one of his chief confidants, never once suspecting him a spy. When Saitō informed Kondō and Hijikata of Itō's plot, the two leaders took immediate and drastic action.

Itō had previously requested a large sum of money from Kondō to finance espionage activities against Chōshū. Kondō, of course, knew that Itō had no intention of spying on Chōshū. On the afternoon of November 18, Kondō sent a messenger to Itō's headquarters at Gesshin'in Temple, inviting him to the home of his mistress. Kondō's invitation was under the pretext of providing Itō with the money he had requested and discussing national affairs with him. Itō accepted the invitation. He had no reason to doubt Kondō's good intentions. He had managed to maintain good relations with the Shinsengumi, if only ostensibly. (The idea that Kondō was privy to his plot must not have occurred to him, or he certainly would not have gone to meet Kondō alone.) When Itō arrived at Miyuki's house the same afternoon, he was greeted warmly by Kondō and Hijikata. Delicacies were served. Saké was poured freely. Kondō assured Itō that the money he had requested would come from Aizu the next morning, when he should return to collect it. Itō readily acquiesced. The men drank and talked until after nightfall. When Itō took his leave at around eight o'clock, he was intoxicated. He thought that the cold winter air would clear his head. He was wrong. Kondō's hit men, including Ōishi Kuwajirō, Miyagawa Nobukichi, and probably Saitō Hajimé, waited in the moonlight along a narrow lane, just beyond which point Shichijō-dōri crossed Aburakoji Street in the southwestern part of the city.

The attack came suddenly as Itō approached the crossroads. Itō was cut from his left ear to his chin by an assailant he did not even see. Blood spurted from the wound. A second assailant came. As the expert in the Hokushin Ittō style staggered in vain to save himself, he saw several others, drawn swords in hand, approaching fast. Before they could reach him, Itō collapsed. He summoned a final burst of strength to scream his dying word—"Traitors!" The assassins dragged the body to the nearby crossroads. The name of the crossroads, Aburakoji-Shichijō, would become synonymous with the notorious assassination. So cold was the night air that soon after the assassins fled the scene, the blood on Itō 's clothes had frozen solid.

Kondō Isami had already laid plans to eliminate the remnants of the Kōdaiji Faction on the same night—with the noted exception of Tōdō Heisuké. Kondō, in fact, had issued instructions to his men to spare Tōdō's life. He had also arranged for the local authorities to inform the men at Gesshin'in Temple of their leader's death, expecting they would come immediately to retrieve the body.* The plan worked. At around two o'clock in the morning, just hours after the assassination, seven of the Guard of the Imperial Tomb rushed to the scene. Among them were Shinohara, Suzuki, and Tōdō. "We were shocked and angry," Shinohara recalled of their reaction to hearing of Itō's murder.

Hiding in a restaurant near the crossroads were Nagakura, Harada, Ōishi, Shimada, Saitō, and numerous others of the Shinsengumi.† They watched silently as Itō's men arrived at the crossroads, carrying a palanquin for their leader's body. As the guardsmen attempted to place the body inside, the Shinsengumi attacked. The Shinsengumi outnumbered the guardsmen by about four to one. An intense and bloody fight ensued in the light of the winter moon.

---

* Of the twelve men who had defected with Itō, ten remained in the faction. Hashimoto Kaisuké had joined the Rikuentai (literally, Land Auxiliary Force), a Loyalist militia led by Nakaoka Shintarō of Tosa. Saitō, meanwhile, had returned to the Shinsengumi.

† The exact number of the Shinsengumi who fought at Aburakoji is unknown. There were probably between thirty and forty.

Three of the guardsmen were killed, including Tōdō. The four others escaped to the Satsuma estate in the north of the city. Several of the Shinsengumi were wounded, including Harada and Ōishi. The sight at dawn was ghastly. Four corpses lay on the street. Fingers were scattered about, and pieces of hairy flesh were strewn near the bloodied walls of nearby houses. The Shinsengumi left the four corpses, including Itō's, at the crossroads for two days, in an unsuccessful attempt to lure the survivors back to the scene of the carnage.

OF OUTRAGE, FURY, AND INEXORABLE FATE

The end of the old order was upon them, and the leaders of the shō-gun's most lethal fighting corps were, as men on both sides of the revolution, consumed by an outrage and fury begotten by inexorable fate. Fate, whether inseparably intertwined with that relentless goddess or an overwhelming force by which their world was changing at break-neck speed, was, despite their steely will to power, beyond their mortal control. After fifteen years of unprecedented turmoil, neither the winners nor the losers—nor, it seemed, that brilliant divinity of their ancient ancestors—would countenance peace in their sacred nation without a final and bloody struggle.

The sweet taste of revenge afforded the Shinsengumi by the blood of Itō and his Guard of the Imperial Tomb was lost neither to the relentless Sun Goddess nor to the architects of the most momentous event in Tokugawa history. On October 14 of the third year of the era of Keiō—November 8, 1867, in Western reckoning—one month before Itō's assassination, the last shōgun, Tokugawa Yoshinobu, announced his abdication and restoration of rule to the emperor. The announcement was made in the Grand Hall of Nijō Castle before representatives of forty feudal domains. This event, which begot the

Meiji Restoration, was the brainchild of Sakamoto Ryōma. In the previous June, while Ryōma's allies in Satsuma and Chōshū promoted their agenda to crush the Tokugawa by military force, the visionary from Tosa had devised a plan to avert civil war. Ryōma's plan, a bold attempt to lay the cornerstone of democracy in Japan, urged the shōgun to restore the emperor to his ancient seat of power. It called for the establishment of two legislative houses of government—an upper and lower—to be filled by men of ability among the feudal lords, court nobles, and representatives of the Japanese people at large. It stated that governmental measures should be decided by the councilors based on public opinion. Ryōma submitted the plan to Gotō Shōjirō, the chief minister of Yamanouchi Yōdō, the powerful Lord of Tosa. Gotō, in turn, presented Ryōma's plan to his daimyō, who endorsed it in October in a memorial to the shōgun.

As Lord Yōdō's chief minister, Gotō wielded significant influence on the political scene in Kyōto. This was why, as he prepared to submit Yōdō's memorial to the shōgun's prime minister, Itakura Katsukiyo, Gotō arranged to be introduced to another influential player in Kyōto. On the night of September 20, he visited the residence of Bakufu Chief Inspector Nagai Naomuné, a close advisor of the shōgun. As they sat in the drawing room, Nagai announced that there was someone he would like Gotō to meet. Gotō, of course, had come to Nagai's house fully expecting to make the acquaintance of Kondō Isami. As Nagai spoke, Gotō saw a man in the next room wearing a long sword at his side. The man very politely and with full decorum introduced himself. Although Gotō had never met the Shinsengumi commander, he knew well of his reputation. After cordially introducing himself, Gotō abruptly told Kondō, "I hate that long sword at your side," then asked him if he wouldn't remove it. Kondō laughed, removed his sword and placed it on the floor next to himself. The two men spent the following few hours discussing the pressing political situation in Japan. They became friends, or so Kondō liked to believe. Kondō had heard that Gotō, who was of course from Tosa, had many allies on the Loyalist side. Among Gotō's allies was Sakamoto Ryōma, an anathema to the Bakufu. But the peasant's son was nevertheless flattered to make the acquaintance of the illustrious samurai. He instructed his men not to harm Gotō. He was aware that Gotō was arranging for a memorial to be presented to the shōgun but did not know the contents of that document. Needless to say, he was more than eager to see it. He requested that Gotō provide him with a copy. Three days after their first meeting, Kondō visited Gotō at the latter's residence. He tried on at least two subsequent occasions to meet Gotō again, who cunningly, though tactfully, rebuffed Kondō's overtures. Gotō did not show the memorial to Kondō.

Even as Yoshinobu accepted Ryōma's plan, the Sun Goddess continued to torment. She now employed the genius of her darling among the nobles, the shōgun's greatest nemesis at the Imperial Court. Iwakura Tomomi, that master of political intrigue, had been plotting with Satsuma to crush the Bakufu.* Had Yoshinobu delayed his decision any longer, he would have found himself confronted by a secret weapon, against which his forces would have been powerless. The secret weapon was an imperial decree, drawn up by Iwakura, instructing the combined forces of Satsuma, Chōshū, and other powerful feudal domains to attack the Tokugawa. The decree was essentially a Tokugawa death warrant, which called for the destruction of the Edo regime, the punishment of the "traitor" Yoshinobu, and the deaths of the Lords of Aizu and Kuwana. Iwakura entrusted the document to Nakayama Tadayasu, the emperor's maternal grandfather.

Meanwhile, the Tokugawa authorities in Kyōto caught word that Satsuma and Chōshū planned to attack the residence of the Lord of Aizu. The Shinsengumi and the Mimawarigumi were immediately placed on high alert, patrolling the city day and night. The Shinsengumi stationed men at the front gate of Nakayama's residence to keep a close watch on anyone entering or leaving the premises. The day before Yoshinobu's announcement, Lord Iwakura had received an imperial rescript from Nakayama, which exonerated the Lord of

---

* Iwakura Tomomi would become one of the most powerful men in the Meiji government.

Chōshū and his heir of their "Imperial Enemy" stigma. Iwakura hid the document inside the clothes of his young son, who carried it through the front gate unnoticed by Kondō's men.

On the very day of Yoshinobu's announcement at Nijō Castle, which was also the day that the imperial seal was affixed to the Tokugawa death warrant, the Shinsengumi spotted samurai of Satsuma and Chōshū entering Nakayama's house. Although Kondō could not know the specific purpose of their visit, he ordered his men to arrest or kill them as they left. The Satsuma and Chōshū men, however, managed to sneak out through the rear exit, bearing the imperial decree. But history shows that even the well-laid plans of an ancient divinity can be foiled by the foibles inherent in human events. Before Satsuma and Chōshū had time to strike, Yoshinobu's decision was sanctioned by the Imperial Court and the theretofore all-powerful secret decree was rendered useless.

Kondō Isami et al., who just four months earlier had been officially received into the Tokugawa hierarchy, were outraged over the shōgun's abdication. Casting a grim pallor over the entire affair, on October 26, just twelve days after Yoshinobu's announcement, Kondō received word from Edo that his adoptive father's end was near. Two days later Kondō Shūsuké died. He was sixty-seven. Kondō was too occupied with the uproar in Kyōto to attend the funeral in Edo.

The Lords of Aizu and Kuwana, for their part, were infuriated with Yoshinobu. Kondō, meanwhile, assailed the Lords of Owari and Fukui, two of the shōgun's closest retainers, as "unfaithful" for pressuring Yoshinobu to abdicate. In the following month the genius visionary who orchestrated the abdication was assassinated. Although it was not the Shinsengumi who assassinated Sakamoto Ryōma, Kondō Isami would certainly not have hesitated to kill him had the opportunity availed itself. "The day Sakamoto Ryōma and Nakaoka Shintarō were cut down, Kondō was sick in bed at my sister's house," Miyuki recalled. "Two or three days after they were killed, he came to my house. He said, 'Since Sasaki Tadasaburō and some others killed Sakamoto, I can enjoy drinking some saké.' He sent for Sasaki, and they had a big party."*

On November 13, five days before the Aburakoji incidents, Itō Kashitarō and Tōdō Heisuké had paid a visit to Sakamoto Ryōma at his hideout in Kyōto. They had gone to warn Ryōma and his comrade-in-arms, Nakaoka Shintarō, of the danger to their lives. The two Tosa men were among the most wanted on a long list of political enemies of the Tokugawa. They had brokered the military alliance between Satsuma and Chōshū, which hastened Edo's demise. And though Ryōma had been the mastermind behind the plan for Yoshinobu's peaceful abdication, both he and Nakaoka were ready, with their comrades in Satsuma and Chōshū, to crush the Tokugawa by military force should the shōgun refuse to abdicate. It was no wonder, then, that diehards within the Tokugawa camp blamed Ryōma and Nakaoka for the overthrow of the government. "Nakaoka listened to my warning," Itō said afterward. "But Sakamoto seemed indifferent and gave no heed to what I told them." Several of Ryōma's friends had been killed by the Shinsengumi, whom he considered nothing more than a band of brutal thugs. Under no circumstances would he listen to the advice of men who had been part and parcel to that band. Two days later Ryōma and Nakaoka were killed at the former's hideout—a second-story room in the house of a soy merchant in Kyōto.

The Shinsengumi was strongly suspected of the murders. In a letter dated November 19, four days after the incident, Ōkubo Ichizō,† the political leader of Satsuma, wrote to Iwakura Tomomi, "I have heard that without a doubt it was the Shinsengumi who killed Sakamoto.... Kondō Isami is the prime suspect." The assassins had left behind two items—a wax-colored scabbard and a pair of wooden clogs—that seemed to incriminate the Shinsengumi. Shinohara Tainoshin and others of the Kōdaiji Faction, hiding in the Satsuma estate in Kyōto, identified the scabbard as that belonging to Harada

---

* Sasaki Tadasaburō, the younger brother of an elite vassal of the Lord of Aizu, commanded the Mimawarigumi—literally, Patrolling Corps. Like their counterparts in the Newly Selected Corps, the swordsmen of the Patrolling Corps were charged with maintaining law and order in Kyōto. Unlike the Shinsengumi, however, the Mimawarigumi consisted mostly of sons of direct Tokugawa retainers, whose families had served the shōgun for generations.

† Later Ōkubo Toshimichi.

Sanosuké. Harada hailed from Matsuyama Han, which bordered Tosa Han on the island of Shikoku. Before succumbing to his wounds two days after the attack, Nakaoka reported that one of his assailants had screamed a profanity in a Shikoku dialect. Equally damning was a pair of wooden clogs engraved with the mark of a nearby inn. When it was discovered the next day that the inn was frequented by men of the Shinsengumi, Ryōma's followers arranged for Kondō Isami to be questioned by Tokugawa authorities. Kondō, of course, testified that his corps had not been involved in the assassination.

Harada was apparently framed by men of the Kōdaiji Faction out of revenge for Itō's murder. But Harada could not have been the murderer. He was an officer of the Shinsengumi. He was an expert with both the sword and spear who had fought in most of the major battles involving the Shinsengumi, including the Ikéda'ya, Aburakoji, and the battle over the defaced bulletin boards at Sanjō Large Bridge. A seasoned warrior such as Harada would not have forgotten the scabbard of his sword after a skirmish of just two or three minutes. And no matter the urgency by which he vacated the scene of the crime, he would not have left behind a pair of incriminating wooden clogs. Both indiscretions would have been in violation of the Code of the Samurai and so, according to Shinsengumi regulations, punishable by seppuku. Further exonerating Harada and the Shinsengumi were the future recollections of a former corpsman: "We were at Kondō's place that night. Harada Sanosuké was with us. When we heard about the assassinations the next day, we said to one another that whoever did it must have been a very skilled swordsman. When we heard that it was Imai who had done it, it made sense. Imai was well known in Edo at that time for his great skill with a short sword. When he was set to attack, it was said that all you could see was his sword. Imai was the only person who could have done such work in such a cramped room in so short a time."*

Ryōma's men were outraged and possessed by a burning desire for revenge. When Kondō Isami denied involvement in the assassina-

---

* See Appendix I (9).

tions, they took matters into their own hands. There could be no doubt that men of the Tokugawa camp had killed their leader. There were three plausible motives for Ryōma's assassination, and all three were interrelated. Ryōma was the mastermind behind the plan for Yoshinobu's peaceful abdication and restoration of power to the emperor. Ryōma had shot at least one man of the Bakufu, and possibly two, during the previous year, when he was attacked and nearly killed at the Terada'ya inn in Fushimi shortly after securing the military alliance between Satsuma and Chōshū. The third motive had to do with the sinking of a ship that Ryōma's men had chartered to run guns for the revolutionaries. The ship, laden with contraband of four hundred rifles, had been run down and sunk by a ship owned by Kii Han. Ryōma was the leader of a band of outlaws, and Kii was one of the Three Branch Houses of the Tokugawa. When Kii refused the outlaw's demand for compensation, the outlaw threatened to sue in a court of international law. Aware of the power of public opinion, Ryōma composed a short jingle to ridicule Kii.* He introduced the jingle at the pleasure houses in the international port city of Nagasaki, where his headquarters were located and where influential men from throughout Japan were gathered.

Ryōma's intuition worked, and soon Kii was the laughingstock of the city. In May 1867, six months before Ryōma's assassination, Kii agreed to pay an indemnity for the enormous sum of 83,000 ryō if Ryōma would drop the suit. Ryōma did drop the suit, and it was assumed that Kii harbored murderous resentment. When Ryōma's men heard rumors that a high-ranking Kii official, Miura Kyūtarō, had instigated the assassination of their leader by the Shinsengumi, they acted accordingly.

But Miura was innocent. He was also aware that his life was in danger. Through the good offices of the Lord of Aizu, he arranged for men of the Shinsengumi to protect him. Having failed in their first attempt on Miura's life, Ryōma's men learned that he would attend a gathering at the Tenman'ya inn, near the scene of the recent Aburakoji bloodbath, on the snowy night of December 7. At ten

---

* See Appendix I (10).

o'clock that night, sixteen men wearing white headbands, all armed with two swords, some packing pistols, entered the inn. One of them, Nakai Shōgorō, was particularly eager for revenge.* An expert in *iai*, the art of sword drawing, Nakai's weapon was engraved with his name and given him by Ryōma. He dashed up the wooden staircase, the others following him.

Miura's room was on the second floor. Accompanying Miura were more than a dozen men, including Saitō Hajimé, Ōishi Kuwajirō, Miyagawa Nobukichi, and four others of the Shinsengumi. They were drinking saké when they heard someone in the hallway outside the room. As one of Miura's men slid open the screen door, Nakai burst into the room. "Miura!" he screamed. He drew his sword, and in the same lightning motion cut Miura about the forehead. Nakai's fifteen comrades now rushed into the room. The lanterns were extinguished amid the ensuing pandemonium, so that the men could not easily distinguish ally from foe. Sword clashed against sword. Blood sprayed in the darkness. Gunfire and guttural screams filled the cramped room. In the chaos, Miura, slightly wounded, managed to escape through a window onto the roof. One of the Shinsengumi, crossing swords with an assailant, fell through the window into a pond in the garden below. "There were now numerous of the enemy around the pond," wrote Nagakura. The corpsman emerged from the pond in pursuit of the enemy, who "scattered in all directions."

Two of the Shinsengumi were killed, including Miyagawa. Three corpsmen, including Saitō, were wounded. Among the assailants, only Nakai was killed. Another man's hand was severed at the wrist; most of the others received minor wounds.

Before fleeing the scene, one of Ryōma's men beheaded Nakai's corpse. But certainly the head was heavy; and certainly its base oozed blood; and certainly this blood befouled the pure water of the well in which it was cast in an attempt to avoid identification of the headless corpse left upstairs. The head, however, was discovered a few days later, and identified by the name engraved on Nakai's sword.

---

* Nakai had been among the first group of rōnin who in the previous year defaced the Bakufu's defamatory bulletin board at Sanjō Large Bridge.

Civil War

The shōgun had indeed announced his decision to abdicate and restore the emperor to power. But a peaceful transition of government was not in the grand plan of that unrelenting goddess. An emperor had not ruled Japan in a thousand years. The Imperial Court was, to say the least, politically inept. To make matters worse, the new emperor was a fifteen-year-old boy. The shōgun's shocking announcement at Nijō Castle, so physically close yet so symbolically far from the Imperial Palace, had reverberated through the inner confines of that ancient and holy estate with so much eye-opening force that the emperor's chief advisors cowered in the face of their colossal responsibilities. While the imperial advisors begrudgingly and finally accepted their fate, the shōgun's closest allies, most notably the Lords of Aizu and Kuwana, and the Newly Selected Corps, did not.

Even after Yoshinobu's momentous decision, the Bakufu still controlled the government. The oppositionists in the Tokugawa camp, including Kondō Isami and Hijikata Toshizō, were determined to preserve that control. They planned to persuade the Imperial Court to leave the administration of government in the experienced hands of the Edo regime. Meanwhile, their enemies planned to destroy them. Troops of Satsuma, Tosa, Hiroshima, Fukui, and Owari seized the gates of the Imperial Palace. By an imperial proclamation arranged by Saigō, Ōkubo, and Iwakura, and backed by the combined forces of Satsuma, Chōshū, and Tosa, the Tokugawa Bakufu was officially abolished and the Imperial Court now ruled Japan. Important Tokugawa posts were eliminated—most notably the Tokugawa magistrates in Kyōto, the protector of Kyōto, and the inspector of the Imperial Court and nobles. The oppositionists, including court nobles and feudal lords who had supported the Tokugawa, were barred from the palace. The Lords of Aizu and Kuwana were ordered to leave Kyōto.

The importance of controlling the emperor, even at the risk of treating his holy personage as a king on the national chessboard, was no more apparent than now. Saigō Kichinosuké, for all means and purposes commander of the forces of the new imperial government, was not convinced at this juncture that he could defeat the Tokugawa in the event of civil war. He composed a letter urging the emperor's removal from Kyōto to a "safe location" before the outbreak of actual fighting. To Saigō, a "safe location" was a place that would afford the new government direct access to the emperor.

When the oppositionists gathered at Nijō Castle to meet with the deposed shōgun, they seethed with anger at Satsuma and Chōshū. They expressed to Yoshinobu their desire to attack the Satsuma estate in Kyōto. To be sure, this was precisely what Satsuma wanted. An unprovoked attack on Satsuma by troops of the fallen regime would provide the imperial forces with the moral high ground from which to attack the Tokugawa—as long as they controlled the emperor. But the crafty Yoshinobu would not fall into the Loyalists' trap. Although he certainly shared his vassals' resentment, he also realized that the battle had been lost before the fight. On the night of December 12, Yoshinobu quietly removed himself to Ōsaka Castle to avoid civil war. He was accompanied by the Lords of Aizu and Kuwana.

While Yoshinobu attempted to preserve the peace in the west, his vassals in the east handed Saigō the excuse he needed to start a war— by attacking and burning Satsuma's estate in Edo. Actually, Saigō and Ōkubo provoked the attack by orchestrating a series of incidents of arson and looting against Bakufu supporters, including an estate of Shōnai Han. The perpetrators of these crimes were Satsuma men. Pro-Tokugawa troops surrounded Satsuma's estate in the Mita district of Edo in late December. They demanded that the perpetrators be handed over. Satsuma, of course, refused. The Tokugawa side opened fire, knowing well that this would trigger a war in Kyōto.

Meanwhile, the Shinsengumi had been ordered by Tokugawa Prime Minister Itakura Katsukiyo to guard Nijō Castle. No sooner had Kondō and his men received this high honor, than it was pulled out from under them. Mito Han had also been assigned to guard the castle. A dispute ensued over which of the two should assume the guard duty. Commander Kondō is said to have barged in on a meeting among Mito men with the gravity of the situation radiating from his steely eyes. "I understand that your han has been assigned to guard Nijō Castle," he said. "Now that the House of Tokugawa faces such a serious crisis, we are resolved to share the duty with you. If the Aizu and Kuwana men decide to stay here and work with us, I am sure we can do this together." But the Mito men would hear nothing of it. They had received direct orders from Yoshinobu to guard the castle and would not share the duty with anyone. Yoshinobu was the son of the late Lord of Mito. Mito was one of the Three Branch Houses of the Tokugawa. Kondō's eyes flashed with murderous intent. He placed his right hand upon the hilt of his sword and refrained from drawing the blade only by his extraordinary willpower. But Commander Kondō had lost the dispute.

With the protector of Kyōto post abolished, the Shinsengumi was informed that their name would be changed to *Shinyūgekitai Oyatoi*— New Mercenary Guerrilla Corps. They apparently preferred their old name, which was synonymous with their five-year iron rule over the streets of the Imperial Capital. "We refused the name of 'New Guerrilla Corps,' and continued to refer to ourselves as 'Shinsengumi,'" Shimada Kai recorded in his memoirs. While they kept their name, they relinquished their rule and now joined Aizu and Kuwana in Ōsaka. Kondō Isami's murderous corps would never return to Kyōto.

* * * * *

Kondō Isami had attained historical immortality in Kyōto. During his five years in the Imperial Capital, he had become a ruthless killer and a tyrant whose will to power knew no bounds. His mind, however, was not completely preoccupied with war. At around this time he sent a sash of purple satin to his daughter in Edo, celebrating the seventh anniversary of her birth. Indeed, the Shinsengumi commander was endowed with a much revered quality in samurai society. That quality was humanity, pure and simple. When in the following January the Shinsengumi would finally return to the east after the Tokugawa's defeat in the west, Kondō could not but feel happy at the prospect of a reunion with his wife and daughter. He told a high-ranking Tokugawa official with whom he was traveling, "I did not expect to ever see them again." But his happiness was overshadowed by a tinge of shame because, as he admitted to the official, happiness was "unbecoming of a warrior in such difficult times as these." The official replied that it was only natural for a man to want to see his family. "That's humanity," the official said. "No matter how strong the warrior, unless he is endowed with humanity, he is no more than a beast."

"When Kondō left Kyōto," Miyuki recalled, "he gave my sister [Otaka] a certain amount of money," perhaps because she had borne his child Oyū and certainly because he was not without a degree of humanity. Otaka eventually went to the port town of Kōbé in search of work, sending Oyū to a foster home. Oyū grew up without any knowledge of her father. Years later Miyuki happened to see Kondō Isami's daughter at a house in the Gion pleasure quarter of Kyōto. Oyū was about fifteen years old at the time. "Out of respect for Kondō's spirit, I wanted to get someone to intervene," Miyuki recalled. "But after her mother had left for Kōbé, there was no word from her at all. Rumor had it that she had gone to Shanghai, Hong Kong, or some other foreign country." Miyuki was acquainted with a certain police officer who had been associated with the Shinsengumi "during the old days." The police officer intervened. "Your father was Kondō Isami," he told Oyū. "He was a great man. Your working at an occupation like this taints your father's name." Since this was the first time Oyū had heard of her father, "I thought she might be surprised or even happy," Miyuki recalled. "But surprisingly enough, she didn't seem to care much at all." Oyū said she preferred to continue working in the pleasure quarters. But the good police officer would hear nothing of it. He knew people in the Tokugawa family who would surely be willing to help Oyū, "because of her father's distinguished service." He offered to arrange a station for her as a maid for the family, who would certainly treat her "as if she were their own daughter." But Oyū refused, and Miyuki once again lost touch with her. Several years passed. As ironic fate would have it, the daughter of the Shinsengumi commander became a geisha in Shimonoseki. She was a favorite among former samurai of the Chōshū and Satsuma clans—elder statesmen of the Meiji government and Kondō Isami's mortal enemies.

* * * * *

As the Shinsengumi and the other oppositionist forces left Kyōto, troops of Satsuma and Chōshū marched into the city and the surrounding area. War was imminent. Upon reaching Ōsaka, Kondō Isami had intended to guard Tokugawa Yoshinobu at Ōsaka Castle. Instead, however, he received orders to join several other Tokugawa units to defend Fushimi, just south of Kyōto, on the way to Ōsaka.

A breakdown in the old order invited chaos within the ranks of the Shinsengumi. Desertion was rampant and unchecked. When the Shinsengumi set up headquarters at the compound of the Fushimi magistrate on December 18, only about fifty corpsmen remained. They were presently joined, however, by an additional eight hundred pro-Tokugawa troops, including three hundred from Aizu.

As tension mounted between the forces of the old regime and the new, travel on the roads between Kyōto and Ōsaka was perilous for both sides. The men of the Shinsengumi—their commander and vice commander in particular—were objects of animosity and revenge among the new leaders of Japan, especially Chōshū, who had lost many men to the "rōnin hunters" over the previous years. Also waiting for the opportunity to strike back at the Shinsengumi were the survivors of Itō's Kōdaiji Faction, staying at Satsuma's estate in Fushimi, and the followers of Sakamoto Ryōma, many of whom were at the Tosa estate in Kyōto. "[Men of] Satsuma, Chōshū and Tosa came near our headquarters every night," wrote Nagakura, "firing their

cannon and thrusting spears through the walls." One morning Nagakura found a sealed letter on the ground at Fushimi headquarters.
The letter was written by a young corpsman named Kobayashi Kei-
nosuké. When Nagakura noticed that it was addressed to Shinohara
Tainoshin of the Kōdaiji Faction, he opened it immediately. The letter contained secret information about the Shinsengumi. Nagakura
brought the letter to Hijikata, who instructed him to fetch Kobayashi.
Meanwhile, Hijikata called in the hulking Shimada Kai. When Nagakura returned with the informant, Hijikata and Shimada were waiting. As the vice commander questioned Kobayashi, Shimada lunged
upon him and strangled him to death.

Around this time, Kondō was summoned to Nijō Castle to discuss
the impending war. He was well aware that the remnants of Itō's faction were after him. He also suspected that although Kobayashi had
been eliminated, Itō's men still had informants among the Shinsengumi. He therefore moved about with appropriate caution. He brought
four men with him to Kyōto, including three corpsmen and a manservant. Among them was Shimada. The party traveled on horseback
along Fushimi-kaidō Road, reaching Nijō Castle without incident.
After the meeting, on December 18, Kondō remounted his horse for
the return journey. Lying in wait on both sides of the road near a place
called Tanbabashi, guns loaded and at the ready, were a group of Itō's
men, including Shinohara Tainoshin and Itō's brother Suzuki Mikisaburō. "We didn't depend on guns back in those days," one of them
recalled years later. "Once we fired, we assumed they would come
charging in the direction of the smoke with their swords drawn."

Shinohara shot Kondō as his party rode southward through the
cold dim of the late wintry afternoon. Shinohara missed his mark,
however, hitting Kondō on the right shoulder. Kondō was badly
wounded but survived the ambush. According to Shinohara, "he paid
no attention to the profuse bleeding," but rather whipped his horse
and made a fast escape. The assailants pursued the others with their
swords and spears, killing one of the corpsmen and Kondō's manservant. When Shinohara reported the incident to the Satsuma men in
Kyōto, one of them, Nakamura Hanjirō, a lieutenant of Saigō's, begrudgingly asked him why he had not shot the horse first.

When word of the incident reached the Lord of Aizu, he dispatched a physician to Kondō's sickbed, along with twenty ryō. Tokugawa Yoshinobu reportedly sent Kondō some of his own personal bedding from Ōsaka Castle. On December 20, two days after the shooting, Kondō went to Ōsaka to undergo treatment from Yoshinobu's private physician and his own personal friend, Matsumoto Ryōjun.

Hijikata wanted revenge. "We decided that if we saw anyone who looked like a samurai, we would kill him," Nagakura wrote. They went out on patrol but did not find "anyone who looked like a samurai." Upon returning to Fushimi headquarters, they encountered "ten men lying in wait." When Nagakura demanded that they identify themselves, the ten men fled. As it turned out, they were from Satsuma. "On the next day, each and every one of them committed seppuku for running away from an enemy," a violation of Bushidō.

Civil war broke out in the area called Toba-Fushimi, at the southern approach to Kyōto, on the evening of January 3, 1868—the fourth and final year of the old era of Keiō and the first of the new reign of Emperor Meiji.* Although the combined forces of the new regime totaled 50,000, only about 3,500 of these, mostly from Satsuma, had been deployed to the Kyōto area. Meanwhile, the Aizu, Kuwana, and Shinsengumi troops stationed at the Fushimi magistrate's compound had been reinforced to more than 10,000 strong. Though the imperial forces were outnumbered threefold, their victory three days later was decisive, although it has been called a "miracle of luck."

The rout of the Tokugawa was in great part due to Yoshinobu's reluctance to fight, despite his clear military advantage. During the two and a half centuries of Tokugawa rule, the morals of the educated classes, including samurai, and wealthy farmers and merchants, were based on the relationship between sovereign and subject. The emperor in Kyōto was the true sovereign of Japan. The Japanese people, including the commander in chief of the expeditionary forces against the barbarians, were his subjects. Fifteen successive heads of the

---

* The era name would not actually be changed to Meiji until September 8.

House of Tokugawa had simply been entrusted with the reins of government, which Yoshinobu himself had returned to the Imperial Court. Yoshinobu's greatest fear, then, was to be remembered in history as an Imperial Enemy, even if he should perish at the hands of the imperial government. Of this his enemies were well aware. And it was for this reason that in December, when the imperial decree was issued authorizing Satsuma and Chōshū to attack the Tokugawa, Ōkubo Ichizō arranged for his mistress in Kyōto to purchase damask of red and white to be made into imperial banners. The banners were part of a plan by Iwakura Tomomi to render the Tokugawa troops morally incapable of opposing Satsuma and Chōshū, which were now perceived as the defenders of the emperor.

Just before noon on the third day of the Battle at Toba-Fushimi, the artillery forces of both sides were holding out well against each other. The imperial banner suddenly appeared from behind the Satsuma and Chōshū line. At first neither side recognized the strange banner, fluttering majestically in broad daylight above the battlefield. Nobody had ever actually seen the imperial banner, although they had read about it in the ancient war chronicles of Japan. When a message reached both sides that this was indeed the imperial banner, the Satsuma and Chōshū men broke out in cheer, their morale bolstered, while their Tokugawa foes seemed suddenly robbed of their fighting spirit. At that moment the Satsuma gunners ceased firing and charged the enemy with drawn swords. The Tokugawa side attempted to counterattack but were forced to retreat by an all-out charge of the entire imperial force. The following night, the sixth of January, Yoshinobu, accompanied by the Lords of Aizu and Kuwana, stole out of Ōsaka Castle to board the Tokugawa warship *Kaiyō Maru*. The shōgun now fled to Edo, leaving his troops without their supreme commander. His defeat in the west was final.

While Kondō Isami convalesced in Ōsaka, his corps, under the command of Hijikata Toshizō, had engaged the enemy from the compound of the Fushimi magistrate. Although they were armed with guns, including one cannon, these expert swordsmen lacked training in artillery techniques. Accordingly, they depended mostly on their swords and spears against the Satsuma artillery forces, who pounded them with cannon fire from a height above the compound. This was the first time that this most dreaded band of swordsmen had faced a modern artillery unit. The outcome was disastrous. The Shinsengumi lost more than thirty men in the one-sided fight. Among the dead were veteran members Inoué Genzaburō and Yamazaki Susumu. Numerous others were wounded. Some deserted.

During the fighting Hijikata ordered Nagakura to lead a charge with drawn swords because "the outcome of battle cannot be decided by gunfire." The Satsuma gunners belied Hijikata's outmoded ideas about war. After several unsuccessful attempts to penetrate the enemy's fortification, Nagakura's swordsmen were forced to retreat. Nagakura wore heavy armor, which impeded his scaling the high fence surrounding the compound of the Fushimi magistrate. Meanwhile, the bullets flew all around him, and Nagakura expected to be killed. Suddenly the giant Shimada Kai appeared at the top of the fence. He extended his rifle down to Nagakura. "Grab on to this," he shouted, and pulled Nagakura up the wall.

The Shinsengumi retreated to Ōsaka, where they were reunited with their commander. In a poem Kondō Isami had composed in Kyōto, he vowed never to return to Edo without accomplishing his great purpose. His great purpose was nothing less than "loyalty and patriotism." He had "polished the long sword of loyalty and patriotism" during his years of kenjutsu training. In Kyōto he had kept this sword "ready at my hip," and used it with great frequency, alacrity, and skill. But when he viewed his badly beaten corps and learned of Yoshinobu's flight to Edo, he finally admitted defeat in the west and asked Hijikata to arrange passage to the east for the 117 remaining corpsmen. Fewer than twenty of them were Shinsengumi veterans, including seven officers—Kondō, Hijikata, Nagakura, Okita, Harada, Saitō, and Ōishi.

On January 11, Kondō Isami, not yet recovered from his wound, boarded the Tokugawa warship *Fujisan Maru* for the return journey to Edo. Accompanying Kondō were Hijikata and those who had been badly wounded in the fighting, including Saitō. Okita also required medical attention—not for battle wounds but for the tuberculosis that was slowly killing him. The physically sound sailed aboard the Tokugawa warship *Jundō Maru*. Three of the wounded men on the *Fujisan Maru* perished during the return journey.

Upon landing at Edo, the wounded men, including Kondō, were hospitalized. Kondō, still heavily bandaged and pale, was again treated by Matsumoto Ryōjun. At this time, a samurai from Sakura Han, whose daimyō was a direct retainer of the Tokugawa, visited Kondō to inquire about his condition. With Kondō was Hijikata. When the Sakura man asked the Shinsengumi commander about the war in Fushimi, Kondō told him to address the question to his vice commander. To this Hijikata is said to have replied with a grim smile, "Swords and spears will no longer be of any use in battle. They are simply no match for guns." Soon after, on February 3, Hijikata procured state-of-the-art breech-loading rifles for the Shinsengumi.

THE PEASANT AS FEUDAL LORD

Their troops had been badly defeated. Their armies had retreated from the field. Their supreme commander and liege lord had surrendered and pledged allegiance to the enemy. He had admonished them to do the same, as had his councilor—who committed suicide in the castle to bolster this admonishment. But still the oppositionists would not give up the fight. Leading the opposition were personages of noble birth and lofty rank within the fallen regime—and, perhaps most notably, the peasants' sons whose claim to historic immortality lay in their lethal swords and a steadfast propensity to use them.

At the end of January, the Shinsengumi set up headquarters at the Edo estate of a former elite Tokugawa official recently relieved of his post. Kondō Isami had recovered from his wound by February 12. It was on this day that Imperial Enemy Tokugawa Yoshinobu moved from Edo Castle to Daiji'in, a subtemple of Kan'eiji, the Tokugawa family temple at Uéno—a hilly region in the northeastern part of the city. At Daiji'in, Yoshinobu confined himself to two modest-size adjacent rooms to demonstrate his "allegiance and penitence" to the imperial government. He set out for the temple before dawn under the vigilant guard of the Shinsengumi, commanded by Kondō Isami.

Rather than marching as a unit, which would have drawn attention to their invaluable charge, the corpsmen concealed themselves along the roadway traveled by the former shōgun.

These warriors of the east, returned in defeat from the west, nevertheless held themselves in the utmost importance. They would guard the former shōgun with their lives. They would fight to restore the rule of the Edo regime. They did not know, however, how long they would remain in the capital; meanwhile, they would indulge in the pleasures of their native land, which they had not enjoyed in five years. Among these pleasures were the houses in the Fukagawa quarter of Edo. At one of these houses Nagakura Shinpachi quarreled with three samurai, two of whom he killed with his sword. Soon after the incident Hijikata summoned Nagakura. "Such behavior will not be condoned," the vice commander admonished his officer, "because you now occupy too important a position."

Before retreating to Uéno, Yoshinobu had purged the oppositionists from the Tokugawa hierarchy. He placed the control of all political and military affairs into the hands of three of his vassals, who supported the imperial government. Two of them were Katsu Kaishū and Ōkubo Ichiō. Ōkubo was Kaishū's mentor, his closest ally in the Tokugawa camp, and future governor of Tōkyō. He was in charge of the administration of the defunct Bakufu. Kaishū, meanwhile, was in control of the military—both army and navy. The two men were the most prominent among a small number of Tokugawa samurai who enjoyed the ear and respect of the leaders of the new government, most notably Saigō Kichinosuké. As the leaders of the reconciliation faction at Edo who had advised Yoshinobu to "pledge allegiance to the imperial government," Kaishū and Ōkubo were despised, however erroneously, as traitors by the majority of oppositionists within the Tokugawa camp, including Kondō and Hijikata.

After their decisive victory at Toba-Fushimi, the imperial government, with an army of fifty thousand marching steadily toward Edo, planned to launch an attack on Edo Castle, and in so doing subject the entire city to the flames of war. Kaishū and Ōkubo were determined to avoid further civil war. They feared that bringing the war to the east would not only endanger the lives and property of Edo's one million inhabitants but also invite foreign aggression. Now that Yoshinobu was out of the way, they struggled simultaneously to pacify both the oppositionists and the bellicose leaders of the new regime, while planning the evacuation of people from the capital.

Meanwhile, Kondō and Hijikata reported to Kaishū and Ōkubo at Edo Castle, carrying false promises. They planned to capture Kōfu Castle, strategically located in the mountains some ninety miles west of Edo. Throughout the 265 years of Tokugawa rule, Kōfu Castle had been one of three major positions for the defense of Edo. From this mountain fortress, Kondō and Hijikata would engage the imperial troops on their eastward march to the capital. But they lied to Ōkubo and Kaishū. They promised that their intentions were peaceful and that by no means would they fight the imperial forces. Rather, they would meet the advance guard at Kōfu to explain to them the shōgun's pledge of allegiance to the imperial government.

This was precisely what Kaishū and Ōkubo wanted. The two Shinsengumi leaders were now promoted to exalted positions within the old regime. Kondō was appointed *wakadoshiyori*—member of the shōgun's junior council—which placed him among the ranks of the feudal lords. Hijikata was promoted to *yoriaiseki*—a high-ranking Tokugawa retainer. Kondō would soon let it be known that he considered his corpsmen as his vassals, just as a daimyō considered the samurai of his feudal domain. But these exalted positions and these high honors were, of course, things of the past. Under the new imperial regime, ranking within the Tokugawa hierarchy was moot. The fact that Kondō and Hijikata even now refused to acknowledge this basic and bitter truth was laden with the tragic fundamentals of their personalities—their conviction of self-importance and their unyielding will to power. Of this Kaishū and Ōkubo were probably aware. But Kondō and Hijikata offered them a sudden flash of hope. Kaishū and Ōkubo provided Kondō's corps with the sizeable sum of 7,500 ryō, two cannon, three hundred breech-loading rifles, and ammunition, and sent them off to Kōfu.*

---

* Hirao indicates 200 rifles; Shimosawa says 500. Shimada writes that they received 225 rifles, including Miniés. According to Nagakura, they received 300 breech-loaders.

On the evening before leaving Edo, the Shinsengumi held a banquet with all present. Kondō Isami announced to his men that Yoshinobu had indicated they could do as they would with Kōfu Castle and the one million koku yield of the Kōfu domain—if they could capture it. Kondō would take 100,000 koku, which would place him among the wealthiest of feudal lords. Hijikata would take 50,000 koku, their senior officers 30,000 each. The junior officers would take 10,000, and each of the rank and file would receive 1,000, which matched the income of high government officials. But the rout at Toba-Fushimi was a reality. If Kondō was not lying again, surely he was indulging himself in hopeless self-deception, misleading those of his men who would be misled. Surely he knew that the end of the Edo regime and that of his own illustrious and violent career had arrived. Even if the Tokugawa Bakufu should somehow miraculously survive, Kondō and Hijikata were the sons of peasants, their officers and men mere rōshi. For the past two and a half centuries the great domain of Kōfu had been ruled by a hereditary lord. Perhaps Kondō saw himself as a warlord of four centuries past, when a man's worth and wealth were determined by his sword.

Since returning to Edo, the Shinsengumi had increased their ranks to two hundred. The new recruits consisted mostly of untrained men. The corps was officially renamed *Kōyōchinbutai*—Pacification Corps—and placed in charge of suppressing uprisings among the people of the Kōfu region. Hijikata cropped his hair and wore Western-style trousers and cloak. He encouraged his men to do the same. Both Hijikata and Kondō assumed aliases to protect their identity. Hijikata called himself Naitō Hayato.[*] Kondō went by the name Ōkubo Yamato.[†] And certainly Kondō took solace from the fact that his wife had recently received three hundred ryō from the Tokugawa coffers.

---

[*] Hayato was Hijikata Toshizō's father's name.
[†] Kondō's initial alias was Ōkubo Tsuyoshi. In the following March Kondō changed his alias to Ōkubo Yamato.

The new corps was prepared to march by the end of February. But Kondō and Hijikata delayed their departure by several days because they expected to be joined by any number of the thousands of Tokugawa retainers in Edo who, like them, viewed the pacifism of Yoshinobu and Kaishū as nothing less than cowardice. Their expectations proved as false as their views. The two hundred men of the Pacification Corps finally departed Edo on March 1, without the expected reinforcements. Under the commander and vice commander, the officers included Nagakura Shinpachi, Harada Sanosuké, Saitō Hajimé, Okita Sōji, and Ōishi Kuwajirō. They moved westward along Kōshū-kaidō Road, through the Tama region in the province of Musashi. They must have been a grand sight—Kondō Isami, the peasant's son, leading the way on horseback through his native village of Kami'ishihara, his soldier's helmet adorned with the three hollyhock leaves of the Tokugawa. Hijikata Toshizō rode immediately behind Kondō. Following the vice commander were the officers of the corps, and behind them the rank and file, each wearing two swords and carrying a gun.* Kondō, overcome with nostalgia and certainly bursting with pride, briefly dismounted at Kami'ishihara to pray at the village shrine.

Much ado was made over these native sons. Celebrations welcomed them along the way. On their second day out, they visited the Hino estate of Satō Hikogorō, on the Kōshū-kaidō. During these past five years, Satō had watched over Kondō's family. Now he formed a small militia, the Kasuga Corps, consisting of local peasants to fight alongside Kondō's men. A banquet was held at Satō's home in honor of Kondō and Hijikata. Saké was served in large quantities. It is said that because of the pain from the gunshot wound on his right shoulder, Kondō was unable to raise his saké cup above his chest with his right hand. Not to be left out of the festivities, he violated protocol and used his left. Satō's eighteen-year-old son, Toshinori, would recall the gathering decades later:

---

* The two cannon had been dismantled and loaded on horseback.

Although they didn't spend the night at Hino, saké was served right away and they told stories of bravery in Kyōto. The blade of the *Kotetsu* sword, which Kondō had used at the Ikéda'ya, was badly nicked so that it could no longer be used. But it nevertheless fit easily into the scabbard. He spoke highly of it, saying what a truly good sword it was.

The young men who studied kenjutsu in the local area [the Tama region], all of whom were peasants, came over. Fifty or sixty of them crammed onto the dirt floor of the kitchen, saying, "We would like to see the master's face." When we told Kondō about this he was very pleased…. He talked to them in the same manner he had when he used to live in Edo, saying, "It is very good that all of you seem so robust. Please take good care of your health." This made the students very happy, so that they wept out loud.

At five different places on Kondō's coat were small images of the three hollyhock leaves [of the Tokugawa]…. The students said that they wanted to go with him, but Kondō would not consent. "There are still many other things for you to do," he said. "Your intentions make me very happy, but I can't allow you to come with us."

But the young men, nevertheless hell-bent on fighting alongside their hero, had already joined Satō's peasant militia. Satō's son was later arrested by the imperial forces for his part in the opposition. He was taken back to enemy headquarters and questioned. "On the third day I was released, with my head still on my shoulders. But they did take away my swords." When Hijikata heard about the incident, he sent new swords to his nephew. "Hijikata was quite a good-looking man," Toshinori recalled. "But he never smiled very much, perhaps because he tended to be a little high-flown and careful. This was why he did not make as good an impression on the fencing students as Kondō did when they stopped by on the way to Kōfu."

Kondō and Hijikata were pleased with their heroes' welcome. They indulged themselves in the festivities, meeting old friends and relatives along the way. Their dalliance proved costly. On March 4, their third day on the Kōshū-kaidō, they marched through a heavy snowstorm. On the following day, as they reached the summit of Sasago Pass, the most forbidding point along the road, word arrived that Kōfu Castle had fallen to some three thousand imperial forces led by Itagaki Taisuké of Tosa. Had Kondō's corps arrived one day earlier, the castle might have been theirs for the taking.

Kondō attempted to boost his troops' morale by lying to them that six hundred reinforcements from Aizu would arrive the next morning. Hijikata rushed back to Edo to get reinforcements from among the hatamoto. Meanwhile, Kondō led his corps westward across the snowy mountainous terrain. Numerous corpsmen, despairing of victory, deserted. They reached the town of Katsunuma, five miles east of Kōfu, on the same day, March 5. Only 121 corpsmen remained. In the mountains they erected a makeshift fortification, where they positioned their two cannon. In the town they constructed a barrier. In the mountains and the roadway they lit fires to intimidate the enemy, and waited for Hijikata's return.

Far from being intimidated, some twelve hundred enemy troops attacked at noon the following day.*

Having been trained in modern warfare, they had the clear advantage over Kondō's corps, both in sheer number and superiority of arms. Meanwhile, Kondō's men, particularly those who had been in Kyōto, enjoyed the advantage of experience in battle, but not in the use of artillery. Amid the smoke from the nearby fires, the Pacification Corps attempted to defend with their two cannon. There was not a man among them, however, with expertise in firing these large guns. In their inexperience, they misfired. As the enemy pounded them with heavy artillery fire, they had to resort to their rifles. The enemy closed in and charged with drawn swords. Satō Hikogorō's peasant militia, consisting of twenty-one men, fought fiercely against the charge, as did the warriors of the Pacification Corps. Kondō's men

---

* The number of imperial troops at Katsunuma differs depending on the source.

could not see for the smoke in their eyes. After two hours of fighting they had no alternative but to scatter into the surrounding mountains, and eventually retreat to Edo in defeat. In the Battle at Katsunuma, the Pacification Corps suffered eight dead and more than thirty wounded. Only one of the enemy was killed, and twelve wounded.

Of Defeat, Disgrace, and Apotheosis

The cherry blossoms were in full bloom when the warriors of the east returned once again in defeat to the ever-dangerous capital. As if to belie the hope inherent in this most promising of seasons, the end was upon them and they knew it. But even now, as if to challenge the will of that relentless goddess, they refused to give up the fight. Power to them meant everything—power founded on courage, which begot honor. And it was by this courage and for this honor that they would fight their enemies to the death.

In the dark eyes of Katsu Kaishū, this honor was false. All-out war in Edo was imminent. Fifty thousand imperial troops were closing in fast. An attack on Edo Castle was planned for March 15. As head of the Tokugawa military, Kaishū was the most powerful man in Edo. This loyal warrior of the House of Tokugawa, who had a fleet of twelve warships at his disposal, wanted nothing more than peace. He was nevertheless determined to burn Edo Castle rather than relinquish it in battle and to wage a bloody civil war against the imperial forces if they should attack. In a final effort to avoid war and to save the House of Tokugawa, on March 5, the day Kondō's corps reached Katsunuma, Kaishū dispatched Yamaoka Tetsutarō on an urgent and dangerous journey to Saigō Kichinosuké's military headquarters in Sunpu, a hundred miles west of Edo. Yamaoka carried a letter from Kaishū addressed to Saigō. In this letter Kaishū wrote that the retainers of the Tokugawa were an inseparable part of the new Japanese nation, and that Tokugawa Yoshinobu and his retainers had pledged allegiance to the emperor and the new imperial government. Instead of fighting with each other, those of the new government and the old must cooperate in order to deal with the very real threat of the foreign powers, whose legations in Japan anxiously watched the great revolution that had consumed the Japanese nation for these past fifteen years.

When Kaishū learned of the deception of the two Shinsengumi leaders, he was furious. When Kondō and Hijikata reported to him at Edo Castle of their intention to continue the fight, he was disgusted. "It is no more than a personal battle," he told them. "If you must fight again, do it on your own."

Despite the hostilities of the oppositionists, including the Shinsengumi, Saigō trusted Kaishū. He readily replied to Kaishū's letter with a set of conditions. Among them: the shōgun's castle, along with all of his weapons and warships, must be surrendered to the imperial government, and all of the shōgun's troops must be removed from the capital. These conditions, Saigō wrote, must be met if the House of Tokugawa was to be allowed to survive, Yoshinobu's life spared, and war avoided. On the thirteenth and fourteenth of March, with the imperial troops at Shinjuku and Itabashi, the western and northwestern outskirts of the city, Kaishū and Saigō—who after all were allies in the truest sense—met at two different locations, at Takanawa and Tamachi, in the south of Edo. Kaishū accepted Saigō's conditions. On March 15 the attack was called off.

Hijikata Toshizō was the only man left whom Kondō Isami could truly trust. Okita Sōji, afflicted with tuberculosis, was on his deathbed in Edo. Many of the rank and file had fled. Other Shinsengumi veterans had abandoned Kondō, including two of his oldest and most trusted comrades—Harada Sanosuké and Nagakura Shinpachi.

In mid-March, Nagakura, Harada, and several others decided to join their allies in Aizu. They obtained five hundred ryō from Matsumoto Ryōjun for military expenditures, then visited Kondō and Hijikata at a hospital in Edo, where the former was again undergoing treatment for his shoulder wound. They invited Kondō and Hijikata to join them. According to Nagakura, Kondō reacted angrily that his subordinates had made war plans without his knowledge. He replied that he would join them under the condition that they serve as his vassals. "All of us took offense," Nagakura recalled. They told Kondō that they would fight alongside him as comrades but would not serve him. They never saw their former commander again.

* * * * *

While the imperial government prepared to occupy Edo Castle, it set itself to the task of eliminating the significant number of Tokugawa retainers and sympathizers in and around the capital who even now refused to surrender. By the end of March the imperial forces had completely surrounded Edo. Meanwhile, one thousand oppositionists who called themselves *Shōgitai*—Corps of Clear Loyalty—were entrenched at Kan'eiji Temple to "protect" Tokugawa Yoshinobu. Others fled to the countryside in the northwest, north, and northeast to plan a concerted uprising with their comrades in the capital.

Prominent among these die-hard oppositionists were Kondō Isami and Hijikata Toshizō. Fewer than fifty men remained in Edo under their command. (Kondō had sent more than twenty men to Aizu to recover from their battle wounds.) Rather than going to Aizu with Nagakura and the others as their equals, Kondō and Hijikata, their will to power now the stuff of tragedy, went to work revising the Shinsengumi. They recruited new men to join forces with the oppositionists in Uéno and the adjacent countryside, from where they would march to Aizu to rally one great army for a final showdown against the new government.

On March 13, unaware that Kaishū and Saigō were on that same day negotiating a solution to impending disaster, Kondō Isami, alias Ōkubo Yamato, and Hijikata Toshizō, alias Naitō Hayato, slipped out of Edo hell-bent on war, just three days after returning from

Katsunuma. With their revised corps of more than one hundred men, they were given temporary quarters and provisions at the private estate of the Kanéko family, a wealthy peasant household with vast landholdings in the countryside just northeast of the capital. Shortly after Kondō's corps had arrived at the Kanéko estate, two messengers appeared on two different occasions. The messengers had been sent by Katsu Kaishū to persuade the Shinsengumi to relinquish their war plans.

But Kondō would not relinquish his war plans. The ranks of the Shinsengumi had been growing with each passing day. Kondō was raring to join his allies in Aizu for the impending great showdown he envisioned. To this end, he now wanted to move to a location more suitable for preparing his new recruits for battle. Through the good offices of Matsumoto Ryōjun, Kondō petitioned the Tokugawa authorities for permission to move. Permission was not granted—a result of direct interference by Katsu Kaishū. By the end of March the Shinsengumi ranks had swelled to 227, greater than their number at the Battle at Katsunuma. Kondō would wait no longer. On April 1 the Newly Selected Corps left the Kanéko estate for a location more appropriate for training the new recruits. Kondō Isami, whom the Kanéko family knew only as Ōkubo Yamato, left behind a photograph of himself, probably taken the previous February at Yokohama, as a token of appreciation for their hospitality.

On the morning of the following day, Kondō and Hijikata set up headquarters at a miso factory in the village of Nagaréyama, near the east bank of the Edogawa in the province of Shimo'usa, about nine miles as the crow flies northeast of the Kanéko estate. The troops were housed at a nearby temple.

At nearly the same time as the Shinsengumi set out for Nagaréyama, three hundred imperial troops, under the command of Staff Officer Kagawa Keizō of Mito,* departed their headquarters at Itabashi with orders to suppress oppositionists in Utsu-nomiya Han, north of Edo. On the day the Shinsengumi reached Nagaréyama,

---

* Kagawa had been involved in the foiled plot by men in Zézé Han to assassinate Shōgun Tokugawa Iémochi.

Kagawa received information from officers on patrol, including Vice Staff Officer Arima Tōta of Satsuma, that an armed unit had set up camp at that village. When some two hundred imperial troops suddenly appeared at Nagaréyama on the following morning, the Shinsengumi recruits were practicing artillery drills in an open field a couple of miles from headquarters. The recruits were taken completely off guard. No sooner did they see the enemy than they threw down their rifles and fled. Kagawa's men now surrounded the nearby Shinsengumi headquarters.

Inside the miso factory Arima and Kagawa found three or four men. One of them, who identified himself as Ōkubo Yamato, had particularly intense eyes, an unusually large mouth, heavy jaw, and full head of thick black hair tied in a topknot. "His demeanor, appearance, and perfect composure were magnificent," Arima recalled more than five decades later in 1923. Although they had never actually seen Kondō Isami in the flesh, they knew his description. Nevertheless, they lacked firm evidence that this man was the hated Shinsengumi commander who had killed so many of their comrades in Kyōto over the past several years. The man who called himself Ōkubo Yamato claimed loyalty to the imperial government. He told the imperial officers that it was not the intention of his corps to oppose them; rather, they had been on a mission to suppress the oppositionists in the north and northeast. The imperial officers would not be so easily deceived. They ordered Kondō to turn over his weapons, disband his corps, and accompany them to their camp at nearby Koshigaya for the night. They informed him that in the morning he would be brought to the imperial military headquarters at Itabashi for questioning. Kondō outwardly acquiesced but inwardly resolved to commit seppuku.

Shimada Kai wrote that Arima also spoke with Hijikata, but neither the vice commander nor any of the other corpsmen were arrested at that time. That evening Kondō met with the enemy officers to surrender three cannon and 118 rifles. Present at that meeting was a samurai of Hikoné Han named Watanabé Kurōsaemon. Watanabé had seen Kondō in Kyōto. He thought that he recognized the man who called himself Ōkubo Yamato as Kondō Isami, commander of the Shinsengumi. Watanabé couldn't believe his eyes. Nor were his superiors, including Kagawa and Arima, inclined to trust his memory when misjudgment might cause trouble later on. The matter was dropped for the time being without mentioning it to Kondō, but the imperial officers nevertheless believed that they had indeed captured the notorious Shinsengumi commander.

Kondō requested time to prepare himself, telling the enemy officers that he would report to their camp that evening. His request granted, he met with Hijikata and informed him of his resolve to die. According to the recollections of Shinsengumi corpsman Kondō Yoshisuké (not related to Kondō Isami) four decades later, Hijikata implored Kondō not to kill himself but rather to report to Itabashi under his alias and stand by his claim of loyalty to the imperial government. "To commit seppuku here would be to die like a dog," Hijikata told him, advising him to "leave the matter to fate." Kojima Shikanosuké, however, recorded a slightly different version of the story. According to Kojima, Hijikata told Kondō that he would accompany him to enemy headquarters. Kondō objected, telling Hijikata that one of them must survive to continue the fight. Either way, Kondō Isami allowed himself to be taken alive, not because he was afraid to die but because dying now would mean certain and utter defeat—defeat not only for himself but also for the Shinsengumi, which had been his reason for living for these past five years.

Arima described the ensuing scene as a prologue to high tragedy:

Night came but Kondō had still not shown up. Considering the situation, I left on horseback [to get him], accompanied by five soldiers and one footman named Sakamoto. There was one sentry without a gun, standing alone beside the gate. I left the soldiers outside the gate and proceeded, accompanied only by Sakamoto. "I've come to see Ōkubo," I said. One of the men who had been with Kondō that morning [now] told me that he was busy and that I should wait for a while inside.

But I felt a bit uneasy going into the house.... I sat down on the edge of the veranda near the study. I lit a lantern adorned

with the Chrysanthemum Crest and waited for a while. Soon
Kondō came and said, "I am very sorry, but I would like to
request a little more time. Won't you please come inside? Since
this is a military headquarters, you need not remove your san-
dals." I couldn't very well refuse, so I went inside with my san-
dals on and waited there for a while, sitting with my legs
crossed. Tea was served. However, since I had heard that men
in the Bakufu would kill people by poisoning their tea, I didn't
drink any. But I was thirsty, maybe from the saké I had drank
a little earlier. I took a drink of water, partly to conceal my
embarrassment for not drinking any tea.

After a short while Kondō appeared dressed in splendid
pleated trousers that made a chaffing sound as he walked. "I
am sorry to have kept you waiting so long," he said. "With so
many people here, I've had much to do. It took me longer
than I realized." Then he called two young men. "They have
been serving under me," he said, then turned to them and
explained repeatedly something to the following effect: "Lord
Yoshinobu is now in confinement. The Son of Heaven is in
Kyōto. In the future you must devote yourselves exclusively
to the Imperial Court." He gave one of them some documents
and a short sword. To the other he gave some documents and
a pistol.

I simply watched the tragic scene, all the while wondering if
this is what happens when one loses a war. I was overcome by
sympathy; tears flowed down my cheeks. Kondō wore an in-
tensely grievous face as he looked at me. He, too, seemed overcome by deep emotion. After that the two young men came
back. "Please allow us to accompany you," they said.

Arima granted their request. "Kondō and I rode on horseback,
he in front, I in the rear. Fifteen soldiers split up into two groups [to
accompany us]—one in back, one in front—and we left." Kondō's
two attendants ran along either side of their master's horse as they

traveled.* The party reached the imperial encampment at Koshigaya at around twelve o'clock the same night.

When Arima awoke the next morning, he discovered that Kondō had been placed in a prisoner's palanquin, covered by a large net. "How could you put the leader of an army of men in a palanquin for a common criminal?" he angrily asked those who had placed him there. "You're truly a disgraceful bunch. Do you actually consider yourselves to be compassionate samurai? Remove the net immediately." According to Arima, he provided Kondō with tobacco, tea, and other accessories for a comfortable journey.

Kondō was transported to enemy headquarters for questioning. At Itabashi he continued to refer to himself by his alias, until the Sun Goddess, now intent on damning him, interfered. At the headquarters happened to be a samurai of Izu Han named Kanō Michinosuké. Kanō was formerly of the Shinsengumi, but lately of Itō Kashitarō's Kōdaiji Faction. Kanō, who had survived the battle at Aburakoji, hated Kondō Isami. When he saw the prisoner, he didn't hesitate to uncover Kondō's identity. "I can still see the look on his face," Kanō reminisced more than three decades later. "He was so very horrified."

Kondō could not have been anything but horrified for still being alive. Bitter and deep must have been his regret for not committing seppuku at Nagaréyama. Arima considered him "a kind of hero." The hero, who cherished honor above all and whose will to power had been unchallenged these past several years, now realized that his end would not be by the dignity of his own sword, but rather by the disgrace of the executioner's. Presently he composed his death song:

Submitting to the will of another,
I have nothing to say on this day.
I value honor above life.

---

* Only one of Kondō's attendants, Nomura Risaburō, traveled as far as the enemy camp. He was subsequently arrested but later was released and rejoined the Shinsengumi at Sendai. Kondō's other attendant returned to Nagaréyama before reaching the enemy camp.

Ah, the long flashing sword
  to which I readily surrender,
  and repay my lord's kindness with my life. *

On the night of Kondō's arrest at Nagaréyama, Hijikata rushed to Edo to visit the home of Katsu Kaishū, whom he still considered a traitor. Hijikata knew that any chance of Kondō's being pardoned rested in Kaishū's hands. "Hijikata Toshizō came [today]," reads the April 4 entry of Kaishū's journal. "He told me the full details of Nagaréyama." Certainly Kaishū was less than pleased. But on the next day a messenger arrived at imperial headquarters in Itabashi. He carried a letter, purportedly written by Kaishū, requesting that Kondō's life be spared. The Shinsengumi was still suspected of Sakamoto Ryōma's assassination. Kondō and Hijikata had lied to Kaishū regarding their intentions for marching to Kōfu. Their subsequent adventurism at Katsunuma jeopardized his peace plans at the eleventh hour. No firm evidence exists to prove that Kaishū actually wrote the letter. Whether or not he did, that the request to spare Kondō Isami's life was flatly rejected is apparent from the fact that the messenger was promptly arrested at Itabashi.

The trial of Kondō Isami began on April 8 at Itabashi headquarters, in the presence of representatives from several of the leading han, including Satsuma, Chōshū, Tosa, Hikoné, and Mito. Most of the representatives, particularly those from Chōshū and Tosa, hated Kondō. To them he was nothing but a brutal thug—the leader of a group of murderers who had killed scores of their comrades in Kyōto. (Staff Officer Kagawa Keizō, who represented Mito, had been hunted by the Shinsengumi.) The Tosa men bore the strongest vendetta against Kondō, whom they held responsible for the assassinations of Sakamoto Ryōma and Nakaoka Shintarō. One of the Tosa men, Tani Tatéki, described Kondō as follows:

---

* By his "lord," Kondō was referring to either the former shōgun, Tokugawa Yoshinobu, or Matsudaira Katamori, the Lord of Aizu.

He was a crafty scoundrel who committed evil for many years and killed a countless number of our men. But now he's been arrested and will die... . The old fox has deceived people. But it's one of the funniest stories ever that the old fox came out during the daytime to be caught so easily. The notorious Kondō Isami arrested without a fight—now all the other foxes will certainly perish.*

According to Tani's account of the trial, Satsuma argued for leniency while Tosa insisted that Kondō be executed. When asked why he had brought his corps to Nagaréyama, Kondō stuck by his original claim of loyalty to the imperial government, testifying that his intention was only to suppress the oppositionist forces in the north and northeast.

After heated argument back and forth between the Satsuma and Tosa sides, the latter prevailed. Kondō Isami was sentenced to die.

※ ※ ※ ※ ※

After Kondō's arrest, most of the Shinsengumi fled north to Aizu. At dawn on April 11, while Kondō awaited death at Itabashi, Tokugawa Yoshinobu quietly vacated his rooms at Kan'eiji Temple to return to the house of his birth in Mito. Yoshinobu's departure from his former capital was aptly timed—later that day Edo Castle was officially handed over to the imperial government. On the same day, amid the ensuing chaos, Hijikata Toshizō joined more than three thousand oppositionist troops in their flight from Edo. He was accompanied by only six of his men, including Shimada Kai. All but one of the six had been with the Shinsengumi since Kyōto.

The oppositionist army was divided into three units. Hijikata was selected as staff officer to lead one of these units north to Utsunomiya. Shimada, marching with Hijikata, carried with three others a great white banner emblazoned with five large Chinese charac-

---

* I have taken poetic license with this metaphoric passage because it does not lend itself to a literal English translation.

ters—*Tōshō Daigongen*—an alternate name for the Tōshōgu Shrine
of Tokugawa Iéyasu.* The oppositionists temporarily occupied Utsunomiya Castle before being driven from that strategic fortress in a
major offensive by imperial forces on April 24. During the fighting
at Utsunomiya, one of Hijikata's men attempted to flee. When Hijikata confronted him, the man insisted that the enemy were too many
to defeat. The Demon Commander saw red. He drew his long sword
and killed the man on the spot. Raising his bloodied sword in the air,
he screamed to his troops, "I'll kill anyone who tries to flee." Their
morale suddenly boosted, Hijikata's men now drew their swords.
They charged the enemy, who fled in great numbers.

During the fighting, Hijikata received a bullet wound to the foot.
Unable to walk, he had to be carried on Shimada's back on their subsequent march to Aizu to continue the fight. On the way to Aizu, near
Nikkō, he arranged a meeting with a childhood friend who was stationed there. When Hijikata told his friend about the fighting at Utsunomiya, tears welled up in the warrior's eyes. "It was pitiful what I
did to that soldier," he said. He handed his friend a packet of gold and
asked him to erect a gravestone for the man who had tried to flee.
Had the warrior lost his propensity to kill? The answer must be a resounding *no*—as he would clearly demonstrate during the ensuing
final year of his short, volatile life.

* * * * *

On April 25, 1868, the day after Hijikata Toshizō had fled Utsu-nomiya, Kondō Isami was placed in a palanquin and brought to
the scaffold near imperial headquarters in Itabashi. The former commander of the Shinsengumi was dressed formally in a lined kimono
of black twill and a black coat adorned with his family crest. He wore
a sash around his waist, probably white. He was barefoot. A slight
beard covered his heavy jaw, a dark but tranquil expression his pallid
face. His arms were bound with heavy rope, tied around his chest like

---

* In 1646, thirty years after Iéyasu's death, the Imperial Court gave him the princely name
Tōshōgu—literally, Shrine (or Prince) of Eastern Light. Thereafter, shrines for Iéyasu
were called Tōshōgu.

so much netting. It had rained the previous night, so that on this sunny spring day the sky was a brilliant blue; the clean scent of the grasses and wildflowers of the Musashi Plain filled the air.

At Kondō's home not fifteen miles to the west, his wife, Otsuné, had heard a rumor that a "ranking Tokugawa samurai" was to be executed on that day. Worried, she sent Kondō's seventeen-year-old nephew, Miyagawa Yūgorō, to Itabashi to find out more. Yūgorō had been betrothed to Kondō's infant daughter since his uncle had gone to Kyōto with the Rōshi Corps. As Kondō Yūgorō, he would succeed Isami as the fifth generational head of the Tennen Rishin style.

Yūgorō hurried to Itabashi. Around noon he saw a palanquin escorted by some thirty guards carrying rifles, "one of them, who looked like the captain, on horseback. As my heart beat rapidly, I took a close look inside the palanquin." The youth was horrified to see his uncle inside. He followed the palanquin to a field by an oak grove. The palanquin stopped near a freshly dug hole—a blood vat—next to which lay a straw mat.

The condemned criminal, Kondō Isami, slowly alighted the palanquin and stood erect atop the mat. The rope around his chest had been removed. He placed his hands on his sash; and as he gazed a final farewell to the sky above Edo, his thoughts must surely have been with Hijikata Toshizō and the war in the north. He uttered a few words to one of the guards standing by, probably a request for permission to shave his face to mitigate the immeasurable disgrace that would be his when his severed head would be mounted atop a stake for public display—by which means his enemies would ensure his absolute destruction, both in life and death. His request was granted, and presently a man appeared carrying a wooden box. It was probably then that Kondō Isami seated himself in the formal position, facing the blood vat. From inside the box the man produced a razor and shaved Kondō's face, because the prisoner could not be trusted with a blade in his hand.

A samurai wielding a long sword now approached from the rear. "He was somewhat thin, around forty-one or forty-two years old," Yūgorō recalled. Kondō's executioner, Yokokura Kisōji, was chief fencing instructor of the Okada domain in the province of Mino.

"I've been a great trouble," Kondō said in a loud clear voice. With the perfect composure of a samurai trained in the protocol of death, Kondō Isami calmly reached behind his head and held up his topknot to facilitate the job of his executioner. The executioner drew his sword. "There was a flash," Yūgorō recalled. A torrent of red gushed from Kondō's neck, and the severed head dropped into the blood vat. The head was retrieved from the hole and washed with a bucket of water, as the youth ran from the scene.

"His countenance was the same as always in the face of death, and he died with composure," Shimada Kai recorded in his memoirs. "Those watching shed tears of sorrow for Kondō. He was truly a great man, unequaled throughout the ages." Whether Kondō Isami was "truly a great man" must necessarily be a matter of subjectivity. That he was "unequaled" throughout the two and a half centuries of the Tokugawa era must be accepted as historical fact—if for no other reason than that the peasant's son had risen to the rank of feudal lord by virtue of his unyielding will to power, unwavering courage, indomitable sword, and unflinching propensity to use it.

Kondō's young nephew ran the entire way home to Kami'ishihara. "Everyone was grieving," he recalled the scene upon his arrival. Kondō's family would not allow the body of their greatest kinsman to remain among the corpses of common criminals at the execution ground. Three days later, through the good offices of a retainer to the elite and illustrious Tayasu family,* not to mention three gold ryō for the official in charge, Kondo Isami's headless corpse was exhumed, placed in a casket, and brought home for a hero's burial at Ryūgenji Temple.

While Kondō Isami was apotheosized at home, his spiked head was displayed for public view at Itabashi. Near the head was erected a signboard, citing his "crimes that are too numerous to count." After three days the head was placed in either alcohol or salt and transported three hundred miles to Kyōto. According to one official, the head was so well preserved as to be "lifelike" when exposed to public

---

* The Tayasu, a Tokugawa Branch House, descended from the second son of the eighth Tokugawa Shōgun. They were in charge of the management of Edo Castle.

derision on the east bank of the Kamogawa at Sanjō Bridge in the ancient Imperial Capital, where the notorious commander and his lethal samurai corps once reigned supreme.

Epilogue:
Hijikata's Last Fight

On April 29, four days after Kondō Isami's execution in Edo, the oppositionist forces reached Aizu-Wakamatsu, the castle town of the Lord of Aizu, where Hijikata Toshizō was treated for a severe foot wound. At Aizu, Hijikata and his six men were reunited with more than one hundred Shinsengumi men who had fled the enemy at Nagaréyama. With their leader incapacitated, the new Shinsengumi, about 130 of them, were under the temporary command of Saitō Hajimé, who now went by the alias Yamaguchi Jirō.

In May twenty-five feudal domains of northern Japan, most notably Aizu, Yonézawa, Shōnai, and Sendai, formed a confederation to fight the imperial forces. By early July, Hijikata, if not completely recovered, was able to rejoin his troops at the front lines. But he was still not well enough to fight and retreated soon after. On August 22 the imperial forces stormed Aizu-Wakamatsu. After a month of heavy fighting, the castle fell. Meanwhile, Hijikata fled to Shōnai, and later to Sendai, to bring the fight farther north. Before leaving Aizu, he placed his men under the command of Ōtori Keisuké, former commissioner of the Tokugawa infantry.

* * * * *

On May 30, while Hijikata convalesced in Aizu, Okita Sōji quietly died of tuberculosis at a private residence in Edo. On his deathbed Okita insisted that he had recovered. "I'll take up my sword to kill the enemy," he said. But Okita had not recovered. Nor was he able to take up his sword with much effect. According to an old woman who nursed him, three days before his death he did feel well enough to get out of bed. He went outside to the garden, where he saw a cat. He tried to kill the cat with his sword, but he was too weak. The next day he tried again, with the same result. "I can't even kill a cat," he screamed in agony, then collapsed. On the following day he uttered his last words: "I'll bet that cat is here." He was twenty-five years old and the Shinsengumi's most gifted swordsman.

* * * * *

At Sendai, Hijikata was reunited with the Shinsengumi, still under Ōtori's command. Only about forty corpsmen remained. Most of the others had either fled or been killed. Saitō Hajimé and twelve other corpsmen refused to abandon their comrades in Aizu, choosing to stay behind for the hopeless fight.

Before Hijikata arrived at Sendai, Enomoto Takéaki, former commissioner of the Tokugawa Navy, had sailed into Sendai Bay, in command of eight Tokugawa warships, including the powerful flagship *Kaiyō Maru*. When Edo Castle was handed over to the imperial government in April, Enomoto had refused to relinquish these warships, which Katsu Kaishū had promised to Saigō. With this fleet, he set sail from Edo in mid-August.

On September 3, a war council was held at Sendai Castle. Present were men of the former Bakufu, including Enomoto, and men from Sendai and the other confederate domains of the north. Hijikata was not invited to participate but rather stayed in an adjacent room while the council convened. Some of the confederate domains inclined toward pledging allegiance to the imperial government. A consensus could not be reached in their war plans. Enomoto suggested that Hijikata, still in the next room, be appointed general of the confederate troops. Enomoto's suggestion was readily accepted, and Hijikata was presently invited to join the council. "He was pale of complexion, and not large of stature," one of the councilors recalled of his impression of Hijikata. "His long, lacquer-like hair was disheveled…. I remember him as a handsome man."

Hijikata agreed to accept the command of the confederate troops—under one condition. "Orders must be strictly obeyed," he said firmly. "If any man defies orders, be he a senior councilor of one of your great domains, I, Toshizō, will have to strike him down with my long sword."* If Hijikata was to serve as general, he essentially demanded the "right to kill or let live." But it was not in the power of any man present to grant that right. It belonged to their respective feudal lords. Until they could receive their lords' permission, they could not accept Hijikata's condition. It is said that "Hijikata firmly stomped out of the room" as the war council adjourned.

Before their lords' permission could be granted or denied, the war council had been rendered moot. The day after the meeting, Yonézawa Han fell to the imperial forces. Six days later Sendai surrendered. By late September most of the other confederate domains had pledged allegiance to the imperial government. The oppositionists could no longer remain in Sendai. On October 12, they sailed aboard Enomoto's ships for the far-northern island of Ezo. When the oppositionists reached Ezo about a week later, the harsh winter snows had already begun to fall.†

Before departing Sendai, Hijikata thought of a way to increase the diminished ranks of the Shinsengumi. Present at Sendai were the Lord of Kuwana (Matsudaira Sada'aki), the Lord of Matsuyama (Itakura Katsukiyo), and the Lord of Karatsu (Ogasawara Nagamichi). It was decided that these lords would sail with the oppositionists to Ezo. Accompanying them at Sendai were numerous retainers who did not belong to the actual fighting forces. With the exception of two or three nonfighting retainers per feudal lord, Enomoto would allow only fighting men aboard his warships. If they remained behind, however, they faced certain capture. Hijikata now urged all of those retainers who wished to accompany their lords to join the Shinsengumi. Thirty-eight men enlisted immediately. Soon the Shinsengumi ranks exceeded one hundred.

---

* The actual wording that Hijikata reportedly used was "a sword three *shaku* in length." A shaku is a unit of measurement just under one foot.

† It was the beginning of December on the Gregorian calendar.

Hijikata was no longer merely the leader of the Shinsengumi. At Ezo he shared with Ōtori Keisuké the command of the entire oppositionist army—about 2,300 strong. Upon landing at Washinoki, on the east coast of southern Ezo, they divided into two large divisions. Most of the Shinsengumi were under Ōtori's command. Shimada Kai and a few other corpsmen stayed with Hijikata. From Washinoki they marched on separate routes toward the port city of Hakodaté, on the southern extremity of the island, facing Tsugaru Strait. Their destination was Goryōkaku, an imposing pentagonal fortress just inland from Hakodaté, occupied by troops of the imperial government. Shaped like a five-pointed star, Goryōkaku had been constructed by the Bakufu along the design of a seventeenth-century citadel at Lille, France, to protect the region after Hakodaté was opened to foreign trade in the previous decade. On October 26, after overcoming slight resistance by imperial forces, the oppositionists captured Goryōkaku without a fight. On the next day they set out for Matsumae Han, on the southern tip of Ezo. On November 6, they occupied Matsumae Castle before driving the remaining imperial forces completely off the island. By late November the forces of the former Tokugawa regime ruled Ezo.

Shortly after these men of the Bakufu had established themselves as the masters of Ezo, Enomoto petitioned the Imperial Court for permission to develop the entire northern island, so abundant in natural resources, and to protect that region from possible foreign aggression. Permission was flatly denied. On November 15, the oppositionists suffered a fatal blow when their flagship *Kaiyō Maru* ran aground and sank in a storm off Esashi, in the Sea of Japan. (Ironically, this day marked the first anniversary of the assassination of Sakamoto Ryōma.) Around the time that the oppositionists lost their flagship, the imperial forces acquired the ironclad *Stonewall Jackson*, which, before its collapse, the Bakufu had ordered from the United States. The *Stonewall* was a formidable warship—1,368 tons, 160 feet long, and equipped with nine cannon. With the outbreak of war, however, the foreign legations in Japan had adopted a policy of neutrality. They would not hand over the ironclad to either side. The

Stonewall therefore remained at anchor off Yokohama until that policy was finally lifted in January. When the imperial forces brought their most powerful warship to the fight in the north the oppositionists were doomed.

In December 1868 the new masters of the far north declared the independence of their short-lived Ezo Republic—where men of the former Bakufu could live in the traditions they still cherished. An election was held. Enomoto was elected president of the republic. Elected to the vice presidency was Matsudaira Tarō, a former vice commissioner of the Tokugawa army. Nagai Naomuné was elected magistrate of Hakodaté. Former Tokugawa naval officer Arai Ikunosuké was chosen as navy commissioner. Ōtori was elected commissioner of the army, and Hijikata his vice commissioner. While the French and British squadrons in Hakodaté conditionally recognized the Ezo Republic, the imperial government at Edo did not. And with the recently acquired *Stonewall Jackson*, it was determined to crush the oppositionists once and for all.

Hijikata Toshizō, vice commissioner of the army of the Ezo Republic, would never give up the fight. At Hakodaté he must have realized that his forces would ultimately lose. He suspected that Enomoto would pursue a peaceful agreement with the imperial government, which by his very nature he opposed. He continuously and intentionally moved into harm's way. He often told people that he should already be dead. He said that the only reason he had not died with Kondō was that he had wanted to clear the false charges laid against the former shōgun. But now Hijikata despaired of ever achieving this goal. If he should make peace with the enemy, he said, he would not be able to look Kondō in the face when they would "meet underground."*

In late January 1869, the second year of Emperor Meiji's reign, the imperial forces controlled the entire northern region of Honshū. They amassed 16,500 troops around Aomori, on the northern end of

---

* The Japanese term *chika*, literally "underground," is sometimes used to mean "afterlife."

Honshū, facing the Tsugaru Strait. All that separated them from the rebels in the far north were the strait and the forbidding cold of a still-early spring. On March 9, the imperial fleet, consisting of eight warships led by the *Stonewall Jackson*, left Edo. On March 20, they reached Miyako Bay, on the northeastern coast of the main island, to acquire provisions for an invasion of Ezo. In order to defend against the impending attack, the oppositionist forces had to command the sea around Ezo. In order to command the sea, they had to disarm the enemy of its most formidable warship. From their fortress at Hakodaté, they now planned the capture of the mighty *Stonewall Jackson*.

By March 21 the forbidding cold of the far north had given way to the warmth of late spring. On that day three warships of the oppositionists' navy—the flagship *Kaiten* leading the *Banryū* and the *Takao*—sailed southward from Hakodaté. Vice Commissioner of the Army Hijikata Toshizō, who had no experience in naval warfare, sailed aboard the *Kaiten* as an observer. The oppositionists' grand plan was to launch an early-morning surprise attack on the imperial fleet in Miyako Bay. The *Banryū* and *Takao* would draw up alongside the anchored *Stonewall Jackson*. Their troops would storm the ironclad with their swords drawn and, before the enemy troops had a chance to defend themselves, capture the ship and crew, returning with them to Hakodaté. That the grand plan failed miserably was on account of rough seas and mechanical failures—cruel fate so inseparably intertwined with that relentless Sun Goddess. Neither the *Banryū* nor the *Takao* made it to Miyako Bay. When the *Kaiten* reached the enemy fleet before dawn on March 25, her crew proceeded with the broken plans on their own. Before entering the harbor, they hoisted an American flag on the mast. But they were unable to position the *Kaiten*, a paddleboat, alongside the *Stonewall*. Rather, they had to approach the ironclad bow-first. Confronted by eight enemy warships, they suddenly replaced the Stars and Stripes with the banner of the Rising Sun and commenced firing. They failed in their first attempt to get close enough to board the *Stonewall*. They succeeded on their second try, bringing their bow to the port side. But the deck of the paddleboat was some ten feet above that of the ironclad, making it difficult for the troops of the *Kaiten* to board her.

Furthermore, the narrow bow approach made them an easy target for the enemy gunners. Although a number of the oppositionists, including Nomura Risaburō of the Shinsengumi, managed to get aboard, they were soon mowed down by the gunners.* Meanwhile, numerous men on the *Kaiten*, including the captain, were killed by gunfire from other enemy ships. The battle at Miyako was over in just thirty minutes, with the *Kaiten* retreating to Hakodaté in defeat. Sixteen oppositionists were killed. "Blood covered the deck," wrote Shimosawa, "corpses were piled high, and pieces of human flesh were scattered about."

There was no stopping the enemy onslaught. Four imperial warships, including the *Stonewall Jackson*, and two transport vessels, carrying some 1,300 troops in all, landed on the southwestern coast of Ezo on April 9. Reinforcements were on their way. The oppositionists, of course, had no reinforcements.

In the face of certain defeat, Hijikata Toshizō fought valiantly. In mid-April he led 230 troops against 600 of the enemy in defense of Hakodaté, at Futamata, just north of the stronghold. After sixteen hours of intense fighting, 35,000 rounds of ammunition spent, and only one among them killed, Hijikata's troops forced the enemy to retreat. The enemy attacked again the next day, only to meet with strong resistance by Hijikata's troops. On the following night Hijikata led his men, swords drawn, on a raid of the enemy camp, setting them to flight. During breaks in the fighting, Hijikata reportedly went through camp handing out saké to encourage his troops.

But Hijikata knew that the end was near. He wrote his death poem:

> *Though my body may decay on the island of Ezo,*
> *My spirit guards my lord in the east.*†

---

* Nomura was the attendant who had accompanied Kondō Isami to the enemy camp after the latter's arrest at Nagaréyama. He had joined the Shinsengumi sometime after June 1867. At Hakodaté he served as assistant to the army commissioner, under Hijikata's command.

† Hijikata's "lord in the east" was none other than the last shōgun, Tokugawa Yoshinobu.

On May 5 Hijikata called his attendant, a seventeen-year-old youth named Ichimura Tetsunosuké, into a private room at Go-ryōkaku. Ichimura had joined the Shinsengumi in the fall of 1867. Hijikata now entrusted Ichimura with his death poem, a photo of himself, a few strands of his hair, two swords, and a letter—and instructed him to bring these mementos to the home of Satō Hikogorō in Hino. At first Ichimura refused. "I asked him to tell someone else to do it, because I had resolved to stay there and die [with him]," Ichimura later reported to Satō. "But he became very angry, saying, 'If you don't follow my orders, I'll cut you down right now.' He had that same menacing look on his face that he always had when angered." Ichimura obeyed Hijikata's orders, leaving Hakodaté soon after aboard a foreign ship bound for Yokohama. "When I left the fortress, I looked back, and in the distance saw someone watching me through a small opening in the gate. I think it was Commander [Hijikata]."

The General Attack on Hakodaté was the oppositionists' last stand, Hijikata's last fight. By May 11 the government forces had driven the rebels back to Hakodaté, where they surrounded them by land and sea. Hijikata retreated to defend the city. He was shot in the belly while on horseback, leading his troops in the fight. The warrior was dead at age thirty-four.[*] The remnants of the Shin-sengumi surrendered four days later. Goryōkaku fell on May 18. The oppositionists were finally defeated.

* * * * *

Kondō Isami and Hijikata Toshizō were glorified as heroes upon their return to Tama in early 1868. In death they were apotheosized. On the expansive grounds of Takahata Fudō Temple in Hino, the stone *Monument of the Two Heroes* was completed in 1888.[†] Over a

---

[*] Ichimura learned of Hijikata's death aboard the ship bound for Yokohama. He reached Hino in July, delivering Hijikata's mementos to Satō's home soon after. When he reported Hijikata's death to Satō and his family and friends, "there was not one among them who did not shed tears."

[†] See Appendix I (11).

century later a bronze statue of Hijikata was erected near the monument. The right hand grips a sword. The left fist is clenched. The eyes … the eyes, battle-ready, are ever prepared for death, "to meet Kondō underground."

APPENDIX I

1. **Katsu Kaishū**
   Katsu Kaishū's ideas were based on sound facts and gleaned from hard-earned experience. During the latter half of the 1850s, Kaishū had been educated in the naval arts and sciences by Dutch naval officers in Nagasaki. In 1860 he captained the warship *Kanrin Maru* on the first authorized overseas journey in the history of the Tokugawa. The tiny schooner sailed to San Francisco, where Captain Katsu and company remained for nearly two months, observing American society, culture, and technology.

2. **The Three Great Fencing Academies in Edo**
   The three great fencing academies during the turbulent final years of the Tokugawa Shogunate were the Chiba Dōjō, the Momonoi Dōjō, and the Saitō Dōjō. These schools served as training halls for young samurai to develop and polish their swordsmanship. They also became venues of political discourse, and from them emerged some of the greatest political leaders of the time. Sakamoto Ryōma, the rōnin from Tosa, served as head of a branch school of the Chiba Dōjō. Takéchi Hanpeita, the Tosa Loyalist leader who masterminded terror on the streets of Kyōto in the early 1860s, served as head of the Momonoi Dōjō. Katsura Kogorō, a leader of the Chōshū Loyalists during the revolution and of the Meiji government afterward, was head of the Saitō Dōjō.

3. **Tosa Han**
   The lower samurai of Tosa Han were completely shut out from participating in government. Like their counterparts in numerous other han, most of them were patriots, self-styled "men of high

purpose" who embraced a specific political agenda—namely, Imperial Reverence and Expel the Barbarians. They eventually advocated the more radical Down with the Bakufu and banded together to form the revolutionary Tosa Loyalist Party. Their leading members included some of the most remarkable heroes of the revolution, including Takéchi Hanpeita, Sakamoto Ryōma, and Nakaoka Shintarō. With the notable exception of Takéchi, the party leader, nearly all of these men fled the confines of Tosa to play out their revolutionary roles on the national stage.*

4. **Ryō**

The ryō was a gold coin that, according to Ernest Satow, interpreter to the British minister in Japan, was equivalent to about 1⅓ Mexican silver dollars. In Edo in 1860, one ryō had the approximate value of $200 in U.S. currency in 2004. This calculation is based on rice prices at the turn of the twenty-first century and in 1860. However, the markets for rice differed in Edo and Kyōto, and prices fluctuated from year to year.

5. **Seppuku (literally, cutting the belly; also called hara-kiri)**

To the samurai, seppuku epitomized a courageous life through a stoic and noble death. Self-disembowelment was not only an agonizing form of suicide, but an opportunity for the samurai to display his inner purity by exposing his bowels, the seat of his courage. It was often a legal form of punishment through which the condemned man could avoid the ignominy of execution. It was a vehicle of apology and a means of absolution for the miscreant to prove his sincerity and redeem honor for himself, his family, his clan, and his liege lord.

Traditionally, the function of the samurai was to accomplish deeds of valor at the risk of his own life. Accordingly, to be well versed in the formal practice of seppuku was part of the samurai's basic education. As far as circumstances allowed, seppuku was

---

* The Tosa Loyalist Party and the discrimination in Tosa society are discussed in detail in *Ryoma* and in *Samurai Tales*.

performed with the ceremony of a highly developed art form.*
Even with a razor-sharp blade, however, it can be difficult to cut
through the human abdomen; the tissue is resilient and tends to
have a springing effect against the tip of a sword. Accordingly,
seppuku demanded of its practitioner absolute composure in the
face of excruciating pain, an unfathomable resolve to plunge in
the blade, and the willpower to cut properly.

The practitioner was most often assisted by a second, in the
person of a trusted friend, disciple, or relative. The role of the
second was every bit as important as that of the practitioner, and
probably more technically difficult. The second had to be an accomplished swordsman who, ideally, would only brandish his
sword after the practitioner had duly sliced open his abdomen.
His task of decapitation demanded unflinching accuracy, impec-
cable timing, and undaunted strength of mind. He had to be certain to strike exactly with the cutting edge, at which instant he
would pull hard on the blade to cut through tough sinew and
bone, and sever the head of a person he cherished. The purpose
of the second was twofold—to minimize the misery of the practitioner and to assist him in accomplishing a beautiful death. Unless performed with perfect precision, self-disembowelment
without a second could be a long, harrowing ordeal, accompanied
by a shameful and sickening scene of protruding intestines. And
just as the second assisted the practitioner, the favor was recipro-
cated. After cutting open his abdomen, the practitioner was obligated to fall forward, his arms extended before him, to facilitate
his second's task. Falling backward or to either side would make
decapitation difficult, if not impossible. It might cause the second
the humiliation of missing his target altogether or striking the
practitioner on the head or, in more extreme cases, shoulder,
back, or elsewhere. And the torrent of blood had to be aimed in
the proper direction or, as the case may be, into a blood vat in
front of the headless corpse, so as not to cause an unsightly mess

---

* A man wounded in battle and facing imminent capture would not have the luxury of
ceremony in committing seppuku.

or cover the second or witnesses with the gore.*

6. **"Just as if you had been wounded from behind"**
Being cut from behind was a blatant violation of Bushidō. Depending on the circumstances, if a man survived such an attack, he might have been placed under house confinement or, in worse cases, stripped of his samurai status, or as in the case of the Shinsengumi, ordered to commit seppuku. If a samurai was killed in an attack from behind, his family line might have been abolished until such time that someone—perhaps a son, brother, or other close relative—could avenge his death by slaying his assailant.

7. **Satsuma's Sea Battle against the British**
In August 1862 a British subject, Charles Lennox Richardson, was brutally murdered by Satsuma samurai. The government of Great Britain demanded that the murderers be tried and executed in the presence of British officers, and that an indemnity of 25,000 pounds be paid to the deceased man's family and three other British subjects who had been hurt in the incident. Satsuma refused. In the following summer, a squadron of seven British warships steamed into the bay off Kagoshima, the capital of the Satsuma domain, to present an ultimatum. The British were met by steely-eyed samurai who manned the batteries and lookout posts in the hills above the bay, and who, like their brethren who had murdered Richardson, were eager to slaughter as many foreigners as possible. They nearly succeeded on the following afternoon, as described in an eyewitness account written a quarter of a century later by Sir Ernest Satow, then-interpreter to the British minister in Japan.

> [A] retinue of forty men came on board, after having exchanged a parting cup of saké with their prince, with the full design of making a sudden onslaught upon the British officers, and killing at any rate the principal ones among them;

---
* From *Samurai Tales.*

they intended in this way to make themselves masters of the flagship. It was a bold conception, and might have been successful but for the precautions taken on our side. Only two or three were admitted into the Admiral's cabin, while the marines kept a vigilant eye upon the retinue who remained on the quarter deck.

For all the bellicosity of the Satsuma samurai, their muzzle-loading cannon were no match for the breech-loading Armstrong guns of the British, which had a firing range four times greater than the Satsuma guns. Five days after their arrival, the British seized three Satsuma steamers. Satsuma retaliated with cannon fire at noon, amid a raging typhoon, immediately decapitating the flag captain and the commander. The British, in turn, looted and burned the captured Satsuma ships and, out of range of the Satsuma guns, pounded the coastline. Satow described the scene: "Rockets were also fired with the object of burning the town, in which we were only too successful. The gale had increased to such a height that all efforts on the part of the townspeople to extinguish the flames must have been unavailing. It was an awful and magnificent sight, the sky all filled with a cloud of smoke lit up from below by the pointed masses of pale fire."

When the fighting finally ended that afternoon, the batteries along the coast had been completely destroyed, many samurai and townspeople killed, and much of the town destroyed by fire. The British casualties totaled eleven dead, including the two officers, and dozens wounded. It might be said that the British suffered a tenuous victory, as indicated by Satow: "The Japanese guns still continued firing at us as we left, though all their shot fell short, and they might fairly claim that though we had dismounted some of their batteries and laid the town to ruins, they had forced us to retreat."

Their obvious technological disadvantage notwithstanding, the Satsuma men gave the British a run for their money. As a condition for peace, Satsuma did pay the demanded indemnity, but stopped short of surrendering Richardson's killers. This final humiliation at the hands of foreigners was an unexpected boon to the Satsuma samurai. They threw off their xenophobia, in name if not in spirit. With the assistance of the British, they modernized their military, and, to the dismay of Edo, embraced Great Britain as their most powerful ally.

8. Sakuma Shōzan's Assassination

As the tension mounted between the Loyalists and the Tokugawa side, still another victim of Heaven's Revenge was felled on the bloody streets of Kyōto. On July 11 Sakuma Shōzan, an advisor to the Bakufu, was cut down on horseback as he rode through the city in broad daylight. Sakuma's knowledge of Western technology was unsurpassed in Japan. He was an expert in the casting and operation of Western-style guns. He was a firm believer in the aphorism "know the enemy," and his cherished slogan was "control the barbarians through barbarian technology." Sakuma was a great admirer of Russia's Peter the Great. In the previous century, after touring Western Europe, Peter the Great had introduced Western technology and culture into Russia and completely overhauled his government and military system. Sakuma was poignantly aware of the dire necessity for Japan to learn from the Russian czar's example. A decade before Perry, around the time of the Treaty of Nanking, which ended the first Opium War in 1842 and through which the British acquired Hong Kong, Sakuma had professed that if Japan expected to survive as a sovereign state in the modern world, it must develop a modern navy, abolish the feudal system, become a unified modern nation, and take its rightful place among the great Western powers. These ideas he imparted to his greatest student, just as he had bequeathed upon him his pseudonym, Kaishū—"Ocean Ship"— which Katsu Kaishū immortalized. His extraordinary foresight notwithstanding, Sakuma was an elitist who believed that the Japanese race was superior to all others, and that he, Sakuma Shōzan, was superior among Japanese. His assassin, a rōnin from the Higo domain, was incensed by Sakuma's progressive ideas (his espousal of Open the Country) and by the Tokugawa advisor's plan (with Aizu) to remove the emperor to nearby Hikoné* and eventually to Edo—to safeguard against a suspected Chōshū plot to kidnap him and as a means for finally securing a Union of Court and Camp. As if to exacerbate the anger of the antiforeign side, the great innovator had been riding through the Imperial Capital dressed in Western clothes and mounted on a Western saddle. He had been attacked from behind, which violated Bushidō. According to the law of Sakuma's native Matsushiro Han, his family line was discontinued. In order to reinstate the Sakuma line, his murder had to be avenged. For this purpose his only son, Sakuma Kakujirō, enlisted in the Shinsengumi.

9. **Assassinations of Sakamoto Ryōma and Nakaoka Shintarō**

It has been conjectured that Ryōma's murder was orchestrated by certain of his allies in the revolution who, convinced that the Tokugawa must be crushed militarily, had opposed Ryōma's peace plan. Iwakura Tomomi and Ōkubo Ichizō—the Machiavellian leader of Satsuma who plotted with Iwakura to obtain the emperor's decree to attack the Bakufu—have been named as suspects in this scenario.

Numerous men claimed to have murdered Sakamoto Ryōma and Nakaoka Shintarō. In February 1870 Imai Noburō, formerly of the Mimawarigumi, was accused of the murders by a captured former Shinsengumi corpsman. Imai testified at the Japanese Ministry of Penal Affairs that he and six others of the Mimawarigumi, including Sasaki Tadasaburō, had committed the murders. But since it was known that Ryōma had shot at least one Tokugawa samurai, albeit in self-defense, at the Terada'ya inn during the previous year, it was determined that the Mimawarigumi had acted legally, according to orders from the Tokugawa authorities in Kyōto. Imai was therefore found innocent and released. The question of Imai's innocence or guilt notwithstanding, neither his testimony nor the subsequent investigation and research have yielded conclusive evidence as

---

* Hikoné was the domain of slain Tokugawa Regent Ii Naosuké.

to the true identity of Ryōma's assassins. The incident must therefore be classified among the most tragic unsolved crimes in Japanese history.

Imai was stigmatized for the rest of his long life. After the Meiji Restoration, many former Tokugawa samurai followed the deposed shōgun into settlement in pastoral Shizuoka, an ancestral home of the Tokugawa. Among them was the man who claimed to have killed Sakamoto Ryōma. Imai lived under constant fear of revenge. He dug a deep tunnel near his house—a means of escape to the nearby riverside in case of sudden attack. Whenever a visitor came, he would hide until he could identify the person. When leaving home, he would carry a club concealed in his trousers.

During the early 1870s it was decided that a small shrine would be built in Imai's village. This shrine would house a wooden image of a Buddhist deity of special favor to the Tokugawa family. Imai was assigned the task of raising the money for construction costs. To this end, he sought the advice of Yamaoka Tesshū (a.k.a. Yamaoka Tetsutarō) in Edo. Yamaoka suggested that Imai enlist the help of two of his friends with connections among business and government circles in Tōkyō. These were Katsu Kaishū and Ōkubo Ichiō, two of a small number of former Tokugawa retainers recruited by the new government. Kaishū had served the Meiji government in various capacities, including head of foreign affairs, the army, and the navy. Ōkubo was then serving as the governor of Tōkyō. When Imai visited Kaishū and Ōkubo, he was met with a cold shoulder. Neither of the great men would help the confessed killer of Sakamoto Ryōma.

10. Ryōma's Jingle

It won't be only money we take
for sinking our ship at sea.
We won't give up until we've taken
the entire domain of Kii.

It won't be only money we take
for sinking our ship at sea.

We won't give up until we've taken
   the heads of all the men of Kii.

11. **Monument of the Two Heroes**

The monument was built twenty years after Kondō Isami's execution, nineteen years after Hijikata Toshizō fell in battle. It was the work of a group of their friends and relatives, including Satō Hikogorō, Kojima Shikanosuké, and Kondō Yūgorō. Their purpose was to clear the names of Kondō and Hijikata, who had been branded traitors by the Meiji government. The group asked the former shōgun, Tokugawa Yoshinobu, to write the inscription. In response to their request, Yoshinobu is said to have simply shed tears, without giving them an answer. The inscription was finally written by Matsudaira Katamori, the former Lord of Aizu. Matsumoto Ryōjun composed the main text.

Appendix II: The Survivors

Kondō Otsuné and Kondō Tamako (Kondō Isami's wife and daughter)
Otsuné and Tamako suffered after Kondō's death, under the stigma of his crimes against the imperial government. They lived with the Miyagawa family, at the home of Kondō Isami's birth in Kami'ishihara Village. Otsuné, the well-bred daughter of a reputable samurai family, did not adjust to life in a farming village. She felt alienated. She firmly rebuffed suggestions that she remarry, by attempting to cut her own throat with a dagger. At age fourteen, Tamako was wed to Miyagawa Yūgorō, her father's nephew who had witnessed his execution. In 1883, fifteen years after Isami's death, Tamako bore a son, Kondō Hisatarō. Three years later she died of natural causes at age twenty-four. Otsuné died in 1892, six years after her daughter, at age fifty-five. It is not clear whether Otsuné died of natural causes or finally succeeded in the suicide she had attempted on numerous occasions. Hisatarō, Kondō Isami's only descendant, perished in the Russo-Japanese War, thus ending the bloodline of his notorious grandfather.

Nagakura Shinpachi
Of the seven men from Kondō's fencing dōjō who enlisted in the Rōshi Corps, only Nagakura survived the Meiji Restoration. After breaking with Kondō and Hijikata, Nagakura, Harada Sanosuké, and some others formed an oppositionist militia consisting of about one hundred men. They called themselves *Seikyōtai*. Nagakura and Harada served as vice commanders, and many of their subordinate officers were former Shinsengumi members. After the surrender of Edo Castle, the Seikyōtai fled north to join the other oppositionists. (Harada returned to Edo. In May he joined the Shōgitai in the fighting

at Uéno, where he was mortally wounded.)

After the Meiji Restoration, Nagakura settled in his ancestral Matsumae on Ezo. He married the daughter of a physician to the former Lord of Matsumae, and took his wife's family name, Sugimura. He served for a number of years as chief kenjutsu instructor at a local prison. In 1876 Nagakura, with the assistance of Matsumoto Ryōjun, erected a shrine in Tōkyō's Itabashi district, near the site of Kondō Isami's execution. He dedicated the shrine to the memory of Kondō, Hijikata, and more than one hundred other Shinsengumi men who had died in the years leading up to and immediately following the Meiji Restoration. During his final years Nagakura held requiems for the souls of his dead comrades. He died of natural causes in the city of Hotaru on Hokkaidō (formerly Ezo) in 1915. He was seventy-six.

During a two-year period starting some four years before his death, Nagakura provided a newspaper journalist with an oral history of the Shinsengumi. Nagakura's oral memoirs were published in serial form by a local newspaper, *Hotaru Shinbun*, over a three-month period in 1913. Since they were given nearly a half century in retrospect and embellished by the vivid imagination of the journalist, the oral memoirs are more a sensationalized account than a faithful historical record of the Shinsengumi. Nagakura's more historically accurate written memoirs constitute the only firsthand account of the five-year history of the Shinsengumi. Long before his newspaper interview, Nagakura had lent his written memoirs to an acquaintance, who had promised to return them. They were never returned to Nagakura, and, in fact, were lost for decades. They were recently discovered, and published in book form in 1998.

Shimada Kai

Shimada Kai was wounded in the fighting at Aizu. When Goryōkaku citadel fell to the imperial forces, Shimada stood alone, his sword at his side, the Tōshō Daigongen insignia wrapped around his waist,* in the face of certain defeat, inciting the startled admiration of the enemy. After his capture, he was imprisoned at a Buddhist temple in

---

* See pages 196–197.

Hakodaté. He was subsequently incarcerated at Nagoya Castle, during which time it is believed that he wrote his famous so-called *Shimada Kai Diary*, which is actually a chronicle of the five-year history of the Shinsengumi and the following one-year period of civil war ending at Hakodaté. After his release in 1873, Shimada returned to Kyōto, where he married a local woman whom he had met during his years in the Shinsengumi. He ignored the urging of his friends to enter service in the Meiji government, instead making a living by working at local shops and teaching kenjutsu. In his old age he served as a security guard at Nishihonganji Temple, the former headquarters of the Shinsengumi. Shimada died of natural causes in 1900, at age seventy-two.

Saitō Hajimé

Saitō Hajimé, alias Yamaguchi Jirō, remained in Aizu to fight to the bitter end—as commander of thirteen of the Shinsengumi who had chosen to stay with him. After the fall of Aizu Castle, Saitō traveled southwest to Takada Han, where he lived quietly for a time. He eventually returned to Tōkyō, changed his name to Fujita Gorō, and married the daughter of a ranking retainer of the former Lord of Aizu. In 1872 he became a career police officer. He died of a stomach ailment in 1915 at age seventy-one. In defiance of death, he expired sitting upright in the alcove of his living room.

Shinohara Tainoshin

Shinohara Tainoshin fought on the Satsuma side in the Battle at Toba-Fushimi. After the Meiji Restoration, he became a businessman and, in later life, a devout Christian. His memoirs describe important events regarding the Shinsengumi, including his assassination attempt on Kondō Isami, the assassination of Itō Kashitarō, and the fighting at Aburakoji. Shinohara died of natural causes in 1911 at the age of eighty-three.

TABLE OF ERA NAMES AND THEIR CORRESPONDING YEARS IN WESTERN CHRONOLOGY

Era Name	Years in Western Chronology
Tenpō 1–14	1830–43
Kōka 1–6	1844–47
Ka'ei 1–6	1848–53
Ansei 1–6	1854–59
Man'en 1	1860
Bunkyū 1–3	1861–63
Genji 1	1864
Keiō 1–4	1865–68
Meiji 1–45	1868–1912

GLOSSARY OF JAPANESE TERMS

Aburakoji: a street in Kyōto, scene of Itō Kashitarō's assassination and the subsequent battle

Aizu: a Tokugawa-related clan in northern Honshū, feudal domain of Matsudaira Katamori

Aizu-Wakamatsu: the castle town of Aizu Han

Akébono-tei: a restaurant in eastern Kyōto

Ansei: an era name (see Table of Era Names)

Ansei Purge: infamous purge of the enemies of Tokugawa Regent Ii Naosuké

Arima Tōta: Satsuma samurai, vice staff officer of imperial forces, arrested Kondō Isami

Asada Tokitarō: Tosa samurai, committed seppuku for violating Bushidō

Bakufu: see Tokugawa Bakufu

Banryū: A warship of the oppositionists in northern Japan

Bunkyū: an era name (see Table of Era Names)

Bushidō: Code of the Samurai

Chiba Dōjō: a prestigious fencing school in Edo

Chōshū: a leading anti-Bakufu feudal domain, ruled by an outside lord, located on the western end of Honshū

chūgokui mokuroku: the third (and middle) rank in the Tennen Rishin

style of fencing

daimyō: a feudal lord

Denzūin: a Buddhist temple in Edo

dōjō: a martial arts training hall

Edo: capital of the Tokugawa Bakufu

Edogawa: a river flowing southward through the province of Shimo'usa

Enomoto Takéaki: former commissioner of the Tokugawa Navy, leader of the oppositionists on Ezo

Ezo: vast undeveloped far northern territory, one of four main Japan-ese islands

Fudō-dō: a village in southwestern Kyōto, location of the Shinsengumi's third headquarters

Fujisan Maru: a Tokugawa warship

Fukui: a Tokugawa-related feudal domain in central Honshū, on the Sea of Japan

Furudaka Shuntarō: an anti-Tokugawa Loyalist in Kyōto, arrested by the Shinsengumi

Fushimi: a town just south of Kyōto

geigi: an entertainer in the Kyōto pleasure quarters, accomplished in the arts of song and dance

geisha: an entertainer in pleasure quarters of Edo and elsewhere, accomplished in the arts of song and dance

Genji: an era name (see Table of Era Names)

Gesshin'in: a subtemple of Kōdaiji, served as headquarters of Kōdaiji

Faction

Gion: a district in eastern Kyōto, near the Kamogawa River

Goryōkaku: a modern citadel near Hakodaté

Gotō Shōjirō: chief minister of the Lord of Tosa

Hagi: primary castle town of Chōshū, located on the Sea of Japan

Hakodaté: a port city on Ezo open to foreign trade, location of oppositionists' last stand

Hamaguri Gate: one of the Nine Forbidden Gates of the Imperial Palace, scene of heaviest fighting in Battle at the Forbidden Gates

han: a feudal clan or domain

Harada Sanosuké: Shieikan swordsman, founding member and officer of the Shinsengumi

Hashimoto Kaisuké: Shinsengumi corpsman, member of Kōdaiji Faction

hatamoto: direct retainers of the shōgun, whose annual rice revenue of less than 10,000 koku did not qualify them as daimyō

Hijikata Toshizō: assistant instructor of the Shieikan, founding member and vice commander of the Shinsengumi

Hikoné: a pro-Tokugawa clan in western Japan, feudal domain of Ii Naosuké

Hino: a post town along the Kōshūkaidō Road in Tama, just west of Edo

Hirama Jūsuké: Shinsengumi officer, member of Serizawa faction, narrowly escaped assassination

Hirao, Michio: a modern Japanese history writer noted for writings about the Shinsengumi and Sakamoto Ryōma

Hirayama Gorō: Shinsengumi officer, member of Serizawa faction, assassinated with Serizawa Kamo

Hiroshima: a feudal domain in southwestern Honshū, on the Inland Sea

Hokushin Ittō style: style of fencing taught at Chiba Dōjō

Honshū: largest of the four main Japanese islands

iai: the art of sword drawing

Ii Naosuké: Lord of Hikoné, Tokugawa regent, assassinated in Edo

Ikéda'ya: an inn in Kyōto, site of notorious battle between Shinsengumi and anti-Tokugawa Loyalists

Ikumatsu: a geigi, lover-spy, and future wife of Katsura Kogorō

Imai Noburō: Mimawarigumi corpsman, suspected assassin of Sakamoto Ryōma and Nakaoka Shintarō

Inoué Genzaburō: Shieikan swordsman, founding member and officer of the Shinsengumi

Ishida: the native village of Hijikata Toshizō, located in Tama

Itabashi: a district in Edo, location of Kondō Isami's execution

Itakura Katsukiyo: Tokugawa prime minister and Lord of Matsuyama

Itō Kashitarō: staff officer of the Shinsengumi, Kōdaiji Faction leader, assassinated at Aburakoji

Iwakura Tomomi: leader of anti-Bakufu faction at the Imperial Court

Jōi: (literally, Expel the Barbarians): a slogan of Imperial Loyalists

Jundō Maru: a Tokugawa warship

Ka'ei: an era name (see Table of Era Names)

Kagawa Keizō: Mito samurai, staff

officer of imperial forces, arrested Kondō Isami

Kagoshima: castle town of Satsuma

Kaikoku (literally, Open the Country): the official policy of the Tokugawa Bakufu after the arrival of Commodore Perry

Kaiten: flagship of the oppositionists in northern Japan

Kaiyō Maru: a Tokugawa warship

Kami'ishihara: the native village of Kondō Isami, located in Tama

Kamogawa: a river in Kyōto

Kan'eiji: the Tokugawa family Buddhist temple at Uéno, served as place of self-confinement of Tokugawa Yoshinobu

Kanéko (family): a wealthy peasant household with vast landholdings in the countryside just northeast of Edo

Katsu Kaishū: commissioner of the Tokugawa Navy, a founder of the Japanese Navy, one of the most valuable personages in the Tokugawa Bakufu

Katsunuma: a town five miles east of Kōfu on the Kōshū-kaidō Road, scene of battle between the Shinsengumi and imperial forces

Katsura Kogorō: political leader of the Chōshū Loyalists, key player in overthrow of the Tokugawa Bakufu

Katsuragawa: a river in Kyōto

Kawaramachi: a district in Kyōto, on the west side of the Kamogawa River

Kawasé Dazai: a Zézé samurai, involved in failed plot to kill Shōgun Tokugawa Iémochi

Keiō: an era name (see Table of Era Names)

kenjutsu (literally, sword techniques): Japanese fencing

Kiheitai (literally, Extraordinary Corps): Japan's first modern militia, founded by Takasugi Shinsaku of Chōshū

Kii: a feudal domain in western Japan, one of the Three Branch Houses of the Tokugawa, native domain of Shōgun Tokugawa Iémochi

kimono: a gown worn by men and women

Kinnō-Tōbaku (literally, Imperial Loyalism and Down with the Bakufu): a slogan of anti-Tokugawa Imperial Loyalists

kirikami: the first rank in the Tennen Rishin style of fencing

Kiyokawa Hachirō: organizer of the Rōshi Corps, outspoken anti-Tokugawa dissident, assassinated in Edo

Kōbé: a port town on Ōsaka Bay

Kōdaiji: a Buddhist temple in the Higashiyama district of Kyōto

Kōdaiji Faction: the name of Itō Kashitarō's group after they defected from the Shinsengumi

Kōfu: a feudal domain strategically located some ninety miles west of Edo, ruled by a hereditary lord

Kojima Shikanosuké: leader of Onoji Village in Tama, close friend and patron of Kondō Isami

koku: bushel of rice (equivalent to 44.8 U.S. gallons)

Kōmei: a Japanese emperor, chronic xenophobe, ruled 1846–67

Kondō Isami: master of the Shieikan, founding member and commander of the Shinsengumi

Kondō Otsuné: Kondō Isami's wife

Kondō Shūsuké: Kondō Isami's fencing instructor and adoptive father

Kondō Tamako: Kondō Isami's daughter

Kondō Yūgorō: see Miyagawa Yūgorō

Kōshū-kaidō: a main road connecting Edo and Kōfu

Kotetsu: Kondō Isami's prize sword, which he used at the Ikéda'ya

Kumamoto: a feudal domain in west-central Kyūshū, ruled by an outside lord, hotbed of anti-Tokugawa Imperial Loyalism

Kuwana: a Tokugawa-related clan in central Honshū, feudal domain of Matsudaira Sada'aki

Kyōto: Imperial Capital

Kyō'ya: an inn in southeastern Ōsaka

Kyūshū: one of four main Japanese islands, located southwest of Honshū

Maekawa (residence): headquarters of the Shinsengumi at Mibu

makoto (literally, sincerity): symbol of the Shinsengumi

Man'en: an era name (see Table of Era Names)

Masu'ya: shop of Furudaka Shuntarō, served as hiding place of Chōshū-led rōnin in Kyōto

Matsudaira (Houses of): ruling families of Aizu, Kuwana, and Fukui clans, Related Houses of the Tokugawa

Matsudaira Chikaranosuké: chief fencing instructor at the Bakufu's Military Academy in Edo, helped establish Rōshi Corps

Matsudaira Katamori: Lord of Aizu, protector of Kyōto, master of the Shinsengumi

Matsudaira Sada'aki: Lord of Kuwana, inspector of the Imperial Court and nobles, younger brother of Lord of Aizu

Matsumae: a feudal domain on the southern tip of Ezo, ruled by an outside lord

Matsumoto Ryōjun: personal physician to the shōgun, befriended and treated Kondō Isami

Meiji: an era name (see Table of Era Names), name of the emperor who ruled during that era

menkyo: the fourth rank in the Tennen Rishin style of fencing, a license to serve as assistant instructor

Mibu: a district in western Kyōto, location of the first Shinsengumi headquarters

Mibu Rōshi: derogatory term for men of the Rōshi Corps and the Shinsengumi

Mimawarigumi (literally, Patrolling Corps): a Tokugawa security force in Kyōto

Minakuchi: a feudal domain, ruled by a hereditary lord

Mito: a feudal domain northeast of Edo, one of the Three Branch Houses of the Tokugawa, native domain of Tokugawa Yoshinobu, birthplace of Imperial Loyalism

Miura Kyūtarō: a high-ranking samurai of Kii Han, falsely suspected of orchestrating assassination of Sakamoto Ryōma

Miyabé Teizō: a rōnin from Kumamoto, Loyalist leader, perished at the Ikéda'ya

Miyagawa Hisajirō: Kondō Isami's father

Miyagawa Katsugorō: Kondō Isami's name at birth

Miyagawa Nobukichi: Kondō Isami's cousin, Shinsengumi corpsman, killed at the Tenman'ya

Miyagawa Yūgorō: Kondō Isami's nephew, witnessed execution of Kondō Isami, married Kondō Tamako, changed family name to Kondō, succeeded Kondō Isami as head of the Shieikan

Miyako Bay: scene of sea battle between oppositionists and imperial forces, on the northeastern coast of Honshū

Miyuki: a mistress of Kondō Isami in Kyōto

Mochizuki Kaméyata: a Tosa Loyalist and rōnin; perished in the Ikéda'ya Incident

mokuroku: the second rank in the Tennen Rishin style of fencing

Mōri (House of): ruling family of Chōshū

Musashi: a province west of Edo

Nagai Naomuné: a chief inspector in the Tokugawa Bakufu

Nagakura Shinpachi: close associate of the Shieikan, founding member and officer of the Shinsengumi

Nagaréyama: a village near the east bank of the Edogawa in the province of Shimo'usa, location of Kondō Isami's arrest

Nagasaki: an open port city in western Kyūshū on the East China Sea

Naitō Hayato: Hijikata Toshizō's alias

Nakai Shōgorō: a follower of Sakamoto Ryōma, killed at the Tenman'ya inn

Nakaoka Shintarō: a Tosa Loyalist leader, close comrade of Sakamoto Ryōma, assassinated with Ryōma

Nakayama Tadayasu: maternal grandfather and official guardian of Emperor Meiji, confidant of Iwakura Tomomi

Namamugi: a village near Edo, scene of murder of a British subject by Satsuma samurai

Nijō Castle: the Tokugawa stronghold in Kyōto

Nishihonganji: a Buddhist temple in western Kyōto, served as the second headquarters of the Shinsengumi

Nomura Risaburō: Shinsengumi corpsman, Kondō Isami's attendant, accompanied Kondō to Itabashi, killed in battle at Miyako Bay

Ogasawara Nagamichi: Lord of Karatsu and a senior councilor in the Tokugawa Bakufu

Ōishi Kuwajirō: an officer of the Shinsengumi

Okita Sōji: genius swordsman, head of the Shieikan, founding member and officer of the Shinsengumi

Ōkubo Ichiō: an influential official in the Tokugawa Bakufu, close ally of Katsu Kaishū

Ōkubo Ichizō: a Loyalist leader of Satsuma, key player in overthrow of the Tokugawa Bakufu

Ōkubo Yamato: Kondō Isami's alias

Onoji: the native village of Kojima Shikanosuké, in Tama

Ōsaka: mercantile center, located in western Honshū near Kyōto

Otaka: Kondō Isami's mistress in Kyōto, who bore him a daughter

Ōtori Keisuké: former commissioner of the Tokugawa infantry, headed oppositionist army

Ōtsu: a town just east of Kyōto

O'umé: the mistress of Serizawa Kamo in Kyōto

Owari: a feudal domain in central Honshū, one of the Three Branch Houses of the Tokugawa

Oyū: Kondō Isami's daughter, borne by

his mistress Otaka

rōnin: a samurai who did not serve a feudal lord

rōshi: a samurai who did not serve a feudal lord (less derogatory than rōnin)

Rōshi Corps: forerunner of the Shinsengumi

ryō: gold coin and unit of Japanese currency

Saigō Kichinosuké (a.k.a. Saigō Takamori, Saigō the Great): military leader of Satsuma, a key player in overthrow of the Tokugawa Bakufu, commander of imperial forces

Saitō Hajimé: close associate of the Shieikan, founding member and officer of the Shinsengumi

Sakamoto Ryōma: a Tosa Loyalist and rōnin, a key player in overthrow of the Tokugawa Bakufu, assassinated in Kyōto

saké: an alcoholic beverage made from rice

Sakuma Shōzan: a leading scholar of Western thought, teacher of Katsu Kaishū, assassinated in Kyōto

samurai: a warrior who generally served a daimyō

Sanbongi: a pleasure quarter in Kyōto, near the western bank of the Kamogawa

Sanjō-dō ri: a main thoroughfare in Kyōto

Sanjō Large Bridge: a bridge in Kyōto spanning the Kamogawa River

Sanjō Sanétomi: leader of the Seven Banished Nobles

Sanjō Small Bridge: a bridge in Kyōto spanning the Takaségawa Canal

Sasaki Tadasaburō: leader of the Mimawarigumi, a suspected assassin of

Kiyokawa Hachirō, Sakamoto Ryōma, and Nakaoka Shintarō

Satō Hikogorō: leader of Hino Village in Tama, brother-in-law of Hijikata Toshizō, close friend and patron of Kondō Isami

Satsuma: a leading anti-Bakufu feudal domain in southern Kyūshū, ruled by influential Outside Lord Shimazu Hisamitsu

Sei'i'taishōgun (literally, commander in chief of the expeditionary forces against the barbarians, generally called shōgun): title of the military ruler of feudal Japan

Sendai: a feudal domain in northern Japan, ruled by an outside lord

seppuku (literally, cutting the belly; also called hara-kiri): an honorable form of suicide practiced by samurai

Serizawa Kamo: Mito rōnin, founding member and commander of the Shinsengumi, assassinated in Kyōto

shaku: a unit of measurement just under one foot

shamisen: a three-stringed musical instrument resembling a banjo

Shiba Tsukasa: Aizu samurai, committed seppuku for violating Bushidō

Shibata Hikosaburō: Shinsengumi corpsman, forced to commit seppuku for deserting

Shieikan: Dōjō of Kondō Isami

Shikoku: smallest of the four main Japanese islands, located in south, east of Kyūshū

Shimabara: a pleasure quarter in western Kyōto

Shimada Kai: Shinsengumi veteran, followed Hijikata Toshizō to Ezo

Shimazu (House of): ruling family of Satsuma

Shimazu Hisamitsu: father of Satsuma daimyō, influential de facto Lord of Satsuma

Shimoda: an open port southwest of Yokohama

Shimonoseki: a port in Chōshū on the western tip of Honshū

Shimonoseki Strait: strait between Honshū and Kyūshū

Shimosawa, Kan: a modern Japanese history writer and novelist noted for writings about the Shinsengumi

Shimo'usa: a province northeast of Edo

shinan menkyo: fifth and highest rank in the Tennen Rishin style of fencing, a license to open a dōjō and teach one's own students

Shinmi Nishiki: nominal commander of Shinsengumi, later demoted to vice commander, member of Serizawa faction, forced to commit seppuku for violating corps regulations

Shinohara Tainoshin: Shinsengumi officer, close confidant of Itō Kashitarō, member of Kōdaiji Faction, shot Kondō Isami

Shinsengumi (literally, Newly Selected Corps): a Tokugawa security force in Kyōto

Shintokuji: a Buddhist temple in Mibu, served as headquarters for Rōshi Corps

Shintō Munen style: style of fencing practiced by Serizawa Kamo

shishi: men of high purpose

Shōgitai (literally, Corps of Clear Loyalty): an oppositionist corps at Uéno

shōgun: see sei'i'taishōgun

Shōnai: a feudal domain in northern Japan

Sonnō-Jōi (literally, Imperial Reverence and Expel the Barbarians): a slogan of Imperial Loyalists

Sumi'ya: a house of pleasure in Shimabara, Kyōto, frequented by the Shinsengumi

Sumiyoshi: a pleasure house in Ōsaka

Suzuki Mikisaburō: Shinsengumi officer, younger brother of Itō Kashitarō, member of Kōdaiji Faction

Takahata Fudō: a Buddhist temple in Hino

Takao: a warship of the oppositionists in northern Japan

Takaségawa: a canal in Kyōto

Takasugi Shinsaku: revolutionary commander of Chōshū Army

Takéchi Hanpeita: leader of Tosa Loyalist Party

Takéda Kanryūsai: Shinsengumi officer, suspected traitor, murdered in Kyōto

Tama: a region in Musashi province, just west of Edo

Tamagawa: a river in Tama

tatami: thickly woven straw mats perfectly fitted together and covering the floor in traditional Japanese rooms

Ta'uchi Tomo: Shinsengumi corpsman, forced to commit seppuku for violating corps regulations

Tenmanbashi: a bridge in Ōsaka

Tenman'ya: an inn in western Kyōto

Tennen Rishin style: style of fencing taught at the Shieikan

Tenpō: an era name (see Table of Era Names)

Terada'ya: an inn in Fushimi

Toba-Fushimi: area at the southern approach to Kyōto where civil war broke out between the imperial forces and oppositionists loyal to the Tokugawa Bakufu

Tōdō Heisuké: Shieikan swordsman, founding member and officer of the Shinsengumi, member of Kōdaiji Faction, killed at Aburakoji

Tokugawa (House of): ruling family of feudal Japan

Tokugawa Bakufu (a.k.a. Edo Bakufu, Bakufu): military government at Edo which dominated the Japanese nation

Tokugawa Iémochi: child-lord of Kii, fourteenth Tokugawa Shōgun

Tokugawa Iésada: feebleminded thirteenth Tokugawa Shōgun

Tokugawa Iéyasu: founder of the Tokugawa Bakufu, first Tokugawa Shōgun

Tokugawa Yoshinobu (a.k.a. Hitotsubashi Yoshinobu): fifteenth and last Tokugawa Shōgun, abdicated and restored the emperor to power in 1867

Tosa: a feudal domain on the Pacific coast of southern Shikoku, ruled by influential Outside Lord Yamanouchi Yōdō

Tsugaru Strait: strait between Honshū and Ezo

Tsushima: a feudal domain located in the strait between the Korean Peninsula and Kyūshū, ruled by an outside lord

Uchiyama Hikojirō: official at the Ōsaka magistrate's office, assassinated by the Shinsengumi

Uéno: a hilly region in the northeastern part of Edo, location of Tokugawa Yoshinobu's self-confinement

Utsunomiya: a strategically located feudal domain north of Edo

Yagi (residence): residence of the Shinsengumi leaders at Mibu

Yagi Gennojō: master of the Yagi residence

Yamaguchi: secondary castle town of Chōshū

Yamanami Keisuké: assistant instructor of the Shieikan, founding member and officer of the Shinsengumi, defected before committing seppuku

Yamanouchi (House of): ruling family of Tosa

Yamanouchi Yōdō: influential Lord of Tosa

Yamaoka Tetsutarō (aka Yamaoka Tesshū): low-ranking Tokugawa samurai, expert swordsman, close friend of Kiyokawa Hachirō, an overseer of Rōshi Corps

Yamato'ya: a silk wholesaler in Kyōto

Yamazaki Susumu: Shinsengumi officer and spy

yarijutsu: the art of the spear

Yodogawa: a river in Ōsaka

Yokohama: a port city on Edo Bay west of Edo, location of foreign settlement

Yonézawa: a feudal domain in northern Japan, ruled by an outside lord

Yoshida Shōin: archetype of Japanese revolutionaries, martyred teacher of Chōshū Loyalists

Yoshida Toshimaro: a Chōshū Loyalist and student of Yoshida Shōin, perished in the Ikéda'ya Incident

Yoshida'ya: an inn in the Sanbongi pleasure quarter of Kyōto; also the name of a pleasure house in Ōsaka

Zézé: a feudal domain in western Japan, ruled by a hereditary lord

Bibliography

Akama, Shizuko. "Shinsengumi Taishi no Tsuma to Aijintachi." *Rekishidokuhon: Bakumatsu Ishin wo Ikita 13-Nin no Onnatachi.* Shinjinbutsu Ōraisha, winter 1979.

Carlyle, Thomas. *Thomas Carlyle: Historical Essays* (Chris R. Vanden Bossche, ed.). University of California Press, 2002.

Craig, Albert M. *Chōshū in the Meiji Restoration.* Harvard University Press, 1961.

Furukawa, Kaoru. *Takasugi Shinsaku.* Sōgensha, 1971.

Hillsborough, Romulus. *Ryoma—Life of a Renaissance Samurai.* Ridgeback Press, 1999.

—. *Samurai Tales: Courage, Fidelity and Revenge in the Final Years of the Shogun,* Tuttle, 2010.

Hinoshi Furusato Hakubutsukan, ed. *Shinsengumi Furusato Hino: Kōshū Dōchū Hino to Shinsengumi.* Shinsengumi Festa in Hino Jikko Iinkai, 2003.

Hirao, Michio. *Kaientai Shimatsuki.* Chūōkōronsha, 1976.

—. *Rikuentai Shimatsuki.* Chūōkōronsha, 1977.

—. *Ryōma no Subété.* Kōchi Shinbunsha, 1985.

—. *Teihon: Shinsengumi Shiroku.* Shinjinbutsu Ōraisha, 2003.

Kaionji, Chōgorō. *Saigō Takamori.* Vols. 3, 8, and 9. Asahi Shinbunsha, 1976, 1978.

Katsu Kaishū. "Bakufu Shimatsu." *Katsu Kaishū Zenshū.* Vol. 11. Keisō Shobō, 1975.

—. "Bakumatsu Nikki." *Katsu Kaishū Zenshū.* Vol. 1. Kōdansha, 1982.

—. *Hikawa Seiwa.* Hiroiké Gakuen Shuppanbu, 1967.

—. "Kainanroku." *Katsu Kaishū Zenshū.* Vol. 11. Keisō Shobō, 1975.

—. *Kaishū Zadan.* Iwanami Shoten, 1983.

—. "Shokan to Kengen." *Katsu Kaishū Zenshū.* Vol. 2. Kōdansha, 1982.

—. "Suijinroku." *Katsu Kaishū Zenshū.* Vol. 6. Kōdansha, 1977.

Katsubé, Mitaké. *Katsu Kaishū.* Vols. 1 and 2. PHP Kenkyūsho, 1992.

Keene, Donald. *Emperor of Japan: Meiji and His World, 1852–1912.* Columbia University Press, 2002.

Kikuchi, Akira. *Hijikata Toshizō no Shōgai.* Shinjinbutsu Ōraisha, 2003.

Kikuchi, Akira, Seirō Itō, Tatsuya Yamamura, eds. *Shinsengumi Nisshi (Compact).* Vols. 1 and 2. Shinjinbutsu Ōraisha, 2003.

Kimura, Sachihiko, ed. *Shinsengumi Nikki: Nagakura Shinpachi Nikki, Shimada Kai Nikki wo Yomu*. PHP Kenkyūsho, 2003.

—. *Shiden Hijikata Toshizō*. Tokyo: Gakushū Kenkyūsha, 2001.

Kojima, Masataka. *Bujutsu: Tennen Rishinryū*. Kojima Shiryōkan, 1978.

—. *Shinsengumi Minigaido*. Kojima Shiryōkan, 2001.

—. *Shinsengumi Yodan*. Kojima Shiryōkan, 1990.

—. "Tennen Rishinryū to Kondō Isami." *Kondō Isami no Subété*, Shinjinbutsu Ōraisha, 1993.

Konishi, Shirō. *Kaikoku to Jōi*. Chūōkōronsha, 1974.

Konishi, Shirō, Takeshi Yamamoto, Fumio Etō, Saichirō Miyaji, Kijūrō Hirotani, eds. *Sakamoto Ryōma Jiten*. Shinjinbutsu Ōraisha, 1988.

Matsumoto, Kenichi. *Bakumatsu no Sanshū*. Kōdansha, 1996.

—. *Hyōden Sakuma Shōzan*. Vol. 1. Chūōkōronsha, 1990.

Matsuura, Rei. *Shinsengumi*. Iwanami Shoten, 2003.

Miyaji, Saichirō. *Nakaoka Shintarō*. Chūōkōronsha, 1993.

—, ed. *Sakamoto Ryōma Zenshū*. Kōfūsha Shuppan, 1982.

Nagakura Shinpachi. *Shinsengumi Tenmatsuki*. Shinjinbutsu Ōraisha, 1998.

Nihon Rekishi Gakkai, ed. *Meiji Ishin Jinmei Jiten*. Furukawa Kōbunkan, 1981.

Nihonshi Yōgo Jiten Henshū Iinkai-hen. *Nihonshi Yōgo Jiten*. Kashiwa Shobō, 1979.

Ozaki, Hideki. "Ryōma Ansatsu no Shinsō." *Sakamoto Ryōma*. Ōbunsha, 1983.

Satō, Akira. *Kikigaki Shinsengumi*. Shinjinbutsu Ōraisha, 1972.

Satow, Ernest. *A Diplomat in Japan*. Oxford University Press, 1968.

Shiba Ryōtarō. *Hitokiri Izō*. Tokyo: Shinchōsha, 1988.

Shimosawa, Kan. *Shinsengumi Shimatsuki*. Chūōkōronsha, 1977.

Shinmura, Izuru, ed. *Kojien*. Iwanami Shoten, 1955.

Shinsengumi: Bakumatsu no Seishun. "Serizawa Kamo no Bōsatsu." Purejidentosha, 1981.

Shinsengumi: Bakumatsu no Seishun. "Tenryō Bushū Tama-gun." Purejidentosha, 1981.

Shinsengumi Daijiten. Compact. Shinjinbutsu Ōraisha, 1999.

Shinsengumi Shashinshū. Shinjinbutsu Ōraisha, 1974.

Shinsengumi Saizensen. Vol. 1. Shinjinbutsu Ōraisha, 1998.

Shinsengumi Shiryōshū (Compact). Tokyo: Shinjinbutsu Ōraisha, 1998.

Tani Haruo, "Hino to Shinsengumi (2): Satō Hikorgorō to Hijikata Toshizō," Hino Tōmonkaihō, No. 6.

Tominari, Hiroshi. *Shinsengumi: Ikéda'ya Jiken Tenmatsuki*. Shinjinbutsu Ōraisha, 2001.

Tōyama, Mitsuru. *Bakumatsu Sanshūden*. Shimazu Shobō, 1990.

Ushiyama, Eiji. *Yamaoka Tesshū no Isshō*. Shunpūkan, 1967.

Yamaoka, Tesshū and Katsu Kaishū. *Bushidō*. Kadokawa Sensho, 1971.

Source Notes

Historical Background

p. 34   Katsu Kaishū quote: "Bakufu Shimatsu," *Katsu Kaishū Zenshū* (Keisō Shobō), vol. 11, p. 256.

p. 32   comparison between Chōshū and Satsuma: *Saigō Takamori*, vol. 9, pp. 212–13.

p. 34   Ii Naosuké's thoughts: *Kaikoku to Jōi*, p. 122.

Loyal and Patriotic Corps

p. 36   *Shinsengumi Nisshi*, vol. 1 p. 50; *Teihon: Shinsengumi Shiroku*, pp. 29, 30; *Shinsengumi Shimatsuki*, p. 34; *Shinsengumi Daijiten*, p. 231.

p. 41   for the first time in its history, the Tokugawa Bakufu officially recruited rōnin: *Shinsengumi*, p. 3.

p. 46   *Shinsengumi Shimatsuki*, pp. 27–29, 31; *Shinsengumi*, pp. 7, 9; *Yamaoka Tesshū no Isshō*, p. 125; *Bakumatsu Sanshūden*, p. 108.

p. 43   about Matsudaira Chikaranosuké: *Shinsengumi Shimatsuki*, p. 27; *Shinsengumi Nisshi*, I, p. 41.

p. 46   *Shinsengumi*, pp. 7–8.

p. 46   number of corpsmen: *Teihon: Shinsengumi Shiroku*, p. 29.

p. 44   desecration of statues: *Kaikoku to Jōi*, p. 266.

p. 44   distance between Kamogawa and Mibu: *Shinsengumi Saizensen*, vol. 1, p. 162.

p. 44   *Teihon: Shinsengumi Shiroku*, p. 33; *Shinsengumi Yodan*, pp. 39–40; *Shinsengumi Shimatsuki*, pp. 40–41; *Shinsengumi*, p. 11.

pp. 46–47   *Shinsengumi Nisshi*, vol. 1, pp. 67, 165–66; *Shinsengumi Shimatsuki*, p. 77; *Teihon: Shinsengumi Shiroku*, pp. 46–47; *Shinsengumi*, pp. 15–16, 20; *Shinsengumi: Ikéda'ya Jiken Tenmatsuki*, p. 153.

p. 47   Kiyokawa assassination: *Teihon: Shinsengumi Shiroku*, pp. 41–42; *Shinsengumi Shimatsuki*, pp. 49–60.

pp. 46–47   treatment of Kiyokawa's corpse: *Shinsengumi Shimatsuki*, pp. 60–63.

Newly Selected Corps

pp. 49–51   *Bujutsu Tennen Rishinryū*, pp. 183–84; *Shinsengumi Nisshi*, vol. 1, pp. 12, 16–17; *Hijikata Toshizō no Shōgai*, p. 10; *Shinsengumi: Bakumatsu no Seishun*, p. 70.

p. 51   rank in Tennen Rishin style: *Hijikata Toshizō no Shōgai*, p. 15.

p. 51   anecdote about robbers: *Bujutsu: Tennen Rishinryū*, pp. 185–86.

pp. 52–53   *Shinsengumi Nisshi,* vol. 1, pp. 13, 22; *Kondō Isami no Subété,* pp. 62, 67–68; *Shinsengumi Shimatsuki,* pp. 19–20; *Shinsengumi Yodan,* p. 23.

p. 53   "vent [his] long-held indignation": *Shinsengumi Tenmatsuki,* p. 29.

p. 54   footnote: *Hijikata Toshizō no Shōgai,* p. 14.

pp. 54–55   *Shinsengumi Shimatsuki,* pp. 23–24, 105; *Teihon: Shinsengumi Shiroku,* p. 22; *Shinsengumi Daijiten,* p. 94; *Shinsengumi Yodan,* p. 14, *Hijikata Toshizō no Shōgai,* p. 14.

p. 55   footnote: *Shinsengumi Yodan,* p. 47.

pp. 55–57   *Hijikata Toshizō no Shōgai,* pp. 9–25; *Shinsengumi Shimatsuki,* pp. 24–25; *Teihon: Shinsengumi Shiroku,* p. 22.

pp. 57–58   Okita's background: *Hijikata Toshizō no Shōgai,* p. 25; *Shinsengumi Nisshi,* vol. 1, pp. 14–15; *Shinsengumi Daijiten,* p. 63; *Shinsengumi,* p. 27.

p. 57   Nagakura's background: *Shinsengumi Tenmatsuki,* pp. 15–17, 28–29, 266–67.

p. 58   Yamanami's background: *Shinsengumi Daijiten,* p. 256; *Hijikata Toshizō no Shōgai,* p. 25.

p. 58   Inoué's background: *Shinsengumi Daijiten,* p. 36; *Shinsengumi,* p. 27.

p. 58   Tōdō's background: *Shinsengumi Daijiten,* p. 175; *Hijikata Toshizō no Shōgai,* p. 25.

p. 58   Harada's background: *Shinsengumi Daijiten,* p. 203.

p. 59   Saitō's background: *Shinsengumi Shashinshū,* p. 173; *Shinsengumi,* p. 28; *Hijikata Toshizō no Shōgai,* p. 25; *Shinsengumi Nikki* ["Shimada Kai Nikki"], p. 241.

pp. 59–60   about Serizawa: *Shinsengumi Tenmatsuki,* pp. 72–73; *Teihon: Shinsengumi Shiroku,* p. 63; *Shinsengumi Shimatsuki,* p. 36; *Shinsengumi: Bakumatsu no Seishun,* pp. 95, 99; *Shinsengumi Daijiten,* pp. 144–45.

p. 60   Serizawa's syphilis: *Teihon: Shinsengumi Shiroku,* p. 47.

p. 61   Shimosawa quote about Serizawa: *Shinsengumi Shimatsuki,* p. 36.

p. 61   about Serizawa: *Shinsengumi Shimatsuki,* pp. 34–38.

p. 61   anecdote about Serizawa and tiger: *Shinsengumi Nisshi,* vol. 1, p. 118.

p. 61   *Shinsengumi Shimatsuki,* pp. 81–83; *Shinsengumi Nikki* ["Shimada Kai Nikki"], p. 186.

pp. 61–62   *Teihon: Shinsengumi Shiroku,* p. 32; *Shinsengumi Daijiten,* p. 250.

p. 62   *Shinsengumi Yodan,* pp. 38–39.

pp. 62–63   *Teihon: Shinsengumi Shiroku,* pp. 48, 53; *Shinsengumi Shimatsuki,* p. 101.

pp. 63–64   rōnin phenomenon: *Saigō Takamori,* vol. 8, pp. 461–62.

p. 68   *Shinsengumi,* pp. 31–32.

p. 66   Chōshū's attack on foreign ships at Shimonoseki: *Kaikoku to Jōi,* pp. 275–76; *A Diplomat in Japan,* p. 95.

p. 66   foreign ships shelling of Shimonoseki: *Kaikoku to Jōi,* p. 276.

pp. 67–68   *Shinsengumi,* pp. 32–34, 38.

p. 68   number of armed Loyalists: *Chōshū in the Meiji Restoration,* p. 206.

p. 68   quote describing Chōshū warriors: *Kaikoku to Jōi,* p. 306.

p. 68   *Shinsengumi Yodan,* p. 55.

p. 68   *Shinsengumi: Ikéda'ya Jiken Tenmatsuki*, p. 156.

p. 69   "patrol the city day and night": *Teihon: Shinsengumi Shiroku*, p. 58.

p. 69   one gold ryō reward: *Teihon: Shinsengumi Shiroku*, p. 58.

p. 69   Shinsengumi prohibitions: *Teihon: Shinsengumi Shiroku*, pp. 48–49; *Shinsengumi Shimatsuki*, pp. 85–86.

p. 69   footnote: *Shinsengumi Nisshi*, vol. 1, p. 312.

pp. 69–70   *Shinsengumi Shimatsuki*, pp. 194–200; *Teihon: Shinsengumi Shiroku*, p. 131–32; *Shinsengumi Nisshi*, vol. 2, pp. 15–16; *Shinsengumi Daijiten*, p. 149.

p. 70   about Shibata Hikosaburō: *Shinsengumi Nisshi*, vol. 2, pp. 21–22; *Shinsengumi Daijiten*, p. 120.

pp. 71–72   Nagakura quote about Yamanami: *Shinsengumi Tenmatsuki*, p. 124.

p. 71   *Shinsengumi Yodan*, p. 45.

p. 71   rivalry between Hijikata and Yamanami: *Shinsengumi Shimatsuki*, p. 181.

pp. 71–72   Yamanami's defection: *Teihon: Shinsengumi Shiroku*, pp. 125–26; *Shinsengumi Nisshi*, vol. 1, pp. 293–96; *Shinsengumi Shimatsuki*, pp. 178–81.

p. 71   footnote: *Shinsengumi Nisshi*, vol. 1, p. 295.

p. 72   Yamanami's seppuku: *Shinsengumi Tenmatsuki*, p. 125.

p. 72   *Shinsengumi Shimatsuki*, p. 289; *Kondō Isami no Subété*, p. 262.

p. 73   Nagakura quote about Chōshū men's hate for Shinsengumi: *Shinsengumi Tenmatsuki*, p. 78.

p. 73   This August 25 date is from *Shinsengumi Tenmatsuki*, p. 78.

p. 73   Kondō quote about killing Chōshū men: *Shinsengumi Tenmatsuki*, p. 82.

p. 73   Kondō quote: *Shinsengumi Tenmatsuki*, p. 79.

pp. 73–74   *Shinsengumi Tenmatsuki* pp. 78–84; *Shinsengumi Shimatsuki*, pp. 108–10.

Of Insult and Retribution

p. 75   acclaimed teller of samurai history and lore: *Saigō Takamori*, vol. 3, p. 398.

pp. 76–77   incident with sumo wrestlers in Ōsaka: *Shinsengumi Shimatsuki*, pp. 89–92; *Teihon: Shinsengumi Shiroku*, p. 54; *Shinsengumi Tenmatsuki*, pp. 55–58, 61–63.

pp. 76–79   trouble between Serizawa and girls of pleasure quarter: *Shinsengumi Tenmatsuki*, pp. 63–69.

The Purge

pp. 81–82   *Shinsengumi Tenmatsuki*, pp. 48–49, 50.

p. 82   *Shinsengumi Tenmatsuki*, pp. 50–52.

pp. 82–83   *Shinsengumi Tenmatsuki*, pp. 50–55; *Shinsengumi Shimatsuki*, pp. 88–89.

pp. 83–84   *Shinsengumi Shimatsuki*, p. 112; *Shinsengumi Tenmatsuki*, p. 69.

pp. 84–85   Yamato'ya incident: *Shinsengumi Shimatsuki*, pp. 96–97; *Teihon: Shinsengumi Shiroku*, pp. 63–64; *Shinsengumi Nisshi*, vol. 1, pp. 105–08.

p. 85   footnote: *Shinsengumi Nisshi*, vol. 1, p. 108.

p. 86   incident of Serizawa at palace gate: *Shinsengumi Shimatsuki*, p. 103;
             Shinsengumi: Bakumatsu no Seishun, p. 96.

p. 87   Shinmi's seppuku: *Shinsengumi Shimatsuki*, p. 112; *Shinsengumi Dai-
             jiten*, p. 191; *Shinsengumi Tenmatsuki*, p. 70.

p. 87   Nagakura quote about Kondō: *Shinsengumi Tenmatsuki*, p. 69.

p. 87   footnote: *Shinsengumi Nisshi*, vol. 1, pp. 122–24; *Shinsengumi*, p. 220.

p. 88   about Hirayama and Hirama: *Shinsengumi Daijiten*, p. 209.

p. 89   assassination and funeral of Serizawa: *Shinsengumi*, pp. 42–43; *Shin-
             sengumi Tenmatsuki*, pp. 70–71; *Teihon: Shinsengumi Shiroku*, pp. 63–
             64; *Shinsengumi Shimatsuki*, pp. 111–15; *Shinsengumi Nisshi*, vol. 1, p.
             124; *Rekishidokuhon: Bakumatsu Ishin wo Ikita 13-Nin no Onnatachi*,
             p. 254.

A Propensity to Kill

p. 91   Katsu Kaishū quote: *Kaishū Zadan*, pp. 59–60.

pp. 91–92   *Teihon: Shinsengumi Shiroku*, pp. 70–74.

pp. 91–92   *Shinsengumi*, pp. 43–44; *Shinsengumi Shimatsuki*, pp. 111, 227; *Tei-
             hon: Shinsengumi Shiroku*, p. 71; *Shinsengumi Tenmatsuki*, p. 84.

p. 93   footnote about hatamoto: *Katsu Kaishū Zenshū*, vol. 6, p. 6.

p. 93   footnote about value of ryō: *Shinsengumi Nisshi*, vol. 1, p. 26.

p. 94   Katsu Kaishū quote about hatamoto: *Bakumatsu Sanshūden*, p. 258.

pp. 94–95   *Shinsengumi Shimatsuki*, pp. 176–78, 226–27; *Teihon: Shinsengumi
             Shiroku*, p. 129.

p. 95   Every day the men would go out and cross swords with the enemy:
             Shinsengumi Shimatsuki, p. 183.

p. 96   quote of Kondō's mistress: *Shinsengumi Shimatsuki*, p. 187.

pp. 96–97   screening process: *Shinsengumi Shimatsuki*, pp. 213–14.

p. 97   message on bulletin boards: *Shinsengumi Shimatsuki*, p. 212.

p. 97   unpopularity of Shinsengumi and Aizu samurai in Kyōto: *Shinsengu-
             mi Nisshi*, vol. 1, p. 177.

pp. 98–99   *Shinsengumi Shimatsuki*, pp. 211–18; *Shinsengumi Tenmatsuki*, pp.
             128–30; *Shinsengumi Nisshi*, vol. 2, pp. 24–26; *Shinsengumi Nikki*
             ["Nagakura Shinpachi Nikki"], pp. 103–6; *Shinsengumi Daijiten*, p. 201.

pp. 99–100   Uchiyama's assassination: *Shinsengumi Shimatsuki*, pp. 93–95; *Teihon:
             Shinsengumi Shiroku*, pp. 54–55; *Shinsengumi Nisshi*, vol. 1, pp. 172–
             73.

Slaughter at the Ikéda'ya

p. 101   *Shinsengumi Shimatsuki*, p. 122, *Shinsengumi Tenmatsuki*, p. 86.

p. 102   *Shinsengumi*, p. 51; *Kaikoku to Jōi*, pp. 324–31.

p. 103   *Shinsengumi: Ikéda'ya Jiken Tenmatsuki*, p. 153; *Shinsengumi Nisshi*,
             vol. 1, pp. 165–66; *Shinsengumi*, p. 54.

pp. 103–04   *Shinsengumi: Ikéda'ya Jiken Tenmatsuki*, p. 156; *Shinsengumi Nisshi*,
             vol. 1, p. 176; *Shinsengumi Shimatsuki*, p. 119; *Shinsengumi Nikki*
             ["Nagakuru Shinpachi Nikki"], pp. 77–78.

p. 104   footnote, "another source": *Kaikoku to Jōi*, p. 321.

p. 104   *Shinsengumi: Ikéda'ya Jiken Tenmatsuki*, pp. 161–63.

p. 104–05   Miyabé's background: *Shinsengumi Nisshi*, vol. 1, p. 175; *Shinsengumi Shimatsuki*, pp. 132, 138; *Meiji Ishin Jinmei Jiten*, p. 971; *Shinsengumi: Ikéda'ya Jiken Tenmatsuki*, p. 159.

p. 105   *Shinsengumi: Ikéda'ya Jiken Tenmatsuki*, p. 166; *Shinsengumi Nisshi*, vol. 1, p. 175.

p. 105   corpsmen involved in Masu'ya raid: *Shinsengumi: Ikéda'ya Jiken Tenmatsuki*, p. 171; *Shinsengumi Daijiten*, p. 155.

pp. 105–06   Furudaka's interrogation: *Shinsengumi Tenmatsuki*, pp. 85–86; *Shinsengumi Shimatsuki*, pp. 119–23; *Teihon: Shinsengumi Shiroku*, pp. 85–86; *Shinsengumi: Ikéda'ya Jiken Tenmatsuki*, p. 174.

p. 106   *Shinsengumi Shimatsuki*, pp. 122–23; *Kido Takayoshi Autobiography*, quoted in *Shinsengumi Shimatsuki*, p. 130; *Teihon: Shinsengumi Shiroku*, pp. 86–87; *Shinsengumi Nisshi*, vol. 1, pp. 176–206.

pp. 106–07   number of corpsmen available for service on night of Ikéda'ya Incident: *Shinsengumi Nisshi*, vol. 1, p. 189; *Shinsengumi: Ikéda'ya Jiken Tenmatsuki*, pp. 187–88.

p. 107   footnote: Kondō assigned more men to Hijikata's group than to his own: Kondō Isami letter, quoted in *Shinsengumi: Ikéda'ya Jiken Tenmatsuki*, p. 187.

p. 107   festivities in vicinity of Sanjō Small Bridge: *Shinsengumi Tenmatsuki*, p. 88.

pp. 107–08   chain mail: *Shinsengumi Yodan*, pp. 24–25.

p. 107   footnote, weight of Kondō's chain mail: *Shinsengumi Yodan*, p. 25.

p. 107   Kondō entered first, followed by others: *Shinsengumi Tenmatsuki*, p. 88; *Shinsengumi Nikki* ["Nagakura Shinpachi Nikki"], p. 72.

p. 107   Description of beginning of Ikéda'ya battle: *Shinsengumi Nikki* ["Nagakura Shinpachi Nikki"], p. 72–73.

p. 108   Nagakura's "cornered rats" quote: *Shinsengumi Tenmatsuki*, p. 89.

p. 108   Nagakura's "blood ran into his eyes" quote: *Shinsengumi Tenmatsuki*, p. 90; *Shinsengumi Nikki* ["Nagakura Shinpachi Nikki"], p. 73.

p. 108   Nagakura quote about his nearly being wounded: *Shinsengumi Tenmatsuki*, p. 91.

p. 108   Nagakura's "blood sprayed as he fell" quote: *Shinsengumi Tenmatsuki*, p. 91.

pp. 108–09   *Kaikoku to Jōi*, p. 322; *Shinsengumi: Ikéda'ya Jiken Tenmatsuki*, pp. 237–38; *Teihon: Shinsengumi Shiroku*, pp. 87–88, 92.

p. 109   Miyabé's seppuku: *Shinsengumi Shimatsuki*, p. 132; *Shinsengumi: Ikéda'ya Jiken Tenmatsuki*, p. 198.

p. 109   Miyabé's relation with Yoshida Shōin and Kiyokawa Hachirō: *Shinsengumi: Ikéda'ya Jiken Tenmatsuki*, pp. 16, 18–19.

p. 109   Nagakura's "Kondō fought furiously" quote: *Shinsengumi Tenmatsuki*, p. 91.

p. 109   Nagakura's "[Kondō] was nearly cut three different times" quote: *Shinsengumi Nikki* ["Nagakura Shinpachi Nikki"], p. 74.

p. 109   When Harada, Inoué, and Takéda burst into the house: *Shinsengumi Nikki* ["Nagakura Shinpachi Nikki"], p. 74; *Shinsengumi Tenmatsuki*, p. 91.

p. 109   Nagakura's "Takéda cut him" quote: *Shinsengumi Nikki* ["Nagakura Shinpachi Nikki"], p. 74.

p. 109   Kondō's letter quoted: *Kaikoku to Jōi*, p. 322.

p. 110   about Yoshida Toshimaro: *Shinsengumi Shimatsuki*, p. 132.

p. 110   footnote, Yoshida Toshimaro's corpse: *Shinsengumi: Ikéda'ya Jiken Tenmatsuki*, p. 202.

pp. 110–11   Mochizuki's seppuku: *Kaientai Shimatsuki*, pp. 77–78.

pp. 110–11   about Katsura Kogorō: *Shinsengumi: Ikéda'ya Jiken Tenmatsuki*, pp 11–12; 121.

p. 111   proprietor's escape, and Harada's killing of fleeing rebels: *Shinsengumi Nikki* ["Nagakura Shinpachi Nikki"], p. 74–75; *Shinsengumi Shimatsuki*, p. 133; *Shinsengumi Tenmatsuki*, p. 93.

p. 111   Nagakura's quote about aftermath of Ikéda'ya: *Shinsengumi Tenmatsuki*, p. 92.

pp. 111–12   scene outside Ikéda'ya: *Shinsengumi Nisshi*, vol. 1, p. 202.

pp. 111–12   eyewitnesses' report of aftermath of Ikéda'ya: *Shinsengumi: Ikéda'ya Jiken Tenmatsuki*, p. 241.

p. 112   footnote: *Shinsengumi Nisshi*, vol. 1, p. 202

p. 112   Nagakura's "Had the Shinsengumi not achieved a great victory" quote: *Shinsengumi Tenmatsuki*, p. 94.

p. 112   Nagakura's "a crowd of tens of thousands" quote: *Shinsengumi Tenmatsuki*, p. 92.

p. 112   Hijikata smiled at every step: *Shinsengumi Shimatsuki*, p. 134.

p. 113   Shimosawa's quote about composure of Kondō and Hijikata: *Shinsengumi Shimatsuki*, p. 134.

p. 112   Shinsengumi casualties at Ikéda'ya: *Teihon: Shinsengumi Shiroku*, p. 87.

p. 113   Shinsengumi men rewarded after Ikéda'ya: *Teihon: Shinsengumi Shiroku*, pp. 90–91.

p. 113   footnote: *Shinsengumi Nisshi*, vol. 1, p. 207; *Shinsengumi Nikki* ["Nagakura Shinpachi Nikki"], pp. 80–81.

A Tale of Bushidō

p. 115   quote about Shinsengumi surveillance: *Teihon: Shinsengumi Shiroku*, pp. 94–95.

p. 115   *Shinsengumi Shimatsuki*, p. 159.

pp. 115–16   *Teihon: Shinsengumi Shiroku*, pp. 94–97; *Meiji Ishin Jinmei Jiten*, p. 20; *Shinsengumi Shimatsuki*, pp. 159–63; *Shinsengumi Tenmatsuki*, pp. 93–94; *Shinsengumi Nisshi*, vol. 1, pp. 214–21.

pp. 117–18   Katsu Kaishū quote about Bushidō: *Hikawa Seiwa*, pp. 264–65.

Battle at the Forbidden Gates

pp. 119–20   *Rikuentai Shimatsuki*, pp. 78–79; *Takasugi Shinsaku*, p. 140; *Shinseng-*

umi Shimatsuki, p. 148; Teihon: Shinsengumi Shiroku, p. 98; Rikuentai Shimatsuki, pp. 79, 81; Teihon: Shinsengumi Shiroku, p. 107; Takasugi Shinsaku, p. 140; Nakaoka Shintarō, pp. 137–38.

p. 121   Martial Prohibitions: Shinsengumi Shimatsuki, pp. 150–52; Teihon: Shinsengumi Shiroku, pp. 99–100; Shinsengumi Daijiten, p. 89.

pp. 121–22   Shinsengumi defend south of city: Teihon: Shinsengumi Shiroku, p. 99; Shinsengumi Nisshi, vol. 1, p. 227.

pp. 122–23   Battle at the Forbidden Gates: Shinsengumi Shimatsuki, pp. 149, 151; Rikuentai Shimatsuki, pp. 83–84; Kaikoku to Jōi, p. 332; Nakaoka Shintarō, p. 141; Shinsengumi Nisshi, vol.1, pp. 238–39; Hirao quote: Teihon: Shinsengumi Shiroku, p. 109; Katsu Kaishū quote: Hikawa Seiwa, pp. 33–34; Kaikoku to Jōi, pp. 332–33; Takasugi Shinsaku, p. 145.

p. 123   Shinsengumi Nisshi, vol. 1, pp. 218–19.

p. 123   Shimosawa quote: Shinsengumi Shimatsuki, p. 156.

pp. 123–24   eyewitnesses' account: Shinsengumi Shimatsuki, pp. 155–58.

p. 124   Ernest Satow quote: "The [Chōshū] batteries had been destroyed": A Diplomat in Japan, p. 95.

p. 125   shelling of Shimonoseki by allied squadron: Kaikoku to Jōi, p. 294; A Diplomat in Japan, p. 112.

p. 125   footnote: A Diplomat in Japan, pp. 112–13.

p. 125   Ernest Satow quote: "The Japanese could not stand our advance": A Diplomat in Japan, p. 113.

p. 125   peace between Chōshū and foreign nations: Kaikoku to Jōi, p. 296.

Return of a Hero

pp. 127–28   trouble between Kondō and men: Shinsengumi Tenmatsuki, pp. 112–15; Shinsengumi Nisshi, vol. 1, p. 256.

pp. 128–29   about Ikumatsu: Rekishidokuhon: Bakumatsu Ishin wo Ikita 13-Nin no Onnatachi, pp. 131–32, 141; Shinsengumi Shimatsuki, p. 186; Shinsengumi: Ikéda'ya Jiken Tenmatsuki, pp. 135–36.

p. 129   footnote: Rekishidokuhon: Bakumatsu Ishin wo Ikita 13-Nin no Onnatachi, p. 131.

p. 129   Katsu Kaishū had numerous mistresses: Katsu Kaishū, vol. 1, p. 44.

p. 129   respect shown for Katsu Kaishū's wife: Katsu Kaishū, vol. 1, pp. 27–49.

p. 130   Katsu Kaishū quote about sexual desire of great men: Hikawa Seiwa, pp. 235–36.

p. 130   about Sakuma Shōzan: Hyōden Sakuma Shōzan, vol. 1, p. 185; Katsu Kaishú, vol. 2, p. 47; Shinsengumi Nisshi, vol. 1, p. 263.

p. 130   footnote: Katsu Kaishú, vol. 2, p. 498.

pp. 130–31   Kondō's description: Shinsengumi Shimatsuki, pp. 192–93.

p. 131   Shimada quote about Kondō: Shinsengumi Shimatsuki, p. 185.

p. 131   Miyuki quote about first meeting with Kondō: Shinsengumi Shimatsuki, p. 186.

p. 131   Shinsengumi Shimatsuki, pp. 184–87.

p. 131   Miyuki quote about Kondō's relationship with her sister: Shinsengumi Shimatsuki, pp. 184–90.

p. 132　　　about Komano: *Rekishidokuhon: Bakumatsu Ishin wo Ikita 13-Nin no Onnatachi*, p. 252.

p. 132　　　Miyuki quote about Shinsengumi's money: *Shinsengumi Shimatsuki*, p. 187.

p. 132　　　about Hijikata and women: *Shinsengumi Shimatsuki*, p. 187; *Shinsengumi Yodan*, pp. 41, 45–46.

pp. 133–34　*Shinsengumi Shimatsuki*, p. 166; *Kaikoku to Jōi*, pp. 342–43; *Shinsengumi Shimatsuki*, pp. 166–67.

p. 134　　　Kondō decides to travel to Edo: *Shinsengumi Shimatsuki*, pp. 163–67; *Teihon: Shinsengumi Shiroku*, p. 115; *Shinsengumi Nisshi*, vol. 1, pp. 259, 261.

pp. 134–35　Kondō and others travel to Edo: *Shinsengumi Shimatsuki*, pp. 167–68; *Shinsengumi Nisshi*, vol. 1, pp. 258, 261; *A Diplomat in Japan*, pp. 194, 207.p. 102

p. 135　　　*Shinsengumi Yodan*, pp. 62–63; *Shinsengumi Nisshi*, vol. 1, p. 264; *Shinsengumi Shimatsuki*, p. 168; *Kaikoku to Jōi*, p. 268.

p. 135　　　Kondō's comparison of samurai in east and west: *Shinsengumi Shimatsuki*, pp. 170–71.

pp. 135–36　about Itō Kashitarō: *Shinsengumi Shimatsuki*, pp. 169–71; *Teihon: Shinsengumi Shiroku*, p. 117; *Shinsengumi Nisshi*, vol. 1, pp. 257–58, 265.

p. 136　　　about Matsumoto Ryōjun: *Katsu Kaishū*, vol. 1, pp. 459–60.

pp. 136–37　Matsumoto Ryōjun quote: *Shinsengumi Nisshi*, vol. 1, p. 270.

pp. 136–37　Matsumoto Ryōjun's ideas: *Shinsengumi*, p. 92.

p. 137　　　*Shinsengumi Nisshi*, vol. 1, pp. 272–74; *Shinsengumi Shimatsuki*, p. 171.

Endings and Transformations

pp. 139–40　*Teihon: Shinsengumi Shiroku*, pp. 117–18; *Kaikoku to Jōi*, pp. 345–51.

p. 142　　　*Shinsengumi Shimatsuki*, pp. 207–09; *Shinsengumi Nisshi*, vol. 1, pp. 360–71; *Shinsengumi Yodan*, p. 73.

p. 142　　　*Shinsengumi Shimatsuki*, pp. 208, 270; *Shinsengumi Nisshi*, vol. 1, pp. 371–72; *Teihon: Shinsengumi Shiroku*, pp. 134, 137.

p. 142　　　Kondō quote about hatamoto: *Kaikoku to Jōi*, p. 406.

p. 142　　　Kondō quote about leniency toward Chōshū: *Kaikoku to Jōi*, p. 406.

pp. 142–43　Sakamoto Ryōma's quote about Chōshū: *Sakamoto Ryōma Zenshū*, pp. 47–48.

p. 143　　　Kondō's second trip to Chōshū: *Shinsengumi*, p. 127.

pp. 143–44　incident involving samurai of Zézé Han: *Teihon: Shinsengumi Shiroku*, pp. 134–36; *Shinsengumi Nisshi*, vol. 1, pp. 319–23; *Meiji Ishin Jinmei Jiten*, p. 308.

pp. 144–46　*Shinsengumi Daijiten*, p. 193; *Teihon: Shinsengumi Shiroku*, pp. 112–13; *Shinsengumi Shimatsuki*, pp. 182–83; *Teihon: Shinsengumi Shiroku*, pp. 125–27.

p. 146　　　reorganization of Shinsengumi: *Shinsengumi Shimatsuki*, pp. 173–78; *Teihon: Shinsengumi Shiroku*, pp. 127–29; *Shinsengumi Nisshi*, vol. 1, pp. 311–12.

p. 146   Shinsengumi regulations declared official: *Shinsengumi Nisshi*, vol. 1, p. 312.

pp. 146–47   Katsu Kaishū reinstated: *Kaishū Zadan*, p. 65–66.

p. 147   Katsu Kaishū's meeting with Saigō Kichinosuké: *Katsu Kaishū*, vol. 2, pp. 53–57.

p. 147   Katsu Kaishū's letter to Lord Katamori: *Katsu Kaishū*, vol. 2, p. 73.

p. 147   Katsu Kaishū quoted about meeting with Lord Katamori: *Kaishū Zadan*, pp. 66.

p. 148   number of Shinsengumi corpsmen: *Shinsengumi Nisshi*, vol. 2, p. 61; *Shinsengumi*, p. 139.

p. 149   Shinsengumi corpsmen granted hatamoto status: *Shinsengumi Shimatsuki*, p. 227; *Teihon: Shinsengumi Shiroku*, pp. 160–61; *Shinsengumi Nisshi*, vol. 1, pp. 59–61; *Shinsengumi*, p. 139.

p. 149   only Kondō given direct access to shōgun: *Shinsengumi Nisshi*, vol. 2, p. 53.

p. 149   Kondō's political comments: *Teihon: Shinsengumi Shiroku*, pp. 173–76.

Blood at the Crossroads

pp. 151–52   *Shinsengumi Shimatsuki*, pp. 218–21; *Teihon: Shinsengumi Shiroku*, pp. 158–60; *Shinsengumi Nisshi*, vol. 2, pp. 12–15, 31–32.

pp. 152–53   anecdote about drinking bout: *Shinsengumi Tenmatsuki*, pp. 131–33.

p. 153   about Miyagawa Nobukichi: *Shinsengumi Daijiten*, p. 242.

p. 153   footnote: *Shinsengumi Nisshi*, vol. 2, p. 47.

pp. 153–54   *Shinsengumi Shimatsuki*, pp. 221–24; *Teihon: Shinsengumi Shiroku*, pp. 158–60; *Shinsengumi Nisshi*, vol. 2, pp. 47, 67–68; *Shinsengumi*, p. 138.

pp. 154–55   circumstances of assassinations of Ito's men: *Shinsengumi Nisshi*, vol. 2, p. 48; *Shinsengumi Shimatsuki*, pp. 228–31, 235; *Teihon: Shinsengumi Shiroku*, pp. 162–64; *Shinsengumi Nikki* ["Nagakura Shinpachi Nikki"], pp. 114–20; *Teihon: Shinsengumi Shiroku*, p. 164.

p. 155   Shinsengumi convince priests: *Shinsengumi Shimatsuki*, pp. 183–84; *Shinsengumi Nikki* ["Nagakura Shinpachi Nikki"], p. 116.

p. 155   description of new headquarters: *Shinsengumi Shimatsuki*, p. 193; *Shinsengumi*, pp. 144–45.

p. 156–57   murder of Takéda Kanryūsai: *Shinsengumi Shimatsuki*, pp. 197–201; *Shinsengumi Nisshi*, vol. 2, pp. 58–59.

p. 158   *Shinsengumi*, pp. 147–53; *Shinsengumi Nikki* ["Nagakura Shinpachi Nikki"], p. 122.

pp. 158–59   Itō Kashitarō assassination: *Shinsengumi*, pp. 148–49; *Shinsengumi Shimatsuki*, pp. 234–36; *Teihon: Shinsengumi Shiroku*, p. 170; *Shinsengumi Nikki* ["Nagakura Shinpachi Nikki"], pp. 122–23; *Shinsengumi Nisshi*, vol. 2, p. 84; *Shinsengumi Tenmatsuki*, pp. 140–42.

pp. 159–60   battle at Aburakoji: *Shinsengumi Shimatsuki*, pp. 236–40; *Teihon: Shinsengumi Shiroku*, pp. 170–72; *Shinsengumi Nikki* ["Nagakura Shinpachi Nikki"], pp. 123–26; *Shinsengumi Nisshi*, vol. 2, pp. 91–92.

Of Outrage, Fury and Inexorable Fate

p. 162   Ryōma's plan: *Kaientai Shimatsuki*, pp. 168–73.

pp. 162–63   *Shinsengumi Nisshi*, vol. 2, pp. 70, 72–73; *Ryōma no Subété*, pp. 348, 384–86; *Teihon: Shinsengumi Shiroku*, p. 185; *Shinsengumi Shimatsuki*, pp. 255–56.

p. 164   *Shinsengumi Nisshi*, vol. 2, pp. 75–76; *Meiji Ishin Jinmei Jiten*, p. 127; *Kaikoku to Jōi*, pp. 476–78; *Teihon: Shinsengumi Shiroku*, pp. 186–88.

p. 164   Kondō Shūsuké's death: *Shinsengumi Shimatsuki*, p. 173; *Shinsengumi Nisshi*, vol. 2, pp. 77–78.

p. 164   Kondō assailed the Lords of Owari and Fukui: *Teihon: Shinsengumi Shiroku*, p. 185.

pp. 164–65   Miyuki's quote: *Shinsengumi Shimatsuki*, p. 189.

p. 165   Itō's quote about Ryōma and Nakaoka: *Teihon: Shinsengumi Shiroku*, p. 190. Ōkubo Ichizō letter quoted: *Ryōma no Subété*, p. 383.

pp. 165–66   Shinsengumi suspected of Ryōma's assassination: "Ryōma Ansatsu no Shinsō," *Sakamoto Ryōma*, p. 112; *Ryōma no Subété*, p. 393; *Shinsengumi Nisshi*, vol. 2, pp. 96–97; *Shinsengumi Shimatsuki*, pp. 245–46; *Teihon: Shinsengumi Shiroku*, p. 191; *Kaientai Shimatsuki*, pp. 224–25.

p. 166   about Harada and Imai: *Shinsengumi Nisshi*, vol. 2, p. 97; "Ryōma Ansatsu no Shinsō," *Sakamoto Ryōma*, p. 112; *Teihon: Shinsengumi Shiroku*, p. 193; *Ryōma no Subété*, pp. 383–84.

pp. 167–68   Tenman'ya incident: *Shinsengumi Shimatsuki*, pp. 251–54; *Kaientai Shimatsuki*, pp. 158–68, 227–31; *Teihon: Shinsengumi Shiroku*, pp. 194–95; *Shinsengumi Nikki* ["Nagakura Shinpachi Nikki"], pp. 128–29.

p. 168   footnote: *Shinsengumi Shimatsuki*, p. 212.

Civil War

p. 170   *Teihon: Shinsengumi Shiroku*, p. 199.

p. 170   Saigō letter: *Saigō Takamori*, vol. 9, pp. 15–16.

p. 170   *Shinsengumi Shimatsuki*, pp. 256–57; *Teihon: Shinsengumi Shiroku*, pp. 199–200.

p. 171   *Saigō Takamori*, vol. 9, pp. 20, 22; *Emperor of Japan*, p. 125; *Teihon: Shinsengumi Shiroku*, pp. 201–02.

p. 171   Shimada Kai quote: *Shinsengumi Nikki* ["Shimada Kai Nikki"], p. 219.

pp. 172–73   *Shinsengumi Shimatsuki*, pp. 190–92, 268; *Kondō Isami no Subété*, pp. 48, 217–18.

p. 173–74   *Shinsengumi Shimatsuki*, pp. 256–57; *Shinsengumi Nikki* ["Nagakura Shinpachi Nikki"], pp. 141–42; *Shinsengumi Nikki* ["Shimada Kai Nikki"], p. 219; *Teihon: Shinsengumi Shiroku*, pp. 200–02; *Shinsengumi Nisshi*, vol. 2, p. 108, 110–11; *Shinsengumi Tenmatsuki*, pp.156–57.

pp. 174–75   assassination attempt on Kondō: *Shinsengumi Shimatsuki*, pp. 259–62; *Shinsengumi Nikki* ["Nagakura Shinpachi Nikki"], pp. 142–43, 147; *Shinsengumi Nikki* ["Shimada Kai Nikki"], p. 219; *Teihon: Shinsengumi Shiroku*, pp. 203–05; *Shinsengumi Nisshi*, vol. 2, pp. 112–14.

p. 175   Nagakura quotes: *Shinsengumi Nikki* ["Nagakura Shinpachi Nikki"], pp. 143–44.

pp. 175–76   *Saigō Takamori*, vol. 9, pp. 19, 43, 53–54, 59–61; *Emperor of Japan*, p. 126.

pp. 176–77   Shinsengumi fighting at Fushimi: *Shinsengumi Shimatsuki*, p. 263; *Teihon: Shinsengumi Shiroku*, pp. 208–09; *Shinsengumi Nikki* ["Nagakura Shinpachi Nikki"], p. 150.

p. 177   Kondō's poem: *Shinsengumi Yodan*, p. 59.

p. 177   *Shinsengumi Nisshi*, vol. 2, pp. 128, 130, 137; *Shinsengumi Shimatsuki*, pp. 264, 269; *Teihon: Shinsengumi Shiroku*, pp. 209–11.

The Peasant as Feudal Lord

pp. 179–80   *Shinsengumi Shimatsuki*, p. 267; *Teihon: Shinsengumi Shiroku*, p. 214; *Shinsengumi Nikki* ["Shimada Kai Nikki"], p. 225.

p. 180   Nagakura's fight: *Shinsengumi Shimatsuki*, pp. 267–68.

pp. 180–82   *Shinsengumi Shimatsuki*, pp. 269–70; *Teihon: Shinsengumi Shiroku*, p. 215; *Katsu Kaishū*, vol. 2, p. 163; *Shinsengumi Nisshi*, vol. 2, pp. 132–33; *Shinsengumi Nikki* ["Nagakura Shinpachi Nikki"], pp. 159–60, 162; *Shinsengumi Nikki* ["Shimada Kai Nikki"], p. 225; *Shinsengumi*, pp. 170, 174, 179–80; *Katsu Kaishū Zenshū*, vol. 11, "Kainanroku," pp. 373–74.

p. 182   footnote about Hijikata's father's name: *Hijikata Toshizō no Shōgai*, p. 12.

p. 182   footnote about Kondō's alias: *Shinsengumi Nikki* ["Nagakura Shinpachi Nikki"], p. 170; *Shinsengumi Nisshi*, vol. 2, p. 159.

p. 182   footnote: *Kondō Isami no Subété*, p. 176.

p. 183   *Kondō Isami no Subété*, pp. 175–77, 236; *Shinsengumi Shimatsuki*, pp. 269, 270–71 *Teihon: Shinsengumi Shiroku*, p. 215; *Katsu Kaishū*, vol. 2, p. 163; *Saigō Takamori*, vol. 9, p. 175; *Shinsengumi Nisshi*, vol. 2, pp. 140–42, 144–45; *Shinsengumi Yodan*, p. 78.

p. 184   Toshinori quote: *Shinsengumi Shimatsuki*, pp. 273–74.

pp. 185–86   *Shinsengumi Shimatsuki*, p. 271; *Teihon: Shinsengumi Shiroku*, pp. 219–20; *Shinsengumi Nisshi*, vol. 2, pp. 144–48, 152–53; *Shinsengumi Nikki* ["Nagakura Shinpachi Nikki"], pp. 163–64; *Shinsengumi Nikki* ["Shimada Kai Nikki"], p. 226; *Kondō Isami no Subété*, pp. 180, 183–84; *Shinsengumi Yodan*, pp. 83–84; *Shinsengumi*, p. 174.

Of Defeat, Disgrace and Apotheosis

pp. 187–88   *Bushidō*, pp. 80–86; *Bakumatsu no Sanshū*, pp. 75–78, 88–100; *Teihon: Shinsengumi Shiroku*, p. 225; *Katsu Kaishū Zenshū* vol. 11, "Kainanroku," pp. 373–74.

p. 189   *Shinsengumi Nikki* ["Nagakura Shinpachi Nikki"], pp. 173–74; *Teihon: Shinsengumi Shiroku*, p. 224; *Shinsengumi Nisshi*, vol. 2, p. 155.

pp. 190–92   *Teihon: Shinsengumi Shiroku*, pp. 225–27; *Bakumatsu Sanshūden*, p. 320; *Kondō Isami no Subété*, pp. 195–208; *Shinsengumi Nisshi*, vol. 2, pp. 155–56, 159–60, 163–67; *Shinsengumi*, pp. 181, 183; *Katsu Kaishū Zenshū*, vol. 2, p. 118; *Shinsengumi Nikki* ["Shimada Kai Nikki"], p. 227; *Shinsengumi Nikki* ["Nagakura Shinpachi Nikki"], p. 178; *Shinsengumi Shimatsuki*, p. 280.

pp. 192–93   Arima quote: *Shinsengumi Nisshi*, vol. 2, pp. 168–69.
p. 194   footnote: *Shinsengumi Nisshi*, vol. 2, p. 169.
p. 194   *Teihon: Shinsengumi Shiroku*, pp. 227–28; *Shinsengumi Shimatsuki*, pp. 171, 282.
p. 194   Arima quote about Kondō as "a kind of hero:" *Shinsengumi Nisshi*, vol. 2, p. 184.
pp. 194–95   Kondō's death poem: *Shinsengumi Shimatsuki*, p. 283; *Teihon: Shinsengumi Shiroku*, p. 233; *Shinsengumi Yodan*, pp. 89–90.
pp. 194–95   *Shinsengumi Nisshi*, vol. 2, p. 169; *Katsu Kaishū Zenshū*, vol. 1, p. 233; *Shinsengumi Nisshi*, vol. 2, pp. 174–75; *Shinsengumi*, pp. 184–85.
p. 196   Tani quote: *Teihon: Shinsengumi Shiroku*, p. 228.
p. 196   Kondō's trial: *Teihon: Shinsengumi Shiroku*, pp. 229–33.
pp. 196–97   *Teihon: Shinsengumi Shiroku*, p. 237; *Shinsengumi Nikki* ["Shimada Kai Nikki"], pp. 231–32; *Shinsengumi Nisshi*, vol. 2, pp. 177–78, 186, 192, 198; *Shinsengumi Yodan*, pp. 97–98; *Hijikata Toshizō no Shōgai*, pp. 223–25, 228–29, 232–33.
pp. 197–98   Kondō's execution: *Shinsengumi Shimatsuki* pp. 283–85; *Teihon: Shinsengumi Shiroku*, pp. 233–36; *Shinsengumi Nikki* ["Nagakura Shinpachi Nikki"] p.180; *Shinsengumi Nisshi*, vol. 2, p. 194; *Kondō Isami no Subété*, p. 236.
p. 199   Shimada quote: *Shinsengumi Nikki* ["Shimada Kai Nikki"], vol. 2, p. 228.
p. 199   footnote: *Bakumatsu no Sanshū*, p. 99; *Teihon: Shinsengumi Shiroku*, p. 233.
pp. 199–200   *Shinsengumi Shimatsuki* p. 285; *Kondō Isami no Subété*, p. 257; *Teihon: Shinsengumi Shiroku*, p. 234; *Shinsengumi Nisshi*, vol. 2, pp. 195–96.

Epilogue: Hijikata's Last Fight
p. 201   *Teihon: Shinsengumi Shiroku*, pp. 237–38; *Shinsengumi Daijiten*, p. 56; *Shinsengumi*, p. 190; *Shinsengumi Nikki* ["Shimada Kai Nikki"], p. 235; *Hijikata Toshizō no Shōgai*, pp. 244–48.
pp. 201–02   Okita's last days: *Shinsengumi Daijiten*, p. 63; *Shinsengumi*, p. 192.
pp. 203–04   *Teihon: Shinsengumi Shiroku*, p. 238; *Shinsengumi*, pp. 193–95; *Emperor of Japan*, p. 155; *Shinsengumi Daijiten*, p. 48; *Hijikata Toshizō no Shōgai*, pp. 253–55, 258–60, 263–65.
pp. 205–07   *Shinsengumi Daijiten*, pp. 99, 242–43; *Hijikata Toshizō no Shōgai*, pp. 258–60, 263–65, 274–76; *Teihon: Shinsengumi Shiroku*, p. 238–39; *Emperor of Japan*, pp. 165–66; *Shinsengumi*, pp. 197–99; *Shinsengumi Shimatsuki*, pp. 286–88.
p. 207   footnote: *Shinsengumi Daijiten*, p. 198.
p. 208   *Shinsengumi*, pp. 199–201; *Shinsengumi Daijiten*, pp. 31, 200–01, 214; *Hijikata Toshizō no Shōgai*, pp. 276–77, 279–81, 285, 287; *Teihon: Shinsengumi Shiroku*, p. 239; *Kikigaki Shinsengumi*.
p. 208   footnote: *Kikigaki Shinsengumi*.

Appendix I

p. 212   ryō: *Shinsengumi Nisshi*, vol. 1, p. 26.

pp. 214–15   Satsuma's sea battle against the British: Ernest Satow quotes *A Diplomat in Japan*, pp. 85, 88, 89.

pp. 216–17   Sakuma Shōzan assassination: *Katsu Kaishū*, vol. 2, p. 497; *Teihon: Shinsengumi Shiroku*, p. 107; *Shinsengumi Nisshi*, vol. 1, pp. 262–63; *Bakumatsu no Sanshū*, pp. 47–48; *Hyōden Sakuma Shōzan*, vol. 1, pp. 12–19, 47–48.

pp. 217–18   Assassinations of Sakamoto Ryōma and Nakaoka Shintarō: *Kaientai Shimatsuki*, pp. 220–21; *Katsu Kaishū*, vol. 2, p. 263; *Kaishū Zadan*, pp. 253–55.

pp. 218–19   Ryōma's jingle: *Sakamoto Ryōma Zenshū*, p. 221; *Sakamoto Ryōma Jiten*, pp. 120–21.

p. 219   *Monument of the Two Heroes: Shinsengumi Shashinshū*, p. 194; *Shinsengumi Daijiten*, p. 126.

Appendix II: The Survivors

p. 220   Kondō Otsuné and Kondō Tamako: *Shinsengumi Daijiten*, pp. 103–04; *Shinsengumi Yodan*, p. 104; *Rekishidokuhon: Bakumatsu ishin wo ikita 13-nin no onnatachi*, pp. 253, 292; *Kondō Isami no Subété*, pp. 220–21.

pp. 220–21   Nagakura Shinpachi: *Shinsengumi Tenmatsuki*, p. 268; *Shinsengumi Daijiten*, pp. 182–83; *Shinsengumi Nikki* ["Shimada Kai Nikki"], p. 240; *Teihon: Shinsengumi Shiroku*, p. 237; *Shinsengumi: Ikéda'ya Jiken Tenmatsuki*, pp. 226–27.

pp. 221–22   Shimada Kai: *Shinsengumi Shashinshū*, p. 176; *Shinsengumi Nikki* ["Shimada Kai Nikki"], pp. 187–88; *Shinsengumi Daijiten*, pp. 122–23; *Hijikata Toshizō no Shōgai*, p. 238.

p. 222   Saitō Hajimé: *Shinsengumi Daijiten*, pp. 106–07; *Hijikata Toshizō no Shōgai*, pp. 256–57.

p. 222   Shinohara Tainoshin: *Shinsengumi Daijiten*, p. 120; *Shinsengumi Shimatsuki*, p. 223.

INDEX

Books to Span the East and West

Our core mission at Tuttle Publishing is to create books which bring people together one page at a time. Tuttle was founded in 1832 in the small New England town of Rutland, Vermont (USA). Our fundamental values remain as strong today as they were then—to publish best-in-class books informing the English-speaking world about the countries and peoples of Asia. The world is a smaller place today and Asia's economic, cultural and political influence has expanded, yet the need for meaningful dialogue and information about this diverse region has never been greater. Since 1948, Tuttle has been a leader in publishing books on the cultures, arts, cuisines, languages and literatures of Asia. Our authors and photographers have won many awards and Tuttle has published thousands of titles on subjects ranging from martial arts to paper crafts. We welcome you to explore the wealth of information available on Asia at www.tuttlepublishing.com.

Published by Tuttle Publishing, an imprint of Periplus Editions (HK) Ltd.

www.tuttlepublishing.com

Copyright © 2005, 2020 Jeff Cohen

All rights reserved. No part of this publication may be reproduced or utilized in any form or by any means, electronic or mechanical, including photocopying, recording, or by any information storage and retrieval system, without prior written permission from the publisher.

Library of Congress Control Number: 2005926980

ISBN 978-4-8053-1546-0

25 24 23 22 21 20
10 9 8 7 6 5 4 3 2 1
2009TP

Printed in Singapore

TUTTLE PUBLISHING® is a registered trademark of Tuttle Publishing, a division of Periplus Editions (HK) Ltd.

Distributed by

North America, Latin America & Europe
Tuttle Publishing
364 Innovation Drive
North Clarendon, VT 05759-9436
U.S.A.
Tel: 1 (802) 773-8930
Fax: 1 (802) 773-6993
info@tuttlepublishing.com
www.tuttlepublishing.com

Japan
Tuttle Publishing
Yaekari Building 3rd Floor
5-4-12 Osaki Shinagawa-ku
Tokyo 141 0032
Tel: (81) 3 5437-0171
Fax: (81) 3 5437-0755
sales@tuttle.co.jp
www.tuttle.co.jp

Asia Pacific
Berkeley Books Pte. Ltd.
3 Kallang Sector #04-01
Singapore 349278
Tel: (65) 6741-2178
Fax: (65) 6741-2179
inquiries@periplus.com.sg
www.tuttlepublishing.com